NATURAL WOMEN,
CULTURED MEN

NATURAL WOMEN, CULTURED MEN

A FEMINIST PERSPECTIVE ON SOCIOLOGICAL THEORY

R. A. Sydie

Open University Press
Milton Keynes

Published in Canada and the United States of
America by Methuen Publications, 2330 Midland
Avenue, Agincourt, Ontario, Canada M1S 1P7

Published elsewhere by Open University Press, 12
Cofferidge Close, Stony Stratford, Milton Keynes
MK11 1BY England

British Library Cataloguing in Publication Data

Sydie, Rosalind
    Natural women, cultured men: a feminist
    perspective on sociological theory
    1. Sociology   2. Sex Roles
    I Title
    301'.01   HM24

ISBN 0-335-15513-8
ISBN 0-335-15512-X PBK

Printed and bound in Canada

Contents

Preface

This book is intended as an undergraduate textbook for students in the social sciences and especially in sociology. It is the result of several years of teaching courses in women's studies to undergraduates, as well as to graduate students in sociology. Initially, the courses, especially the undergraduate courses, were vital "eureka" type discoveries as the resurgence of feminism in the 1960s generated a knowledge explosion both within and, most importantly, outside the academy. The rediscovery of past heroines, the re-evaluation of received wisdoms and the general process of seeing the world afresh from a woman's perspective were exciting and provided for stimulating and challenging teaching and research.

The basic feminist point was that women be treated as knowledgable actresses—a revolutionary perspective for all the disciplines, but especially so for the social sciences with their claims of immediate and direct knowledge of the social world. There was great optimism initially that the feminist reassessments of the nature, grounds and conditions of knowledge production would transform the traditional disciplines and knowledge production. It was assumed that by pointing out the biases in the data bases, the data collection, and the conclusions drawn, often by impeccable research methodology endorsed by traditional standards, that intelligent, "objective" seekers of knowledge would see the error of their ways. Specifically, no longer would half the human race be excluded as legitimate subjects rather than objects of knowledge, or their interests ignored or denigrated as too "subjective" compared with the "objectivity" of masculine knowledge. A good part of the optimism was tied to a vision of a more humane world. Millet's conclusion to her book *Sexual Politics* (1969) expressed this optimism.

It may be that a second wave of the sexual revolution might at last accomplish its aim of freeing half the race from its immemorial subordination—and in the process bring us all a great deal closer to humanity. It may be that we shall even be able to retire sex from the harsh realities of politics, but not until we have created a world we can bear out of the desert we inhabit.[1]

Unfortunately, the desert was more resistant to change than the majority thought possible in the initial years.[2]

The enthusiasm of the early years has been tempered by the recognition that "knowledge itself is power," and that the traditional producers and guardians of knowledge have no intention of relinquishing their position as arbiters of what is to count as legitimate knowledge. As Dorothy Smith observed, "The circle of men whose writing and talk was significant to each other extends backwards in time as far as our records reach. What men were doing was relevant to men, was written by men about men for men."[3] The problem was to both break into and break the circle. This realization of the "politics of knowledge"[4] has not decreased the vitality and importance of the feminist critiques. On the contrary. What has happened is that the focus of the critique has changed. The litany of illustrative cases to prove the feminist point has given way to far-reaching and innovative critiques of the epistemological basis of received wisdoms.

Part of this move has involved the critique of the traditions that have governed the discourse among men. In order to locate the feminist critique, students in women's studies courses must have a greater grasp of the fundamental tenets of the various disciplines, and of the social sciences in particular, because of the prescriptive knowledge that they have presumed to dispense. That knowledge has frequently been detrimental to the interests of women in their daily lives, even though it has been "blessed" by the presumed objectivity of the research.

The changes in the nature and reception of feminist inquiry have had a direct impact on the manner in which the information can be disseminated in the academy. This is particularly true for those large undergraduate courses in which many students are introduced to feminism for the first time. It was because of the changes indicated above and the fact that many of the women's studies courses I taught were large undergraduate courses with students from a range of disciplines that the idea for this text arose. The undergraduate courses demanded, first, an introduction to the basics of traditional sociological perspectives and, secondly, a discussion of feminist theoretical and methodological critiques. The interrelationship of these dual requirements was compounded by a particular feature of the feminist critiques: the rejection of traditional academic boundaries. The cross-disciplinary, comparative perspective involved in feminist critiques is one of the most stimulating aspects of the feminist revitalization within the academy.

Out of this complex of needs the present text emerged. It is designed as a preliminary view of the received wisdoms of the sociological fathers. The discussion of the work of the various theorists is not intended to be exhaustive, and the brief critical remarks addressed to each are not to be taken as definitive. It is assumed that the works and the criticisms can provide a basis for class discussion, as well as providing a framework upon which the vast range of empirical research on questions of sex differences and sex relations can be introduced and criticized. In essence, the "words" of the sociological fathers[5] are introduced as the point from which the raft of illustrative examples found in a variety of introductory texts can be meaningfully situated.

The basic organizing framework of the book is the dichotomized, hierarchical framework of knowledge production that has been particularly characteristic of western intellectual thought. The dichotomies applied to the sexes in which "natural" woman is contrasted with "rational," "cultured" man leads to the hierarchical social relations of subordination and domination that, in turn, are seen to be naturally and inevitably unchangeable. The works of the theorists examined in this text take this framework for granted.

The production of this text owes much to the ongoing, ever-stimulating discourse with a number of friends and colleagues, most especially Dallas Cullen, Ann-Marie Decore and Sharon Abu-Laban. In addition, the continuing debates within the Women's Studies Committee at the University of Alberta and with a number of students have provided an important stimulus to the writing of the book. Specifically, thanks must be extended to the reviewers, Angela Miles and Lorna Marsden, whose invaluable criticisms and suggestions contributed significantly to the final manuscript. My thanks also for the library research undertaken by Anita Molzahn for the Durkheim chapter. Last, but not least, my thanks to Valeria Irwin and Shirley Stawnychy for their patience with my constant revisions to the manuscript, often in the face of an impossible deadline.

It is hoped that the examination of these "classics" is a contribution to the feminist goal of, in Dorothy Smith's words, "remaking the relation between the systematically developed knowledge and the thought of the academy—and the everyday lives of womankind."[6]

NATURAL WOMEN, CULTURED MEN

CHAPTER 1

Society/Sociology

The question, "How is society possible?" provides the basic motivation for the construction of sociological theory. How the question is answered is coloured by the initial assumptions made about the nature of the data. For sociology, and for theorists of society, whether historians or philosophers, the assumptions made about the nature of human nature have affected the manner in which the analysis has been conducted. The assumptions have also influenced any subsequent proposals for social change made by theorists. For example, the belief that human nature was such that individuals were governed by continual desire that would invariably come into conflict with the desires of others led Hobbes to the conclusion that society was possible only through the imposition of a strong, central authority.[1] In contrast, the assumption that human nature is eminently reasonable and individuals recognize the need to limit and control desire if life is to be possible led John Locke to the conclusion that a social contract provided the basis for society.[2]

The assumptions made about the nature of human nature have been, theoretically, sex-blind; that is, human nature, whatever it is thought to be, has been used as a universal concept. However, the universality of the concept is usually qualified when the nuts-and-bolts of social organization are discussed. For example, according to Locke, all human beings, male and female, were equal in the state of nature. Both had the right to autonomy and freedom, and any particular differences between individuals could not affect this fundamental right. The organizations of the State evolved as a result of free individuals consenting to be governed by an abstract authority in the interest of protecting their private property.

The contractual agreement that legitimized political authority in

1

Locke's work was not, however, duplicated in the domestic authority of the husband over the wife. As Clark points out:

> There is a curious asymmetry between the sexes with respect to the consequences which follow from the fact that there are differences, natural and otherwise, between one person and another. The presupposition of a fundamental right to autonomy overrides any differences which may exist between individual men.
>
> The natural differences between the sexes, however, override any presupposition of an equal right to autonomy for men and women. *Here and only here a natural difference creates a justified domination of one person by another.*[3]

The "natural" difference that qualified women's autonomy was their reproductive capacity. Locke's presumption that women were unable to provide for their offspring by themselves meant that women were therefore naturally dependent on men.

"Natural" dependency for women was extended by Locke to social and economic dependence through the lack of property rights for a married woman. Since property and its enjoyment free from the predatory actions of others is the central issue in Locke's exposition, and since the right to transmit property without interference to legitimate heirs was critical, then the "natural" dependence of women in marriage was a necessity if property was to pass to the legitimate recipients. As Clark concludes, "If Adam does not own Eve, how can he be sure who his descendants are, and, hence, on whom his apples ought properly to devolve? And if Eve owns her own apples, why should she obey Adam?"[4]

The appeal to a "natural" difference between men and women based on the reproductive capacity of women has provided the framework for dichotomized views of the nature of the sexes and the assumption that hierarchical relations of male superiority and female subordination are justified by the dichotomy. The dichotomies produce a universe of superior men, but this universe remains dependent upon the natural universe of woman: hence the need for men to control women.

The theoretical asexual assumption of the nature of human nature, whether competitive or cooperative, maintains that all human beings are rational, active, creative beings. Humans, in contrast to the rest of the animal world, have the capacity for reflection and self-knowledge and consequently the means to control their life and destiny. Society is therefore an arrangement of social relationships that are more or less consciously designed by humans. In western thought, since the seventeenth century at least, the social arrangements have been generally understood as the result of the need to control and shape the natural world in the interests of human beings.[5] Nature is a force we must conquer rather than accept and accommodate ourselves to. The rational, active, creative human therefore stands in contrast to the natural, passive world of nature, which humans are "divinely ordained" or "rationally constrained" to control for their own ends.

Human actions, however, transform the sex-blind assumptions about human nature. The female is associated with the natural world, and generic Man becomes men who are connected with the world of nature through women. It is woman's biological specificity, her reproductive capacity, that is the reason for her association directly with the world of animal nature.

Generic man, in thought and practice, becomes man-the-measure of culture in contrast to, but dependent upon, woman as the repository of the natural. For example, Aristotle thought that the female was an incomplete version of the male. He suggested that in terms of reproduction, the contributions of men and women differed such that "the body is from the female, it is the soul that is from the male, for the soul is the reality of the particular body . . ."[6] Consequently, since the "rule of the soul over the body, and of the mind and the rational element over the passionate is natural expedient; whereas the equality of the two or the rule of the inferior is always hurtful," it follows that men are fit to rule and women to obey. The duality of male/female was complemented further by the duality of completion/incompletion, active/passive, form/matter, perfection/imperfection, possession/deprivation.[7]

The dualities, or dichotomies, between the sexes are elaborated, with few variations, in subsequent western thought and practice, especially in regard to women's sexual desires and proclivities. For many Renaissance thinkers and medical men, the uterus was the source of women's greater proneness to hysteria; not only did it weaken their rationality, but also increased the incidence and violence of the passions of hate, vengeance, fear and anger. All these emotions were thought to hold greater sway over females, although compassion, pity and love were also more common to women and could soften the effects of the former emotions. The physiological and psychological disabilities—the "frailty of the body" and the resulting "mental and emotional weaknesses"—produced the "natural justification for their exclusion from public life, responsibility and moral fulfillment."[8]

The metaphorical identification of women with nature, as in the connection of women with the fruitfulness of the earth, meant that there could be contrary interpretations of the connection. From a positive viewpoint, women, as a part of the divine plan, were closer to nature than men and could therefore provide men with the means through which they could understand nature, and by extension, the intentions of the divinity. Some of the fifteenth-century neo-Platonic conceptions of love suggested that the contemplation of earthly beauty could be the means by which the human soul could approach an understanding of the divine. As Ficino suggested: "Regaining the memory of the true and divine beauty by the appearance of beauty that the eyes perceive, we desire the former with a secret and unutterable ardour of the mind."[9] The contemplation of beauty, in whatever manifestation, should not be a passive act. To enjoy without seeking "anything beyond the form his eyes can see" is to Ficino the mark of a "dull and corrupt state" that produces the "kind of love that is the companion of wantoness and lust".[10] Consequently, the celebration of women's beauty as a conduit to the understanding of the divine was to be contained by matrimony. Matrimony would provide man with a "domestic republic" that could, in turn, provide him with the necessary skills for command in the political republic. Domesticity could be a training ground for budding politicians. Furthermore, domesticity meant that "man, as if divine, continuously preserved the human race through succession."[11] The prudent rule of the domestic sphere could also ensure mankind's future status in heaven:

> If you wish to be men and lawful sons of God, increase the human race legitimately, and, just as you are like God, so in the fashion of God, beget sons like yourselves . . . And remember! In family affairs, which need to be so carefully directed, have due regard to yourselves: gain skill and acquire authority in the earthly commonwealth; be worthy of office in the heavenly commonwealth.[12]

For many theorists, women could prove to be true helpmates for men within the legitimate bonds of matrimony and as long as the latter's regard for them did not involve too much lust. Yet, the very association of women with the natural world that would allow men a glimpse of the divine plan, could, in other more negative interpretations, ensure a swift descent into sin and corruption.

The authors of the *Malleus Maleficarum* (Hammer of Witches) suggested that the major reason for the incidence of more female than male witches was because women were "naturally more impressionable, and more ready to receive the influence of a disembodied spirit;" and as they were "feebler both in mind and body, it is not surprising that they should come more under the spell of witchcraft."[13] According to the pious monks who authored the investigation into witchcraft, the initial formation of women from a "bent rib, that is, a rib of the breast, which is bent as it were in a contrary direction to man," made them an "imperfect animal,"[14] more prone to the lures of the devil. In sum, "All witchcraft comes from carnal lust, which is in women insatiable."[15]

Women's sexuality could be the "devil's gateway," or women's beauty could be the means by which men could learn to "guide the society of mankind itself."[16] Marriage, for men, could ensure love of country, compassion, endurance and the ability to conquer adversity; in short, marriage in which the wife was dutifully submissive to the husband was part of the natural law of mankind. Alternatively, marriage could be regarded as a necessary evil for men unable to resist the desires of the flesh. Whatever the interpretation, women were men's opposites, and the opposition was a necessary but potentially negative one.

The distinction between the nature of the female as opposed to the male, and the consequent dichotomized social universe derived from this distinction, provide a basic framework for the examination of the social organization of sex relationships in the western European context. In general, the competitive, exploitive and individualistic interests of men are, ideally, tempered by the cooperative, nurturing and communal interests of women—as long as women are controlled within the legitimate bonds of marriage, or kept within the domestic sphere. The private, domestic world of women can be contrasted with the public world of action in which men order and control nature. This dichotomy is exemplified in the conclusion drawn by another fifteenth-century Italian author:

> Men are by nature of a more elevated mind than women. They are more suited to struggle with arms and with cunning against the misfortunes which afflict country, religion, and one's own children. The character of men is stronger than that of women and can bear the attacks of enemies better, can stand strain longer, is more constant under stress. Therefore, men have the freedom to travel with honor in

foreign lands, acquiring and gathering the goods of fortune. Women, on the other hand, are almost timid by nature, soft, slow, and therefore more useful when they sit still and watch over things. It is as though nature thus provided for our well-being, arranging for men to bring things home and for women to guard them.[17]

The distinctions drawn between the sexes continue in western social theory and are generally similar to those elaborated above. For example, Hegel maintained that a woman's sphere was marriage and that a woman "in the feeling of family piety realizes her ethical disposition." Family piety for women was

the law of nature, which realizes itself subjectively and intuitively, the law of an inner life, which has not yet attained complete realization, the law of the ancient gods, and of the underworld, the eternal law, of whose origin no one knows, in opposition to the public law of the state. This opposition is in the highest sense ethical, and hence also tragic, it is individualized in the opposing natures of man and woman.[18]

Schopenhauer felt that women had a natural need to be controlled by men because of their deficiency of reason. In his view, "woman is by nature meant to obey . . . she needs a lord and master. If she is young, it will be a lover; if she is old, a priest."[19] Unfortunately, according to Schopenhauer, men were often innocent of the true nature of women because of their sexual needs.

It is only the man whose intellect is clouded by his sexual impulses that could give the name of *the fair sex* to that undersized, narrow-shouldered, broad-hipped, and short-legged race; . . . Instead of calling them beautiful, there would be more warrant for describing women as the unaesthetic sex.[20]

Finally, Darwin's conclusions on sex differences provided a "scientific" basis for many traditional assumptions. Darwin's belief that men were "more courageous, pugnacious and energetic than women, and [had] a more inventive genius," was accepted by many nineteenth-century thinkers, including social scientists. More recent variations on the same theme can be found in the work of sociobiologists. Using animal research, usually dealing with the large primates, and the assumption that evolutionary, functional universals have been discovered, sociobiology attempts to substantiate the claim that male dominance is a constant feature of both animal and human society. It is a "natural" phenomenon and therefore tampering with this arrangement would produce conflict and be dangerous to the natural well-being of both sexes. As a twentieth-century variation of this theme, Morris suggests that

> Behind the facade of modern city life there is the same old naked ape. Only the names have been changed: for "hunting" read "working", for "hunting ground" read "place of business", for "home base" read "house", for "pair-bond" read "marriage", for "mate" read "wife", and so on.[21]

The belief in the ideas illustrated above regarding the sexual dichotomy and the resultant natural superiority of men over women have been, and continue to be, subject to variations. In any daily interaction, modifications are made by both men and women no matter how patriarchal the society. Private domesticity has, for example, never contained all women or even, for a good part of western European history, the majority of women. The public arena of action and decision has rarely been the place in which all men, or the majority of men, could assert significant control over the events of the material and/or social world. In many ways the ideas regarding the nature of the sexes have been changeable blueprints, superimposed on an equally changeable frame of social-structural arrangements. In addition, the particular structural and ideological mixes characteristic of the western European experience have not been universal, although sociologists and others have, on occasion, assumed that they were.

The assumption that there are critical differences between the sexes, which results in the allocation of different tasks to women and men, as well as to different evaluations of the sexes and the products of their labour, is common to most societies. But the sort of assumptions made and the sort of tasks allocated differ greatly among societies. For example, in some societies the dichotomy is used as a basis for a much more rigorous separation between the sexes than has been characteristic of western European societies. The segregation, concealment and confinement of many women in Middle Eastern societies show greater adherence to the idea of the private, domestic place for women than has ever characterized most European societies. In contrast, in Africa, Yoruba women are traders in the marketplace and are the lynchpins of the economy.[22] Among the Mbuti of Zaire, both men and women plan and participate in hunting, and female elders have considerable power.[23] And although the hunting activities of the male Ilongots of the Philippines are more highly valued than the gardening of the women, the "two modes of production are seen as complementary and the division of labour is not strict." In fact, "during the day, when women are gardening, men spend long hours with their children."[24]

Whatever the specific nature of the variations among societies in the allocation of tasks to the sexes, there appears to be a general asymmetry in the cultural evaluations of men and women. The asymmetry is most clearly understood in terms of the public/private, cultural/natural, labour/domestic dichotomy. In general, tasks in the public sphere are assigned to males, and they receive more prestige or status than the tasks undertaken by women. The association of women with domestic life has stemmed from the biological fact that women reproduce. However, as de Beauvoir pointed out, biology itself is a cultural and historical artifact; woman's reproduction can be, and has been, interpreted in a variety of ways and has given rise to a range of behaviours associated with the conception, carrying, birthing and subsequent care of the offspring.[25] "The bearing of maternity upon the individual life, regulated naturally in animals by the oestrus cycle and the seasons, is not definitely prescribed in women—society alone is the arbiter."[26]

Understanding the nature and the consequences of the dichotomized social reality that has characterized past western European thought is critical to a critique of past sociological theory. There, the dichotomy was largely taken for granted, along with the resulting "natural" hierarchy of authority and power between the sexes. The recent burgeoning of feminist critical analysis of received wisdoms has recognized the dichotomized perspective as a problem, along with the assumption that social reality is sufficiently accounted for by examining what men do, decide and think. For example, Oakley pointed out that the work of the housewife was invisible to traditional sociologists. In fact, women only registered in the sociological accounts when the family was examined and even then ". . . the largest segment of sociological literature concerning women is focused on their roles as wives, mothers and housewives—but not on the housewife's role as houseworker."[27] A brief sociological reference to housework in the early 1960s can be found in Caplow's *The Sociology of Work*. He suggested that:

One of the reasons for the widespread maladjustment of housewives

may be inferred from the circumstance that the same job requirements are imposed on morons and women of superior intelligence.
There is no age requirement either. Girls of ten years and upwards
may be able to keep house competently, and it is frequently done by
women in their eighties.[28]

Caplow's description is culturally relative as well as an inaccurate
generalization for all North American women. Household tasks
encompass more than some basic cooking and cleaning, which
Caplow's remarks imply. Housework is affected by the class and
status position of the household, the number of household
members, their age, and a variety of other considerations, as Oakley
and others have demonstrated.[29] To regard housework in the same
undifferentiated way that Caplow does is possible only if the work
is defined as non-work in the context of the prevailing dichotomy
that defines paid labour as work, but unpaid domestic labour as
something other than work.

Sociology has generally accepted the idea of a sexual dichotomy
and the assumption that women inhabited, ideally, a privatized
domestic sphere and men the public world of action, decision,
power and authority. Some women might have been found in the
public realm, but their roles were regarded as problematic both to
the men with whom they interacted as well as to themselves. These
"deviant" women could be particularly upsetting to the well-being
of the family. To avoid such a development, Talcott Parsons
suggested that the major status of an adult, urban woman should be
that of housewife, a status symmetrical with the "fundamental
basis of the family's status," which is determined by the occupation
of the husband/father. For those women who follow "the masculine pattern and seek a career in fields of occupational achievement," Parsons warns that most of these women, "whose occupational status is comparable with that of men in their own class, at
least in the upper middle and upper classes, are unmarried, and in
the small proportion of cases where they are married the result is a
profound alteration in family structure."[30] Parsons leaves no doubt
that the profound alteration would be socially, if not personally, for
the individuals involved, destabilizing.

The sociological assumption that the social is defined in terms of
the public sphere in which men interact and towards which the
private sphere (at least ideally) reacts has had significant consequences for sociological theorizing. For example, if the evolution of

society is seen to be defined by the progressive differentiation and specialization of functions, including those between the sexes, in accordance with their biological and mental capacities, then women are likely to be defined out of the public spheres of action in a modern, industrial society—which is precisely the basis of Durkheim's analysis, as we shall discover.

In general, sociology, in accepting the idea of a dichotomized world as natural, has neglected to take into account the private, domestic sphere of women. Instead, sociological theorizing focused on the dynamics of class, status, power, authority and social conflict — all generated by, controlled by and affecting men directly. As a result, social class has been linked to male occupational categories, and the fact of women's paid labour has either been ignored or explained as a special, separate problem; status has been examined in terms of men's interaction and the contribution of women has been acknowledged only in a peripheral sense of "drawing-room" manipulations; power and authority have been seen to refer to the legitimate formal and informal exchanges among men in which women, as power-holders, can appear only as anomalies or as problem cases. The key point is that sociology has had a blinkered, and therefore partial, perspective on the nature of the social world, which has meant the *de facto* exclusion of women's realities from the accounts.

In the following chapters we will examine some of the major theoretical contributions to sociological theory of Durkheim, Weber, Marx, Engels and Freud. They are important to sociological theory in the western European tradition as well as to the manner in which their understanding of patriarchy, class, status and ideology relates to an understanding of sex relations. Although Marx, Engels and Freud are not, strictly speaking, sociologists, their work has influenced sociological thought in important ways. The central perspective brought to bear on all the accounts will be the dichotomy and resulting hierarchy of sex relations that provide the explicit or implicit foundation for classical sociological theory.

We will begin with an examination of Durkheim's work and proceed to that of Weber, Marx and Engels, and then Freud. In our discussion of the five theorists, some important aspects of their work have not been addressed for reasons of space limitations. For example, the work on religion undertaken by Weber, Durkheim and Freud is not discussed, despite the fact that a significant feminist critique could result. More than Weber or Durkheim, it has been Marx, Engels and Freud who have informed the recent feminist critiques and whose works feminist theory has addressed. The reason for this attention is found in the more prescriptive content of their work. Finally, we will examine the process of theorizing from the perspective of feminist critiques of science and sociology.

CHAPTER 2

Durkheim's Science of Sociology and Sex-Role Differences

Emile Durkheim, more than anyone else, is credited with the systematization of the sociological enterprise as a separate discipline and with entrenching sociology within the academy.[1] For this reason, his work is considered first in this text, even though, chronologically, Marx and Engels preceded him.

Durkheim was concerned with defining the relations between the individual and society through the methods of science, continuing the work of his predecessor, Comte. However, whereas Comte's analysis was philosophical, Durkheim wished to give sociology a more systematic, scientific basis. In his view the "vague generalities on the nature of societies, on the relations between the social and biological realms, and on the general march of progress"[2] that had marked previous sociological work had to be replaced with more rigorous scientific methods if sociology was to do more than "paraphrase the traditional prejudices of the common man."[3] Durkheim's ideas are contained in *The Rules of Sociological Method*, the major point being that social facts have to be studied as "things," that is, as detached from individuals and explained in terms of other social facts. The objectivity of the social is the basic theme that runs throughout Durkheim's work.

Despite Durkheim's methodological assumptions and prescriptions he has a dichotomized, hierarchical perspective regarding the sexes. For example, the dichotomies of social organization discussed in *The Division of Labor in Society* have different consequences for the understanding and experience of the dualism of human nature and, by implication, for men as opposed to women. The biological, egotistical nature of "man" is contrasted with his intellectual, moral nature. The realization of the dualism, in terms of social structures and normative regulation, differs according to the degree of social solidarity and the sex of the individual. The nature of these connections will form the substance of the following discussions.

We begin with an examination of *The Division of Labor in Society* and proceed to a discussion of marriage, family and gender roles found in Durkheim's writings.

SOCIAL SOLIDARITY

The unprecedented development of specialization and heterogeneity characteristic of modern, industrializing societies generated considerable concern among nineteenth-century thinkers about the continuing harmony and integration of society. In the celebration of the autonomous individual that accompanied these structural changes, it was feared that the moral regulation and the social solidarity of society would be destroyed, resulting in disorder and even anarchy. As Durkheim pointed out, "If public opinion sanctions the division of labor, it is not without a sort of uneasiness and hesitation. While commanding men to specialize, it seems to fear they will specialize too much."[4] But Durkheim observed that, in reality, the greater the autonomy of the individual, the greater the individual's dependence on society. The central question in *The Division of Labor* is, therefore, "How can he be at once more individual and more solidary?"[5] Durkheim's solution to this contradiction is that social solidarity is transformed by the development of the division of labour; that is, "the division of labor is the source, if not unique, at least principal, of social solidarity."[6]

Since social solidarity is a "moral phenomenon" that cannot be subjected to "exact observation nor indeed to measurement,"[7] then some external index is required to relate the division of labour and social solidarity. The external index Durkheim used was the law.

> Social life . . . tends inevitably to assume a definite form and to organize itself, and law is nothing else than this very organization in so far as it has greater stability and precision. The general life of society cannot extend its sway without juridical life extending its

sway at the same time and in direct relation. We can thus be certain of finding reflected in law all the essential varieties of social solidarity.[8]

His examination of systems of law as expressions of the moral regulation of society was based on the legal sanctions that enforce the moral codes of society. Durkheim identified two types of sanctions: repressive and restitutive. Repressive sanctions are characteristic of penal law, and restitutive sanctions of "civil law, commercial law, procedural law, administrative and constitutional law." The latter, in contrast to penal law, "does not necessarily imply suffering for the agent, but consists only of *the return of things as they were.*"[9] The two types of sanctions are representative of two forms of social solidarity: repressive sanctions are representative of mechanical solidarity, and restitutive sanctions of organic solidarity.

The legal sanctions represent the society's reaction to the "outrage to morality"[10] that the criminal act represents. In the case of repressive sanctions the outrage is greater because of the greater unity and strength of the collectively held moral beliefs. The "collective or common conscience" represents the "totality of beliefs and sentiments common to average citizens of the same society." The collective conscience is held by individuals, but also "has its own life" apart from the particular beliefs and sentiments of the individual members of society."[11] The greater unity and strength of the collective conscience in mechanical solidarity is a consequence of the homogeneity of society, in which the division of labour is minimal. In such societies, "the individual does not appear . . . Individuality is something that society possesses."[12] Consequently, a crime in such society is a crime against the total community and generates the need for a collective, passionate expiation.

In a society characterized by organic solidarity, the increased division of labour results in greater differences between individuals and, consequently, a greater need to regulate the relations between individuals. Therefore, restitutive sanctions that express "the relations governed by cooperative law" predominate. Although the direct effects of the collective conscience are modified by the greater autonomy of the individual in organic society, the collective conscience makes itself felt in the ties that connect the autonomous individuals. The clearest example of the collective conscience at work, according to Durkheim, was to be found in contract law.

Contract law represents the need for individuals to co-operate but, "in order for them to co-operate harmoniously, it is not enough that they enter into a relationship, nor that they feel the state of mutual dependence in which they find themselves."[13] The contract must take account of future consequences of the co-operative venture, and this can only be done on the basis of past experiences of similar co-operative acts. As a result, the contract between two individuals is imbued with the general social experience of such transactions. The individual is therefore connected to the collective conscience under organic solidarity through the contractual ties.

> Even where society relies most completely upon the division of labor, it does not become a jumble of juxtaposed atoms, between which it can establish only external, transient contacts. Rather the members are united by ties which extend deeper and far beyond the short moments during which the exchange is made.[14]

Under mechanical solidarity, the "similitude of consciences gives rise to juridical rules which, with the threat of repressive measures, imposes uniform beliefs and practices upon all." In contrast, the division of labour in organic solidarity "gives rise to juridical rules which determine the nature and the relations of divided functions, but whose violation calls forth only restitutive measures without any expiatory character."[15] As a result, Durkheim maintains that "it is wrong to oppose a society which comes from a community of beliefs to one which has a co-operative basis, according only to the first a moral character, and seeing in the latter only an economic grouping. In reality, co-operation also has its intrinsic morality."[16] In fact, co-operative society "develops in the measure that individual personality becomes stronger."[17] The collective conscience itself in organic solidarity becomes "more and more a cult of that individual," but the morality this embodies is "more human, therefore more rational" than that of mechanical solidarity.

> It does not direct our activities to ends which do not immediately concern us; . . . It only asks that we be thoughtful of our fellows and that we be just, that we fulfill our duty, that we work at the function we can best execute, and receive the just reward for our services. The rules which constitute it do not have a constraining force which snuffs out free thought; but, because they are rather made for us and, in a certain sense, by us, we are free.[18]

The "cult of the individual" that is characteristic of organic solidarity does not imply the free, unregulated reign of egoistic impulses. Freedom is a condition of society, not of its absence. Under mechanical solidarity, social regulation takes the form of maintaining "as intense a common life as possible, in which the individual is absorbed." In contrast, organic solidarity makes "social relations more equitable, so as to ensure the free development of all our socially useful forces."[19] Liberty is found in society because it is "only in so far as man raises himself above things and makes law for them, thus depriving them of their fortuitous, absurd, amoral character" that man can become a social being. "For he can escape nature only by creating another world where he dominates nature. That world is society."[20]

In general, societies progress from mechanical to organic solidarity as a result of increased interaction (moral density) and population growth (social volume). These developments necessitate a greater division of labour, reflected in greater specialization and the differentiation of structure and function in society. The progression from mechanical to organic solidarity can be demonstrated in Durkheim's discussion of the evolution of marital and family relations.

> The history of the family, from its origins, is only an uninterrupted movement of dissociation in the course of which diverse functions, at first undivided and confounded one with another, have been little by little separated, constituted apart, apportioned among relatives according to sex, age, relations of dependence, in a way to make each of them a special functionary of domestic society.[21]

Durkheim makes a critical distinction between marriage and the family regarding the evolution of the division of labour and social solidarity. The modern conjugal family that Durkheim defined as "the husband, the wife, and minor and unmarried children"[22] was the result of progressive contraction of family relations and the increasing regulation of the marital relationship by society in the form of political and legal regulations. Durkheim's account is interesting in that, although changes in the family occur as the division of labour increases in society generally, changes in marital relations seem to reverse the process. In addition, the changes in both family and marital relations have different consequences for the sexes, which leads to the contradictory position that Durkheim is forced to adopt in regard to women when the negative consequences of the conjugal family are examined in his study of suicide.

In terms of the family, as opposed to marriage, Durkheim sees the general "law of contraction or progressive emergence" as being "thoroughly verified."[23] As Mauss suggests, "The dominant theme of the history of family institutions is, according to Durkheim, the reduction in the number of family members and the concentration of family ties."[24] The family contracts with the expansion of specialized, differentiated structures in society that increasingly take over family functions. Initially, the homogeneous clan, formed from the horde and united around the sacred totem, became the family group. In *The Division of Labor in Society*, Durkheim used the Iroquois as his example of such an unspecialized family group. Among the Iroquois, he suggested that "kinship itself was not organized, for we cannot give this name to the distribution of the mass in generations."[25] At the time of Durkheim's writing, he indicated that the Iroquois had some special obligations that united the child with the maternal relatives, but "these relations come to very little and are not sensibly distinguishable from those that bind the child to other members of society." In fact, "originally, all persons of the same age were kin in the same degree."[26]

The separation of smaller groups from the large, relatively undifferentiated clan organization occurs with the progression of society from mechanical to organic solidarity. The clan represented a "family communism," an association in which all property was held in common. This family type gradually contracts in size, along with the communism of property, until in the modern "conjugal family there remain only vestiges of communism."[27] At the conjugal stage, family solidarity is transformed. As Durkheim pointed out, family solidarity rested on two factors, persons and things. "We are attached to our family because we are attached to the people who compose it. But we are attached to it also because we cannot do without material things, and under the regime of familial communism it is the family that possesses these things."[28] When family communism ceases, then the material things no longer serve as a source of solidarity. As a result, "family solidarity becomes completely personal. We are attached to our family only because we are attached to the persons of our father, our mother, our wife, our children."[29]

It is within the conjugal family, with its restricted and personalized basis for solidarity, that Durkheim points to two different contexts in which solidarity is structured and maintained: the marital relationship itself and the family.

The family environment consists of different elements. For the husband and the wife alike the family includes: 1. the wife or husband; 2. the children . . . In other words, the family consists of two different associations: the conjugal group and the family group proper. These two societies have not the same origin, nor the same nature, nor consequently . . . the same effects. One springs from a contract and elective affinity, the other from a natural phenomenon, consanguinity; the former unites two members of the same generation, the latter unites one generation to the next; the latter is as old as humanity, the former was organized at a relatively late date.[30]

The two associations have different functions and are regulated in different ways by society. With regard to the children, the state increasingly intervenes on their behalf and ensures that kinship ties are indissoluble by taking them "under its protection," thus depriving "individuals of the right to break them."[31] At the same time, however, the family has a "less common life" and is "less powerfully integrated" because "all the children sooner or later depart from the (paternal) homestead."[32] The restricted time frame and the small size of the conjugal family meant that the collective consciousness was only weakly represented. "[I]n a family of small numbers, common sentiments and memories cannot be very intense; for there are not enough consciences in which they can be represented and reinforced by sharing them. . . . Small families are also invariably short-lived; and without duration no society can be stable."[33]

One of the ways in which society acted on the family was through the stimulation to work that was generated by dependants. The occupational role, especially for the modern conjugal family, was a means by which the negative effects of egoism were countered and social solidarity reinforced. This was especially the case in regard to inheritance. Although Durkheim felt that inheritance would, in time, be eliminated, he also recognized that something was needed in its place to motivate individuals and counter egoism. Inheritance, that is the transmission of valued goods, was a vestige of the old familial communism. It was familial communism that had accustomed individuals to making inheritance the mainspring of their occupational activities. "Our attachment to work lies in its capacity to enrich the domestic patrimony, to add to the well-being of our children. If this prospect were taken away from us, a powerful moral stimulant would be removed in one fell swoop."[34]

If the family were destined to fail as a moral stimulant to social activity, then it should be replaced by something else. Durkheim then asked, "Could it be matrimonial society?"[35]

Durkheim points out that modern marriage has been strengthened at the same time that family life has weakened. Marriage, in organic society, becomes "well-nigh indissoluble," and "monogamy . . . nearly perfect" and increasingly regulated by domestic law, although "the obligations that result from this are of an eminently positive nature."[36] In contrast to former times when it was probable, according to Durkheim, that there was no such thing as marriage, and sexual relations were somewhat casual affairs "entered into and broken at will without any juridical obligations linking the union," or at best were regulated by "temporary and partial" contract,[37] under organic solidarity, sexual unions and marriage become highly regulated. At the same time, the marital relationship "makes its action felt at each moment and in all the details of life."[38]

The strength of marriage under organic solidarity is limited by two factors. First, it is regulated by the society, and secondly, it is no longer a personal contract. This public contractual character of marriage is consistent with the contractual nature of relationships in organic solidarity. However, the second aspect of the marital relationship contradicts the general trends. The contradiction is to be found in the community of property rule between spouses. The rule might be evaded, but "it exists in full right if there are no contravening conventions." As a result, "while communism was departing from domestic society, it was making its appearance in matrimonial society."[39]

Was it possible, Durkheim asked, that conjugal love could provide the replacement for love of family as the mainspring of moral action? It would seem not, because "conjugal society by itself is too ephemeral, its vistas are too restricted for such results."[40] The moral impetus provided by work results from the belief that the fruits of that labour will survive the individual and be of benefit to those who come after. "But conjugal society . . . is dissolved by death in each generation. Spouses do not long survive each other. Consequently, one of them cannot be a strong enough reason to make the other sacrifice momentary pleasures."[41]

Although marriage and family cannot provide the means to ensure solidarity and protection for the individual from egoism and anomie, they are still important mechanisms for society. Since it is marriage that increasingly provides the "exclusive basis of kinship," then it is marriage that must be regulated by society. Therefore, "any sexual union not contracted under matrimonial regulation is accordingly subversive of duty and of domestic bonds."[42] Irregular sexual union, "free unregulated union," undermines the moral obligations individuals have to one another and produces an "immoral society." This is why "children reared in such environments show so many moral defects—they have not been exposed to a moral environment." For the welfare of the children, as well as society, the juridical regulation of marriage was essential to organic solidarity. "A child cannot have a moral upbringing unless he lives in a society whose every member feels his obligations toward every other member. For outside such a society there is not morality."[43]

The strict regulation of marriage has different consequences, however, for women than for men. These differences illustrate clearly the underlying assumptions about gender differences Durkheim brought to his analyses of marriage and family.

Generally, Durkheim's discussions of marriage and family were similar, in their evolutionary and comparative method, to those of other nineteenth-century evolutionists and ethnographers. Like Engels, Durkheim was indebted to the work of Morgan on kinship systems, but unlike Morgan, Durkheim rejected the idea that the initial human associations were promiscuous hordes, or that kinship regulation was the result of biological instinct. In his view, marriage and family were social institutions of rights and obligations that varied among societies and were regulated by systems of kinship terminology. Kinship relations, in turn, stemmed from the religious and moral beliefs and structures of a society, not from biological connections. For example, Durkheim suggests that "primitive family organization cannot be understood before the primitive religious beliefs are known; for the latter serve as the basis of the former. This is why it is necessary to study totemism as a religion before studying the totemic clan as a family group."[44]

Understanding family organization and marital relations as a social rather than a biologically based phenomenon seems to remove Durkheim from the sort of essentialist arguments that produce the dichotomized understanding of sex roles. However, this is not the case. The progressive division of labour and the increased specialization of functions are also seen to apply to the sexes, both organically and socially. In fact, the strengthening of the marital bond is seen to be tied to the increasing organic differences between the sexes. For example, Durkheim suggested that "the state of marriage in societies where the two sexes are only weakly differentiated thus evinces a conjugal solidarity which is itself very weak."[45]

Durkheim's discussion of the differences between the sexes assumed a biological basis for increased social differentiation. As he pointed out, "The woman of past days was not at all the weak creature that she has become with the progress of morality."[46] Indeed, he suggested that the female form could be regarded as the "aboriginal image of what was the one and only type from which the masculine variety slowly detached itself."[47] Durkheim takes this observation from "travelers' reports," as well as from a scientific study of male and female brains undertaken by a Dr. Lebon. Dr. Lebon claimed to have been able to establish "with mathematical precision this original resemblance of the two sexes in regard to the pre-eminent organ of physical and psychic life, the brain." Durkheim quotes Lebon to the effect that,

> The volume of the crania of man and woman, even when we compare subjects of equal age, of equal height and equal weight, show considerable differences in favor of the man, and this inequality grows proportionally with civilization, so that from the point of view of the mass of the brain, and correspondingly of intelligence, woman tends more and more to be differentiated from the male sex.[48]

The progressive differentiation of anatomy is marked also by the progressive differentiation of economic and political functions as well as personality differences. Durkheim observed that "there is even now a very great number of savage people where the woman mingles in political life," and in some cases women accompany men to war. In general, in more primitive, undifferentiated societies, woman "participates in myriad ways in the men's lives" so that "one of the distinctive contemporary qualities of woman, gentility, does not appear to pertain to her in primitive society."[49]

As the division of labour increases, and the marital union takes on more obligations so that "the union of two people has ceased to be ephemeral," sexual labour also becomes differentiated. At first the difference is limited to sexual functions, but over time the division of labour is extended, so that "long ago, woman retired from warfare and public affairs, and consecrated her entire life to her family. Since then, her role has become even more specialized. Today, among cultivated people, the woman leads a completely different existence from that of the man."[50] The difference between the sexes is both organic, in the sense of physiological and psychological, as well as socially necessary, in the sense of functional, to society. With regard to organic differences, Durkheim again relies on the work of Lebon, who was apparently able to demonstrate not only the differences in height and weight between the sexes but also the differences in the brain that the "progress of civilization" produces. In general, he found the differences in the brain were due to "considerable development of the masculine crania and to a stationary or even regressive state of female crania."[51]

The increasing divergence of the sexes with the progress of civilization is tied to the psychological needs and capacities of the sexes so that "one of the sexes takes care of the affective functions and the other of intellectual functions."[52] The organic, physiological and psychological differences between the sexes are therefore matched with the differences in their social roles and, in line with the general social differentiation of structure and function, the dichotomies are functional to the solidarity of society. Durkheim pointed out that,

> If the sexes were not separated at all, an entire category of social life would be absent. It is possible that the economic utility of the division of labor may have a hand in this, but, in any case, it passes far beyond purely economic interests, for it consists in the establishment of a social and moral order *sui generis*. Through it, individuals are linked to one another. Without it, they would be independent.[53]

Marriage, or conjugal society, is the foremost illustration of the solidarity generated by the division of labour; in fact, the history of conjugal society provides an example of the real function of the division of labour: "to create in two or more persons a feeling of solidarity."[54] He points out that sexual attraction is based on similarity, that it occurs between "individuals of the same type," and that "love generally asks a certain harmony of thought and sentiment," but the real energy and character of sexual attraction is difference. "Precisely because man and woman are different, they seek each other passionately." Yet it is not just a simple contrast but a difference that requires the other for "mutual fruition." It is the sexual division of labour that generates "conjugal solidarity" and makes possible "the strongest of all unselfish inclinations."[55]

This harmonious relationship, so necessary to the moral health of organic society depends upon a strict role differentiation between the sexes. Women undertake the internal, private, affective tasks, and men the external, public, instrumental tasks. The family and conjugal unit is, however, a restricted sphere having shed many of its former functions and been removed from the central activities of social life. As a result, it has different consequences for men, who are involved in social life, compared to women, who are restricted to domestic life. The summary offered by Davy of Durkheim's view of the modern conjugal family is one that, in its positive effects, can apply to the husband and, possibly, the children, but only minimally to the wife and mother.

> [The family] is not only the framework which socially sustains the individual and constitutes the organized defense of certain of his interests. It is also the moral milieu where his tendencies are disciplined and where his aspirations toward the ideal are born, begin to expand, and continue to be maintained . . . in providing a place of refreshment where effort may be relaxed and the will reinvigorated; in fixing for this will and this effort, . . . an end which goes beyond egoistic and momentary enjoyments; in forming, finally, a refuge where the wounds of life may find their consolation and errors their pardon, the family is the centre of morality, energy and gentleness, a school of duty, love and work, in a word, a school of life which cannot lose its role.[56]

The essential role of the family was, however, maintained at the expense of women, especially when they had no means to escape the relationship. As we have seen, the indissolubility of marriage was especially important, in Durkheim's view. It was important in the socialization of future generations as well as in providing individuals—and here it is men who are meant as they are the ones who "work"—with goals that transcended themselves and therefore protected the individual from the negative consequences of anomie and egoism. The recognition of the problem of what the indissoluble conjugal tie might mean to women is first referred to in *The Division of Labor in Society*, in the discussion of the relationship between the division of labour and happiness.

Durkheim was at pains to refute the proposition that the cause of the division of labour was "man's unceasing desire to increase his happiness."[57] He pointed out that happiness is the result of individuals' realization of their nature. Happiness is therefore relative, and so "the happiness of man is not that of woman," just as "that of lower societies cannot be ours."[58] In fact, contrary to the initial proposition, Durkheim found that unhappiness, as measured by suicide rates, increases with the division of labour and, as civilization progresses, unhappiness is likely to increase, especially for men.

> The classes of population furnish suicide a quota proportionate to their degrees of civilization. Everywhere the liberal professions are hardest hit, and agriculture the least. It is the same with the sexes. Woman has had less part than man in the movement of civilization. She participates less and derives less profit. She recalls, moreover, certain characteristics of primitive natures. Thus, there is about one fourth the suicides among women as among men.[59]

The relationship of the sexes to suicide is pursued in more detail in Durkheim's *Suicide*. In general, Durkheim's investigation of suicide rates suggested that modern society was problematic for women to the extent that it was made more congenial for men, but that this situation seemed to be insoluble as long as the organic differences between the sexes were poorly accommodated by social-structural differentiation.

SUICIDE

As stated, the progressive division of labour in society calls for different forms of moral regulation. Under organic solidarity the weight of the collective conscience is muted by the emphasis upon the individual. The solitary egoism of the individual in such a society is, however, overcome by the "rights and duties which link [men] together in a durable way."[60] However, the contractual regulation of social relations may be faulty, especially if "all the conditions for the existence of organic solidarity have not been realized."[61] As a result, a breakdown or the absence of social regulation generates social pathologies such as suicide.

As Lukes points out, the subject of suicide had been of interest to European scholars since the eighteenth century. Many believed that the suicide rates of modern societies were the inevitable result of the "cult of the individual" and the decline in the traditional order of social relations. Suicide, as an index of social instability, was "taken up, with differing emphases, by conservatives, Catholics, Saint-Simonians, Positivists, liberals and socialists."[62] "All agreed in condemning 'l'odieux individualism'—the social, moral and political isolation of self-interes.ed individuals, unattached to social ideas and unamenable to social control; and they saw it as spelling the breakdown of social solidarity."[63]

Suicide was therefore of natural interest to Durkheim and extended his inquiry of social solidarity found in *The Division of Labor*. In addition, an examination of suicide represented an ideal way of demonstrating the distinct subject matter and methods of sociology. The methodological importance of the work will be discussed in more detail below. Suffice it to say here that by selecting the most individual and private of acts as a fit subject for sociological investigation, Durkheim wanted to demonstrate that sociology differed from psychology and had a subject matter of its own. As Durkheim pointed out in his introduction to *Suicide*, "Indubitably for sociology to be possible, it must above all have an object all its own. It must take cognizance of a reality which is not in the domain of other sciences. But if no reality exists outside of individual consciousness, it wholly lacks any material of its own."[64]

Durkheim maintained that locating reality exclusively in the consciousness of the individual is a mistake, because "there can be no sociology unless societies exist, and . . . societies cannot exist if there are only individuals."[65]

In his examination of suicide, Durkheim first looked at the various factors used to explain suicide in previous works. He rejected such factors as insanity, imitation, race and cosmic factors used by others, and instead proposed that suicide rates vary in relation to the degree of social solidarity or social integration. Consequently, each society "has a collective inclination for the act, quite its own, and the source of all individual inclination, rather than their result."[66] The collective inclination is made up of "the currents of egoism, altruism or anomy running through the society under consideration."[67]

Egoism, anomie and altruism are each a measure of social integration in a society. Durkheim's general conclusion was that, "suicide varies inversely with the degree of integration of the social groups of which the individual forms a part."[68] Consequently, in modern, organic societies in which individuality is prized and "the bond attaching man to life relaxes because that attaching him to society is itself slack,"[69] egoistic suicide can result. "Excessive individualism" was the cause of such suicides, whereby the individual personality tended to "surmount the collective personality," and the individual "depends only on himself and recognizes no other rules of conduct than what are founded on his private interests. This is a state of egoism,"[70] and suicide resulting from such individualism is called egoistic suicide.

In contrast to egoistic suicide, altruistic suicide was seen to be more characteristic of mechanical solidarity, since it derived from the excessive integration of the individual into the collectivity. Suicide in this case occurred, because "the ego is not its own property."[71] The individual is completely absorbed by the group, and feels "it is his duty"[72] to die to benefit the collectivity. Although lower societies were seen as "the theatre par excellence of altruistic suicide,"[73] Durkheim suggested that more modern examples persisted in certain highly integrated groups, such as the army, in which individuality is discouraged in the interests of the welfare of the total group.

Egoism and altruism represent opposite phenomena in the integration of the individual into the collectivity. Anomic suicide is the result of the lack of social regulation and contrasts with egoistic and altruistic suicides, which are concerned with "the way in which individuals are attached to society."[74] Anomic and egoistic suicide "have kindred ties" as they "both spring from society's insufficient presence in individuals," but society's absence differs for each type. "In egoistic suicide it is deficient in truly collective activity, thus depriving that latter of object and meaning. In anomic suicide, society's influence is lacking in the basically individual passions, thus leaving them without a check-rein."[75] The conflict between goals and means that the breakdown of social regulations generates was characterized in economic and domestic anomie, both of which could generate suicide.

Economic anomie was first discussed in *The Division of Labor* and was associated with the imperfect organization of organic solidarity. In *Suicide*, Durkheim suggested that in the "sphere of trade and industry" in modern societies, economic anomie was a chronic state. He pointed out that, "for a whole century, economic progress has mainly consisted in freeing industrial relations from all regulation." The consequence of this tactic has been that, "industry, instead of being still regarded as a means to an end transcending itself, has become the supreme end of individuals and societies alike. Thereupon the appetites thus excited have become freed of any limiting authority."[76] The celebration of the idea that it was "man's nature to be eternally dissatisfied" was seen as a mark of "moral distinction," whereas in Durkheim's view, it simply represented "unregulated consciences which elevate to a rule the lack of rule from which they suffer."[77] Consequently, since this was the mark of modern economic relations, the industrial and commercial functions, along with the liberal professions, "furnish the greatest number of suicides."[78]

The lack of regulation that produced anomic suicide was not confined to economic activities, but also applied to domestic relations. Whereas it was generally men who were affected by economic anomie, it was women who were more negatively affected within marriage and the family. As we have seen, the progressive division of labour affected all aspects of social life, including family and sex roles. Generally, women remained within the family, specializing in domestic roles, and therefore, in Durkheim's view, they played a lesser role in the progress of civilization. It was because of such role differentiation that women recalled "certain characteristics of primitive natures" and were generally less prone to suicide than were men. However, although the simpler intelligence of women tended to protect them as a collective group, this protection varied according to the strength of marital and family ties.

The differential suicide rates between men and women were found to be strikingly associated with the regulation of marital relations. In general, Durkheim found that married women tended to commit suicide more than single women and married men where there was no divorce, but that when divorce was available, more men committed suicide than did women. Furthermore, the rate was much lower for single women, especially between the ages of 20 to 45 years, than for comparable single men. Durkheim concluded that marriage "is more favourable to the wife the more widely practiced divorce is; and vice versa,"[79] so that marriage "does her less service than it does man."[80]

The different organic and intellectual capacities of the sexes accounted for their different reactions to the marital bond. As Durkheim pointed out, marriage represents the regulation of sexual relations, but this regulation involves more than simple physical desire. That is, it is not simply the satisfaction of sexual impulse that is regulated, since "love is far more mental than organic." "Moral reasons as well as physical needs impel love. Hence, it no longer has the regular, automatic periodicity which it displays in animals."[81] Because love is "complicated with aesthetic and moral feelings," it requires social regulation. Love must be "restrained by society since the organism has no means of restraining" the impulse. The restraint is found in marriage, which "completely regulates the life of passion, and monogamic marriage more strictly than any other."[82]

The restraint exercised through marriage is, however, of primary benefit to men who, it seems, need it more because of their different physiological and intellectual capacities. Marriage forces "a man to attach himself forever to the same woman," and this means that he has a "definite object" for his need for love and the horizon of infinite desires is therefore closed. It is this that produces the "moral equilibrium from which the husband benefits." By restricting his desires, he "makes it his duty to find happiness in his lot," and although "his enjoyment is restricted, it is assured," because the wife is "forbidden to fail him."[83]

The discipline of marriage therefore provides men with "moral calmness and tranquility." This is in contrast to the lot of the unmarried man, for whom "new hopes constantly awake, only to be deceived, leaving a trail of weariness and disillusionment behind them."[84] The result in this case is a "state of disturbance, agitation and discontent which inevitably increases the possibilities of suicide."[85] This state is potentially that of the married man to the extent that divorce is readily available. In this situation, the enjoyment is "not completely sure: the future less certain." As a result, "where marriage is strongly tempered by divorce, the immunity of the married man is inevitably less."[86]

Whereas men need marriage, and especially indissoluble marriage, women fare better outside marriage. The reason for this difference in Durkheim's view is that "women's sexual needs have less of a mental character because, generally speaking, her mental life is less developed."[87] Women's sexual needs are tied more to their organic base and as a result they are more effectively restrained by biological imperatives than by intellectual preoccupations. "Being a more instinctive creature," woman does "not require so strict a social regulation as marriage, and particularly as monogamic marriage."[88] By enclosing woman in marriage with no hope of divorce, the regulation of a women's sexual needs is unnecessarily stringent, and marriage becomes a "restraint to her without any great advantage." For women there is no hope of change when divorce is unavailable. Although the same restriction applies to men, they are compensated by other advantages as well as by custom that sanctions, to some degree, the double standard, which in turn lessens "the strictness of the regime." For women, however, "monogamy is strictly obligatory."[89]

Durkheim concluded his review of the statistics on marriage, divorce and suicide with the observation that contrary to received wisdom, men benefit more from marriage than do women.

> We reach the conclusion quite different from the current idea of marriage and its role. It is supposed to have been originated for the wife, to protect her weakness against masculine caprice. Monogamy, especially, is often represented as a sacrifice made by man of his polygamous instincts, to raise and improve woman's condition in marriage.[90]

However, the supposed liberty renounced by men turns out to be a "source of torment to him," and it is women "who made the sacrifice" in entering monogamous marital relations.[91] Unfortunately, the increased rate of male suicide in modern societies prompted Durkheim's suggestion that marriage needed to be strengthened rather than made easier to dissolve.

Durkheim pointed out that every society had a "greater or lesser aptitude for suicide" so that a certain level of suicide must be regarded as normal. The question then became, what constituted normality or, more particularly, were the rates for modern European societies abnormal? Durkheim concluded that, "all proofs combine . . . to make us consider the enormous increase in the number of voluntary deaths within a century as a pathological phenomenon becoming daily a greater menace."[92] He proposed various suggestions to counter the trend of egoistic and anomic suicides. The remedies proposed had different consequences for women than for men when it came to the question of domestic anomie.

Durkheim pointed out that "egoistic suicide results from the fact that society is not sufficiently integrated at all points to keep all its members under its control." Therefore, to remedy the situation it is necessary to look to ways of strengthening social groups so that they can "obtain a firmer grip on the individual."[93] Such groups would promote the understanding that the individual "is the instrument of a purpose greater than himself," and so "life will resume meaning in his eyes, because it will recover its natural aim and orientation."[94] What groups could accomplish this task in a modern society? Durkheim rejected the State as "too far removed from the individual to affect him uninterruptedly and with sufficient force."[95] Similarly, religion was no longer seen to have the power or authority sufficient to counter suicide, and even the family (as opposed to the marital or conjugal unit) was rejected as providing certain protection against suicide. As we saw previously, the restricted size and longevity of the modern family made it a weak basis for social solidarity and moral regulation.

> Changes have actually occurred in the constitution of the family which no longer allow it to have the same preservative influence as formerly. While it once kept most of its members within its orbit from birth to death and formed a compact mass, indivisible and endowed with a quality of permanence, its duration is now brief. It is barely formed when it begins to disperse. As soon as the children's first growth is over, they very often leave to complete their education away from home; moreover, it is almost the rule that as soon as they are adult they establish themselves away from their parents and the hearth is deserted.[96]

As a result, the family is reduced to the married couple and, as indicated above, "this union acts feebly against suicide," especially for women.

The social group that Durkheim believed could have sufficient power of prevention was the occupational group or corporation. The corporation was the ideal group, "since it consists of individuals devoted to the same tasks, with solidarity or even combined interests . . . Identity of origin, culture and occupation makes occupational activity the richest sort of material for a common life."[97] Unlike the State, whose influence is remote and "intermittent," the occupational group's control "extends to the greatest part of life." The occupational group "follows the workers wherever they go; which the family cannot do." In contrast to religion in modern society, "occupational life is almost the whole of life," so that it can provide the necessary "collective orientation" that religion supplied for mechanical solidarity.[98] With a reorganization of occupational life to encompass the worker more fully, both egoistic and anomic suicide could, in Durkheim's view, be combatted. "Anomy . . . partially results from the same state of disaggregation from which the egoistic current also springs . . . In both cases the remedy is therefore the same."[99]

Unless Durkheim meant to include women as full partners in the occupational, public realm, then the reorganization of occupational life would be of little benefit to women. On the contrary, one might suppose that the greater the absorption of men into their occupational roles and the more the corporate group satisfied men's needs, the more isolated and socially marginal women were likely to become. Women would be enclosed in the privatized, restrictive sphere of the home, which already made women more suicide-prone.

Nevertheless, Durkheim proposed that marriage (as opposed to family relations) be made even more restrictive in regard to divorce, even though

> the condition of a married woman was, on the contrary, made worse with respect to suicide . . . Not that man is naturally a wicked and egoistic being whose role in a household is to make his companion suffer. But in France where, until recently, marriage was not weakened by divorce, the inflexible role it imposed on women was a very heavy, profitless yoke for them. Speaking generally, we now have the cause of that antagonism of the sexes which prevents marriage favoring them equally: their interests are contrary; one needs restraint and the other liberty.[100]

At this point in his study of suicide, Durkheim reaches an impasse. The suicides of husbands can be reduced by making marriage more indissoluble. But, "what makes the problem especially disturbing and lends it an almost dramatic interest is that the suicides of husbands cannot be diminished in this way without increasing those of wives."[101] As a result, "We seem here confronted with an antimony which is insoluble." Durkheim then asks, "Must one of the sexes necessarily be sacrificed, and is the solution only to choose the lesser of the two evils?"[102] It seems that the answer is yes to both questions and that the lesser evil is to make marriage more indissoluble, at least for the time being and until men and women become "creatures of the same nature."

The basic problem with marriage in relation to suicide, according to Durkheim, lies in the fact that men and women do not share equally in social life. Man is "almost entirely the product of society" while woman is "to a far greater extent the product of nature."[103] Man is therefore a more highly socialized being than woman.

> His tastes, aspirations and humor have in large part a collective origin, while his companion's are more directly influenced by her organism. His needs, therefore, are quite different from hers, and so

an institution intended to regulate their common life cannot be equitable and simultaneously satisfying to such opposite needs.[104]

Women are governed more by their natural, biological impulses, and their mental capacity is seen to be less well developed than that of men. Thus, they are meant to be fulfilled by their domestic role in modern society. But domesticity produces unhappy women. This problem represents a real sociological contradiction. The conjugal family generally provides a positive integrative experience, but women who spend, or are supposed to spend, most of their life within this protective circle seem immune to its positive effects. Men, in contrast, find the conjugal family an important antidote to the anomie that threatens them in their public occupational life. Durkheim was unable to confront the problem he had identified without resorting to a biological argument that it was women's nature that accounted for the problematic difference between the sexes. Durkheim's use of biological differences as an explanation represents a sociological failure, but is explicable given the logic of Durkheim's argument that saw the division of labour, in all aspects of life, as evidence of the progress of civilization. Women simply represented an anomaly that some adjustment to the division of labour could, he hoped, rectify.

Durkheim suggested that although there is "no reason to suppose that woman may ever be able to fulfill the same functions in society as man," she may come to play a "more active and important" role than was presently the case.[105] The role she will play will be "peculiarly her own," in that "the female sex will not again become more similar to the male; on the contrary, we may foresee that it will become more different. But these differences will become of greater social use than in the past."[106] A return to the almost androgynous conception of the sexes that Durkheim had suggested was characteristic of the first human societies is ruled out. The logic of his evolutionary conception of the division of labour demands that the sexes will continue to become more differentiated. However, with greater differentiation the need to monitor closely the distribution and performance of social roles between the sexes would decline. "Woman would not be officially excluded from certain functions and relegated to others. She could choose more freely, but as her choice would be determined by her aptitudes it would generally bear on the same sort of occupations."[107]

The occupations that would be "naturally" selected by women as fitting their capacities and desires would be the traditional domestic roles augmented by aesthetic functions. In fact, Durkheim suggested that men should relinquish aesthetic functions to women in order to concentrate more on "functions of utility." The result would be that "both sexes would thus approximate each other by their very differences. They would be socially equalized, but in different ways."[108]

The directions that the division of labour between the sexes might take seemed to Durkheim to be already occurring. Women seemed to be more differentiated from men in the cities than in the country, and yet "her intellectual and moral constitution is most impregnated with social life in cities."[109] With regard to marriage and the problem of women's anomie, the solution suggested was that women's special capacities be more fully developed to complement those of men. In this way the different responses to marriage for the sexes would be lessened and marriage would "no longer be thought . . . necessarily to favour one to the detriment of the other."[110] From this conservative perspective Durkheim pointed out to "the champions today of equal rights for women" that they must not "forget that the work of centuries cannot be instantly abolished; that juridical equality cannot be legitimate so long as psychological inequality is so flagrant."[111] Reducing the psychological inequality would not reduce the physiological differences upon which that inequality was based, but it might reduce the negative effects on women of the indissoluble marital bond.

Durkheim's conclusions in both *The Division of Labor in Society* and *Suicide* on the nature of the sexes were governed by a dichotomized view of the development of the sexes. The dichotomy was supported by his assumption of the evolutionary divergence of the sexes in biological, psychological and social terms. The dichotomies were seen as "natural" in the sense that the progress of civilization was measured by the progress of the division of labour and specialization of tasks. At the same time, the particular sex-role specialization was also "natural" to the extent that each increasingly fulfilled their natural potential. The dichotomized perspective on sex roles that makes women marginal to society and culture is not altered by their possible assumption of aesthetic functions. In fact, such functions are more likely to confirm the differences and the inequality between men and women in future society, as Durkheim's discussion of the duality of human nature illustrates.

The "constitutional duality of human nature" is a theme that runs through all Durkheim's work. As indicated in the introduction to this work, the dualities and dichotomies applied to the natural and the social world have been major themes in much of western thought, and when applied to the nature and role of the sexes they have resulted in some variation of the equation that "woman is to nature as man is to culture." In Durkheim's discussion, the duality of "human" nature is realized in the sexual dichotomies that in turn produce differentiated social roles.

THE DUALISM OF HUMAN NATURE

Durkheim's discussion of the dualism of human nature expands on his investigation of the origins of religion. In *The Elementary Forms of Religious Life*, Durkheim pointed out that the idea of the sacred soul as distinct from the profane body, but nevertheless located in the body, is at the heart of religious belief. This belief represents an expression of the duality of human nature in that the soul is nothing less than the impersonal, regulating principles of the collectivity.

> So we are really made up of two beings facing in different and almost contrary directions, one of whom exercises a real pre-eminence over the other. Such is the profound meaning of the antithesis which all men have more or less clearly conceived between the body and the soul, the material and the spiritual beings who coexist within us.[112]

Consequently, human nature is double, and "there really is a particle of divinity in us because there is within us a particle of these great ideas which are the soul of the group."[113]

The universality and permanence of the belief in the duality of human nature is not, therefore, an illusion. In fact, psychology has confirmed the duality. According to Durkheim,

> Our intelligence, like our activity, presents two very different forms: on the one hand, are sensation and sensory tendencies; on the other, conceptual thought and moral activity. Each of these two parts of ourselves represents a separate pole of our being, and these two poles are not only distinct from one another but are opposed to one another.[114]

Consequently, we understand ourselves and our actions from two perspectives.

There is in us a being that represents everything in relation to itself and from its own point of view; in everything that it does, this being has no other object but itself. There is another being in us, however, which knows things *sub specie aeternitis,* as if it were participating in some thought other than its own, and which, in its acts, tends to accomplish ends that surpass its own.[115]

This dual understanding, however, gives rise to conflict, so that man is "both 'angel and beast' and not exclusively one or the other."[116] The sensory part of man is "necessarily egoistic," whereas moral activity is subject to universalized rules of conduct which begin "with disinterest, with attachment to something other than ourselves." Consequently, psychic life is marked by the antagonistic duality of the personal and the impersonal.

Not only are these two groups of states of consciousness different in their origins and their properties, but there is a true antagonism between them . . . We cannot pursue moral ends without causing a split within ourselves, without offending the instincts and the penchants that are the most deeply rooted in our bodies.[117]

The question arises, where does the duality come from? "How is it that each of us is, to quote another of Pascal's phrases, a 'monster of contradictions' that can never completely satisfy itself?"[118]

The answer, Durkheim indicated, was already found in his examination of the nature of religion. As he had pointed out, "nearly all the great social institutions have been born in religion"[119] and consequently, "if religion has given birth to all that is essential in society, it is because the idea of society is the soul of religion."[120] The idea of society is the idea of solidarity that produces the moral imperatives that impinge on individual behaviour.

Sacred things are simply collective ideals that have fixed themselves on material objects. The ideas and sentiments that are elaborated by a collectivity, whatever it may be, are invested by reason of their origin with an ascendancy and an authority that cause the particular individuals who think them and believe them to represent them in the form of moral forces that dominate and sustain them.[121]

These moral forces become part of the consciousness of individuals and become personalized in the sense that "each person has his own particular way of thinking about the beliefs of his church, the rules of common morality." They also retain an impersonal force because individuals realize "they represent something within us that is superior to us." As a result, "it is not without reason . . . that man feels himself to be double: he actually is double."[122]

Each individual leads a double life that is represented by both the individual organic tendencies and the collective social imperatives. The conflict between the two is represented by the conflict between "the sensations and sensory appetites . . . and the intellectual and moral life."[123] The sensory tendencies are the source of "passions and egoistic tendencies" and are concerned with the physical needs of the individual. In contrast, what is shared with others represents theoretical and practical activity and includes moral and/or religious ideas. Therefore, society has "requirements quite different from those of our nature as individuals,"[124] and in order for individuals to participate in society they must constantly "do violence to certain . . . strongest inclinations."[125] However, the curb that society imposes on those strong, egoistic inclinations is a positive necessity. "To be free is not to do what one pleases; it is to be master of oneself, to know how to act with reason and to accomplish one's duty."[126]

The increasing realization of duality and the understanding that personal freedom and autonomy are possible only in society and in accordance with society's rules comes about with the progressive division of labour and movement towards organic solidarity. Under mechanical solidarity, "individuality is something which the society possesses," and the link between the individual and society is "analogous to that which attaches a thing to a person." Consequently, the individual conscience "is a simple dependent upon the collective type and follows all of its movements, as the possessed object follows those of its owner,"[127] without being aware of the nature of the duality.

Organic solidarity represents a quite opposite situation. In contrast to the absorption of the individual personality into the collectivity, organic solidarity presumes a distinct personality with its own sphere of action. The collective conscience leaves "open a part of the individual conscience in order that special functions may be established there, functions which it cannot regulate" so that the activity of each individual is "more personal as it is more specialized."[128] The greater the individualism, however, the greater the need for collective coordination and constraint. At the same time, the individual is more conscious of personal autonomy. As a result, Durkheim predicted that the "struggle between the two beings within us" will increase as the progress of organic solidarity, or "civilization," continues.[129]

Increased individuality and the concomitant need for social control were part of the general movement from homogeneity to heterogeneity. This movement was not confined to the social structure but also extended, as we have seen, to the organic constitutions of the sexes. The biological and psychological characteristics of the sexes, according to Durkheim, became increasingly differentiated and associated with divergent spheres of social life.

Although the increasingly dichotomized roles of the sexes is presented as a positive feature of the development of civilization, and the impression is left that both sexes benefit from the progressive realization of their different "natural" abilities, in fact the benefit accrues almost entirely to the male. Both constitutionally as well as socially, women can hardly be seen to have progressed in Durkheim's account. This is especially the case given that women retain their primitive impulses and take less kindly to social regulation than do men, as Durkheim's discussion of marital anomie indicates.

The effects of the duality of human nature on the sexes is made particularly clear with Durkheim's recommendation that the aesthetic functions be taken over by women in order to allow men to concentrate on the instrumental functions. The division between these functions parallels the division between sensory, impulsive, organic *nature* and rational, regulated *culture*. Therefore, further specialization of the sexes under organic solidarity reinforces the constitutional and culturally unequal capacities and abilities of women.

Durkheim had a particular conception of the nature and function of aesthetic activities. He suggested that "aesthetico-moral activity . . . seems freed of all control and limitation because it is not regulated."[130] But, in fact, this freedom is deceptive because such activity must be regulated if it is to remain moral. In his view, the expenditure of "too much energy on the superfluous" means that there is nothing left for the essential, so that "when the place of the imagination in morality is made too great, obligatory tasks are necessarily neglected."[131] Consequently, aesthetic activity is "healthy only if moderated," because it represents a temptation to act under "rules of one's own making." Therefore, "too great an artistic sensibility is a sickly phenomenon which cannot become general without a danger to society."[132] The limits beyond which aesthetic activity becomes a danger to the moral stability of a society or individual will vary according to the developmental stage reached by that society or individual.

> The limit beyond which excess begins is, of course, variable, according to the people or the social environment. It begins so much sooner as society is less advanced, or the environment less cultivated. The workingman, if he is in harmony with his conditions of existence, is and must be closed to pleasures normal to the man of letters, and it is the same with the savage in relation to civilized man.[133]

If women are to take on the aesthetic functions in society, they run a risk with regard to their moral development and, it could be supposed, they represent a general risk to society given their innate propensities to be governed more by their organic constitutions than by the abstract cultural rules and regulations. In fact, because aesthetic activity "moves in the domain of the unreal, of the imaginary," those involved in such activities run the risk of "losing sight of reality" when they "fully experience aesthetic feeling."[134]

Aesthetic activity is dangerous because it deals with an imaginary world conjured up by the individual, and it runs the risk of promoting egoism at the expense of collective, moral action. Morality has to do with the real world. "To act morally is to do one's duty, and all duty is limited."[135] In addition, moral actions transform and improve the world for "beings of flesh and blood." Consequently, the world of aesthetic activity that requires the individual to work in abstraction from what is and to transcend, in the imagination, the reality of the present represents a potential threat to the moral stability of the society. To be moral is not to abstract self from the world. "On the contrary, we have to embrace it and love it, in spite of its ugliness, its pettiness and its meanness. We must not turn away from it towards an imaginary world but, on the contrary, we must keep our eyes fixed upon it."[136]

Aesthetic activity is particularly dangerous when it assumes morality as its subject matter; "by placing before us idealized images of a lofty morality, art makes us live an existence on the level of ideas which, save that it is fictional and imaginary, has the external characteristics of truly moral life."[137] When this occurs, individuals are quite prepared to take the realm of the imagination as reality so that, "We are quite prepared to believe ourselves dutiful because we are capable of eloquently praising duty or because we receive pleasure from hearing others offer such eloquent praise." Morality, or duty, is not learned, according to Durkheim, by "discovering how to combine ideas, or to harmonize phrases, sounds or colours," but only by acting on behalf of society and "creating something of oneself outside of oneself."[138]

If aesthetic activities are potentially problematic to the moral health of a society, it seems somewhat contradictory that those individuals who are "more primitive" in their impulses and therefore need more regulation should be the ones to take charge of these functions. However, it is precisely the primitive nature of women, combined with their specialized domestic roles, that makes them the obvious specialists in this sphere. The aesthetic sphere of sensations and imagination represents the counterpart to the rational, intellectual realm of the occupational, corporate sphere of men.

The duality of human nature is common to men and women, but the dichotomies are unequally developed and represented in the sexes. With increased division of labour and specialization, the dualism becomes more acute for men because the individualism these trends produce can result in anomie and egoism. The problem is particularly significant because the progress of society is paralleled by the progressive development of men's intellectual capacities and therefore by their more accurate understanding of the nature and meaning of the dualism they experience.

> The whole development of individualism has the effect of opening moral consciousness to new ideas and of making it more demanding. Since every advance that it makes results in a higher conception, a more refined awareness of the dignity of man, individualism cannot develop without making social relations which once seemed perfectly just now seem quite unjust.[139]

It is suggested that one reason that men need conjugal and family relationships is that they realize more clearly than women the nature of the duality and the destructive possibilities of too great an investment in individualism or, more precisely, egoism. Because women are primitive intellectually and morally, they are less able to appreciate the problem that this duality generates, and so strengthening the conjugal bond becomes the "lesser of two evils."

Women experience the dualism differently. Since the sensory impulses are precisely those that form the foundation of the aesthetic function, then women are best suited to such activities. In particular, aesthetic activities can be dangerous to society if unrestrained, and since women are restrained in conjugal society it follows that aesthetic activities can be both expressive of women's "natural capacities" as well as controlled and regulated by the restraints of the conjugal bond.

Durkheim's account of the roles and functions of the sexes based on the idea of the "natural" and therefore unchangeable dualities of physiology and psychology is no more than a continuation of a tradition in western social theory. However, it is particularly interesting that Durkheim's sociological imagination deserted him when it came to dealing with the prejudices of his time regarding the capacities and roles of the sexes. As Lukes remarks, Durkheim's views on the family and sexuality were a combination of "sociological acumen with strict Victorian morality."[140]

This blinkered perspective is interesting because Durkheim was one of the theorists who rejected the idea of patriarchy as the fundamental form of social and political organization. Henry Maine's idea that the patriarchal family formed the earliest social bond was influential with nineteenth-century theorists and was seemingly corroborated by Darwin's research. In *The Descent of Man,* Darwin suggested that male dominance, male sexual possessiveness and jealousy existed with the origins of society and that the idea of matriarchy or the existence of such a society was either a result of population imbalance or evidence of a society's primitive, "retrograded" instincts. Durkheim, in contrast, was able to examine the idea of matriarchy as one of the original forms of kinship organization without seeing it as necessarily a pre-social, instinctual aberration. As he indicated,

> It is quite probable, if not absolutely demonstrated, that there was an epoch in the history of the family when there was no such thing as marriage. Sexual relations were entered into and broken at will without any juridical obligations linking the union . . . This is the matriarchial family.[141]

However, such a society was understood as a primitive form from which differentiation in sex roles and capacities developed. Consequently, although Durkheim could speculate on the possibility of the female form as the "aboriginal image" from which the "masculine variety slowly detached itself,"[142] this did not alter the fact that he regarded the subsequent differences as constitutionally and socially natural and necessary.

An explanation for Durkheim's position on the question of sex roles can be found in his conceptualization of the nature of the sociological enterprise. Durkheim was concerned with establishing sociology as a legitimate and relatively autonomous intellectual and pragmatic endeavour. He was therefore most concerned with demonstrating the special subject matter and methods that distinguished sociology from other specialties such as history or political science. An examination of Durkheim's position on the special nature of sociological subject matter and methods will indicate the manner in which the biologically based dualism of the sexes could remain the unexamined basis for the conception of dichotomized roles and functions of women and men.

THE SUBJECT OF METHOD OF SOCIOLOGY

Durkheim acknowledged that the development of sociology as a new science was indebted to many earlier thinkers, in particular to Montesquieu, Saint-Simon and Comte. "Saint-Simon had been its harbinger; but Comte is its father, for through him it received the beginnings of its existence."[143] Comte "defined its method and established its framework."[144] However, according to Durkheim, his work remained at the level of "philosophical generalities."

Thus Durkheim intended to establish sociology as a science akin to the natural sciences. In order to do this he had to establish a subject matter separate from the other sciences and ensure the same objective reality that the subject matter of the natural sciences had for its investigators. As he indicated in the Preface to *Suicide*, "Indubitably for sociology to be possible, it must above all have an object all its own. It must take cognizance of a reality which is not in the domain of other sciences."[145] For example, if there is nothing other than the individual consciousness, then psychology, not sociology, is the only possible science. But, as Durkheim points out, although there *"can be no sociology unless societies exist,"* it is equally the case that *"societies cannot exist if there are only individuals."*[146]

Society is, for Durkheim, a *"reality sui generis"* and has an objective reality apart from the individuals that compose that society.

> It is upon this principle . . . that all sociology has been built. This science, indeed, could be brought into existence only with the realization that social phenomena, although immaterial, are never-

theless real things, the proper objects of scientific study. To be convinced that their investigation was legitimate, it was necessary to assume that they had a definite and permanent existence, that they do not depend on individual caprice, and that they give rise to uniform and orderly relations.[147]

In the investigation of social life, the sociologist must therefore treat social facts as "things." In doing this, the investigator will be able to approach the subjects of study objectively in the same manner as the natural scientist.

The sociologist ought, therefore, whether at the moment of the determination of his research objectives or in the course of his demonstrations, to repudiate resolutely the use of concepts originating outside of science for totally unscientific needs. He must emancipate himself from the fallacious ideas that dominate the mind of the layman; he must throw off, once and for all, the yoke of these empirical categories, which from long continued habit have become tyrannical.[148]

Social facts become visible to the sociologist because of their two characteristics, exteriority and constraint. That is, a social fact has an existence "independent of the individual forms" and can be "recognized by the power of external coercion which it exercises or is capable of exercising over individuals."[149] The constraint exercised by a social fact is recognized by the "existence of some specific sanction or by the resistance offered against every individual effort that tends to violate it."[150] The independence of social facts from the particular individuals meant also that social facts had to be explained in terms of other social facts not as caused by "the states of individual consciousness."[151] Therefore, the objectivity of the observation would be secured in the same manner as the natural sciences.

It is a rule in the natural sciences to discard those data of sensation that are too subjective, in order to retain exclusively those presenting a sufficient degree of objectivity. Thus the physicist substitutes, for the vague impressions of temperature and electricity, the visual registrations of the thermometer or the electrometer. The sociologist must take the same precautions.[152]

Social facts can be explained sociologically in two ways: causally and functionally. The two explanatory forms are clearly distinguished by Durkheim. "When, then, the explanation of a social phenomenon is undertaken, we must seek separately the efficient cause which produces it and the function it fulfills."[153] The term *function* is used because Durkheim wishes to distinguish the nature of social facts from the intentions or purposes that apply to individual human acts. Function refers to the "correspondence between the fact under consideration and the general needs of the social organism." The correspondence has an existence apart from whether it was intentional or not. As Durkheim remarked, "All these questions of intention are too subjective to allow of scientific treatment."[154] Consequently, "the function of a social fact ought always to be sought in its relation to some social end."[155]

The two forms of explanation are related in the sense that discovering the causes of social phenomena enables the investigator to understand the functions of the phenomena and to determine whether the existence of such phenomena is normal or pathological. As Durkheim explained,

> After having established by observation that a particular fact is general, he will go back to the conditions which determined this generality in the past and will then investigate whether these conditions are still given in the present or if, on the contrary, they have changed. In the first case he may properly designate the phenomenon as normal; and, in the second, refuse it this designation.[156]

The "normal," that is, healthy social state can be established by a classification of types in terms of the functions that the type fulfils. Consequently, mechanical solidarity requires a different form of morality than organic solidarity, and what is normal, for example, with respect to crime and punishment in one type would be abnormal for the other.

The social fact that enabled Durkheim to classify types of solidarity and estimate what was functional and therefore normal were the legal rules. The legal codes indicated that for organic solidarity the normal, healthy society required associations based on specialized roles rather than on the similarity of members. This division of labour meant that it was functional and normal for women to specialize in marital, family and, possibly, aesthetic roles and for men to concentrate on economic-political roles. The key factor in Durkheim's approach is the operation of the social in contrast to the individual. Therefore, the fact that the roles assigned to women had negative effects on an individual basis, as the suicide study pointed out, must be interpreted as a temporary pathology that can be corrected by assigning aesthetic functions to women and, as a result, allowing men to specialize more in their particular roles.

The idea that the division of labour need not automatically relegate women to the private domestic realm or that biological differentiation of the sexes does not necessarily involve inequality does not occur to Durkheim. The possibility is not entertained because it is the needs of the social, not of the individual, that is the focus of Durkheim's inquiry. It is society, in the interests of its moral health, that requires the division of labour between the sexes.

> The moral importance of the wife's role increased to the degree that domestic life had a greater place in the context of life in general; the conjugal association became more strongly organized. For the family is unexcelled as a territory for feminine activity. But . . . it is inevitable that, at least at a given moment in history, the matrimonial bond cannot become tightly constricting and the family cannot hold together without a resulting legal subordination of the wife to her husband. *For this subordination is a necessary condition of family unity.*[157]

The subordination of women in such a conjugal unit could well be altered at some future date to "allow each of the spouses his (or her) legal individuality," but this can only be a "later development" dependent on changes in *society's needs.*[158]

Social solidarity is a social fact in that it pervades society, is external to the individual, but exercises a coercive power over that individual. From this perspective, resistance to the social is futile if not immoral. "[M]an is a moral being only because he lives in society, since morality consists in being solidary with a group and varies with this solidarity."[159] The power of society restrains and checks the egoism of the individual and "makes him a moral being."[160] The fact that the power and demands of society may be the demands of a special interest group is obscured by the absolute division Durkheim makes between the individual and society. As a result, the fact that the ties that bind women to their specialized marital and family roles are in the interests of the moral health of men and that, to strengthen the conjugal tie under organic solidarity is to make women's lot worse, is simply passed off as an unfortunate stage in social development. The connection is simply not made that the negative consequences for women are the result of the privileged position and role assigned to men—which men would be reluctant to relinquish.

The reification of the social thus obscured the nature of sex-role relationships. The emphasis on the social was, as we have indicated, an important means by which Durkheim attempted to demonstrate the difference between sociology and psychology. But in making this distinction, the dichotomy between society and the individual became overly rigid.

The dichotomy was also associated with other dichotomies, as Lukes demonstrates. The dichotomy of society/individual was matched by the dichotomies of moral rules/sensual appetites, conceptual thought/sensory thought and feelings, and the sacred/ profane. The social-cultural product was contrasted with the biological, pre-social product, and the latter needed regulation by the former in the interests of the moral health of both the individual and the collectivity. Society took on an abstract but controlling position in Durkheim's work, and its abstract needs determined the functions and roles required.

For women the problem with the reification of society and the dichotomy between society and the individual remains obscure as long as human nature is undifferentiated with regard to sex. But, because the explanation of the family and marriage in organic solidarity depends on the assumption of biological and cultural dichotomies between men and women, the consequences of the reification become clear. "Society" is, in fact, a code word for the interests and needs of men as opposed to those of women. These needs and interests are rationalized on the basis of the biological differences between the sexes.

Women's "sensibility is rudimentary rather than highly developed" and, therefore, "society is less necessary to her because she is less impregnated with sociability. She has few needs in this direction and satisfies them easily."[161] Women do not understand the necessity for social regulation because they are less intelligent than men and are guided by their instincts. Therefore, "women can endure life in isolation more easily than man," as the case of old, unmarried women is seen to demonstrate. "With a few devotional practices and some animals to care for, the old unmarried woman's life is full."[162] Men are infinitely more fragile creatures because they are "more complex" and can only maintain their equilibrium through extensive social supports: "he can maintain his equilibrium only by finding more points of support outside himself, and it is because his moral balance depends on a larger number of conditions that it is more easily disturbed"[163]

Men experience and understand the dualism of human nature, whereas women, because they are more firmly fixed in their biology, experience this duality very little and comprehend it even less. As we will discover in our discussions of other theorists, civilization seems often to depend upon the maintenance of the "natural," in the sense of the biological, capacities of women. In addition, it is precisely the control of nature that is regarded as a mark of the progress of mankind. It seems to follow that civilization advances to the extent that man controls nature, and this includes women as human representatives of the natural because of their unique biological capacity to reproduce. This equation is often obscured, as it is in Durkheim's account, by the idea that equality can be achieved through difference. That is, "woman should seek for equality in the functions which are commensurate with her nature."[164] From this position Durkheim suggested,

> who does not feel that whatever may contribute to the weakening of the organic unity of the family and of marriage must inevitably dry up the source of woman's rise to a higher status? The feelings of respect that have directed her way and have become more and more pronounced with the further progress of history originate, in large part, in the religious respect inspired by health and home.[165]

Durkheim continued with the observation that this "religion" cannot survive if "family life should cease being regarded as something more than a precarious cohabitation between two beings who can at any moment separate if they so desire, who for the duration of the partnership each have their centre of interests and concerns."[166]

In response, therefore, to the turn-of-the-century feminist movement, Durkheim suggested that the greater role women wanted in public life would be achieved at the expense of a diminished domestic stature, and the "gains she will settle for with the acquisition of rights claimed in her behalf will be offset by important losses."[167] Some of these losses could give cause for grave concern since the domestic sphere did appear to control some of the more problematic impulses to which women were subject. For example, although widows seem to fare better than widowers in regard to suicidal tendencies, they nevertheless suffer more "in matters of a moral nature." A widow's "tendency toward crime and towards misdemeanors is . . . much more intensified than it is in the other sex." This proves, once more, that "woman's moral sense is less deeply rooted than man's," because she is "less strongly socialized" than man.[168]

Durkheim's reification of society is not simply a problem in the analysis of sex-role relationships. Durkheim's theoretical assumptions and methodological procedures have represented one of the sociological traditions that feminist sociologists have reacted against most strongly. As a general rule, the reactions have concentrated on the structural-functional tradition in North American sociology that took much of its inspiration from the Parsonian account of Durkheim's work. The major feminist criticisms take the form of a reaction against positivism as a methodology capable of giving an objective account of social reality. The nature of this debate will be examined in more detail in Chapter 7. At present, it is sufficient to note that the positivist approach that treats the subject matter of sociology as an object that can be studied in a neutral way by the researcher seems to break down when it comes to the question of sex-role relationships. For Durkheim, as for the structural-functional school, in general, women seem inseparable from their uniquely confining biological nature. The feminist critique has suggested that this perspective is a consequence of the objectification of social reality inherent in the positivist approach. Positivism is not, however, the only theoretical and methodological approach to the study of social reality that is guilty of a blinkered perspective on sex-role relationships, as our discussion of Weber, Marx and Engels shows.

In the next chapter we will examine the work of Max Weber, a contemporary of Durkheim. In many ways, Weber is seen as Durkheim's antithesis in his theoretical perspective and methodological approach. Although both theorists advocated a comparative and historical approach to sociology and both used ideal types in their work, the intentions and possibilities of sociology were understood differently. Bendix points out that both wanted to understand human behaviour through "scientific rationalism," but they differed to the extent that

> Durkheim modeled his sociology after the natural sciences, Weber did not. Durkheim was confident that this new discipline would greatly extend man's control over society. Weber did not share this

optimistic view of progress through science. Durkheim was a social evolutionist who conceived of change as a sequence of social species or types. Weber considered such theories as heuristic devices only, which should not be confused with a historical development.''[169]

The organic and mechanical forms of social solidarity represented objective social facts for Durkheim and were the means by which the health or pathology of the society could be gauged.

For Weber types of society are mental constructs which are indispensible aids in the analysis of selected empirical data. He would have considered Durkheim's distinction between normal and pathological aspects of a social type unscientific, because it claimed scientific status for ethical judgements based on uncertain biological analogies.[170]

Despite the differences illuminated by Bendix, Weber and Durkheim have in common a particular understanding of sex differences. For both sociologists, their analysis of sex roles is coloured by their understanding of natural dichotomies between the sexes. This belief in the invariable significance of biological difference means that the hierarchies of power in society, which relegate women collectively to a subordinate status to men, are taken as givens that do not require sociological analysis.

Durkheim saw patriarchy as a particular historical form of family and marital relations, best exemplified by ancient Roman practices. The patriarchal family form represented a stage in the progressive personalization of family ties and the consequent restriction of kinship relations and moral obligations. For Weber, patriarchy was less significant as a form of family relations than as an expression of power relations that happened to have a basis in the household and marital arrangements. We turn now to Weber's analysis of patriarchy and power.

CHAPTER 3

Weber, Patriarchy and Power

Weber's analysis of patriarchy and power has been largely ignored in recent feminist theory. Part of the explanation may be his association of patriarchy with a particular form of power—traditional power, which, some have assumed, has an historical rather than current relevance to feminist issues and concerns. In fact, Weber's ideas are very relevant to feminist concerns, particularly with regard to the definition of patriarchy as the power of men over women, experienced on a day-to-day basis by all women, and transcending particular modes of production.

Richardson suggests that "patriarchialism is to culture as a rhythm section is to a band. Sometimes it overrides the melodic theme and sometimes it is hushed—but it is always there."[1] The concept of patriarchy as the "rule of men"[2] over women and as a universal form of domination has had considerable use in feminist theory. However, when the term is used in this general sense it becomes ahistorical and interchangeable with "sexism." Consequently, it can be said that women in feudal Europe lived in a patriarchal system just as women of other societies, past and present, live under patriarchy. In general, patriarchy denotes male power, but this being said, it must be recognized that the organization and the experience of patriarchy are different historically and cross-culturally.[3]

In examining the work of Max Weber, we will consider his definition of patriarchy and his analysis of traditional power and how these relate to family, household and sex relations. Finally, we will look at the implications of Weberian analysis for current feminist theory. Before embarking on our analysis, a short note regarding Weber's methodology is in order.

IDEAL TYPES

In contrast to Durkheim, who stated that "when the individual has been eliminated, society alone remains" and who therefore sought the "explanation of social life in the nature of society itself,"[4] Weber defined sociology as "a science which attempts the interpretive understanding of social action in order thereby to arrive at a causal explanation of its course and effects."[5] The action referred to is behaviour that has subjective meaning for the individual actor or actress:

> Action in this sense may be either overt or purely inward or subjective; it may consist of positive intervention in a situation, or of deliberately refraining from such intervention or passively acquiescing in the situation. Action is social in so far as, by virtue of the subjective meaning attached to it by the acting individual (or individuals), it takes account of the behaviour of others and is thereby oriented in its course.[6]

The method to be used by sociology was "interpretive understanding." In contrast to Durkheim, Weber maintained that society cannot "act." Only individuals act. Therefore, the method to be used by sociologists was different from that of the natural sciences and, in a significant way, superior in the acquisition of knowledge to natural science.

> In the case of social collectivities, precisely as distinguished from organisms, we are in a position to go beyond merely demonstrating functional relationships and uniformities. We can accomplish something which is never attainable in the natural sciences, namely the subjective understanding of the action of component individuals . . . We do not "understand" the behaviour of cells, but can only observe the relevant functional relationships, and generalize on the basis of these observations.[7]

One of the methodological devices to be used by the sociologist was *verstehen*, either "direct observational understanding" or explanatory understanding. The intent is to make sense of social behaviour by understanding the meaning and motives of the participants, and in this way the seeming association of events, which might even be confirmed by statistical correlation, can be established as causally linked. There is, however, a difference, as Weber recognized, between understanding behaviour and a causal explanation. More particularly, the sociologist is not able to comprehend directly the meaning of any one person's behaviour. However, to the extent that such behaviour is "typical," given the situation, the sociologist can develop generalizations that provide the basis for causal linkages.

> A correct causal interpretation of typical action means the process which is claimed to be typical is shown to be both adequately grasped at the level of meaning and at the same time the interpretation is to some degree causally adequate. If adequacy in respect to meaning is lacking, then no matter how high the degree of uniformity and how precisely its probability can be numerically determined, it is still an incomprehensible statistical probability, whether dealing with overt or subjective processes.[8]

At the same time adequate meaning can only have causal significance to the extent that the action usually takes the form that has been observed to be meaningful. "For this there must be some degree of determinable frequency of approximation to an average or a pure type."[9] The pure type, or the ideal type, is thus a methodological device that enables the sociologist to make sense of social reality. The task of sociology is therefore "to formulate type concepts and generalized uniformities of empirical process. This distinguishes it from history, which is oriented to the causal analysis and explanation of individual actions, structures, and personalities possessing cultural significance."[10]

The ideal type does not represent preferred descriptions of reality or utopian visions, but rather is the result of isolating significant characteristics of the phenomenon under investigation. In this way sociology is tied to history through the development of the ideal types that help to provide a basis for comparative historical analysis.

The ideal type is an abstraction constructed from empirical, historical manifestations of the phenomenon to be studied and emphasizes the central or core elements of the phenomenon. In contrast again to Durkheim, whose types are assumed to represent a fundamental social reality, Weber's types represent one way, admittedly the "typical" way, of understanding that reality. At the same time this means that no ideal type is a mirror image of reality, or that any type can be absolutely true or false. For example, when examining the phenomenon of power and domination, Weber's ideal types emphasize distinctive, typical characteristics to provide models of "pure" power in various social and historical contexts. In this sense, the ideal types represent a departure from reality, since they are "pure" or uncontaminated by the compromises and adjustments that the day-to-day exercise of power entails.

The ideal type is a methodological tool designed to prevent confusion that could arise with a variety of definitions of the same phenomena. As Weber remarked:

> The same historical phenomena can in one respect count as "feudal", in another as "patrimonial", in yet another as "bureaucratic" and in another still as "charismatic." In order that these terms should have a clear meaning, the sociologist must for his part formulate "pure" or "ideal" types of systems of the relevant kind which exhibit the internal coherence and unity which belongs to the most complete possible adequacy on the level of meaning. Just because of its internal coherence, however, this ideal of pure form is perhaps as little likely to be found in the real world as a physical reaction calculated on the assumption of an absolute vacuum.[11]

In the development of ideal types, however, a static picture of the phenomena is obtained. This is problematic, because the reality of the operation of power, for example, can be grasped only through the actions of the powerful, and these compromise the purity of the type. In fact, as we will discover, it is often the deviations from the pure type that are the most interesting sociologically. One of the critical elaborations in our discussion of power and domination that deviates from the pure types involves the relationship of women to the process of power.

Although Weber recognized the fact that the construction of sociological concepts depends upon the position and interests of the investigator and that the sociological account cannot be static, one phenomenon that he took to be an unchangeable feature of social life was the "natural inequality" between the sexes. Weber saw power as essentially an arrangement among men. In addition, he regarded the access to power and domination by men as natural, inevitable or simply right.

Most discussions of power overlook the fact that if men do hold power as a general rule, this is often a consequence of the very factor that is seen to explain women's absence from power positions, namely, women's reproductive capacity. Rather than assuming that women's reproductive capacity is necessarily and at all times a hindrance to her ability to act in society, it makes more sense to look at the manner in which both men and women have manipulated the fact of women's reproduction in the organization of social life. In this context we can see, when discussing traditional forms of domination in Weberian terms and relating the type to historical evidence, that the powerful women of traditional society were not entirely unusual. The day-to-day exercise of power produces compromises and expedient action and modifies the supposedly ideal type relationship of women to power.

Ideal types are constructed with the intention of illuminating social-historical reality and thus they must refer back to that reality; they must be tested on the evidence of empirical reality in order to ensure conceptual precision. Weber himself indicated that when the empirical historical reality diverged too greatly from the ideal type, then the type should be abandoned. However, theoretical concepts, once formulated, tend to have an independent life that makes their refutation extremely difficult. In the case of Weber's ideal types of domination, the difficulty in reformulating, refining or simply abandoning the types is compounded by the problem that the person who asks the questions and poses the problems affects the construction of theory. As various feminist theorists have pointed out, much sociology has been concerned with issues and problems of significance to men. "Social theorists, like societal members, tend to define a society and discuss its social organization in terms of what men do, and where men are located in that society."[12] Weber's ideal type patriarchy and his discussion of traditional power are not immune, as we will discover, from such theoretical relativity.

In the rest of this chapter we will outline Weber's ideal type patriarchy and traditional domination and then confront the type with specific historical data that are relevant when women are the subject of our concern. The question to be addressed is whether Weber's analysis of patriarchy and traditional domination provides us with a more precise means of understanding power relations between the sexes. This question must be considered in the light of the preconceptions Weber brought to his definition of patriarchy and the nature of domination and, consequently, the value of Weber's conceptualization of patriarchy.

PATRIARCHY Radical

Weber's analysis of patriarchy occurs in the context of his more general analysis of power. Power is defined as the "probability that one actor within a social relationship will be in a position to carry out his own will despite resistance, regardless of the basis on which this probability rests."[13] This is a general definition that could apply to "social relations in a drawing room as well as in the market, from the rostrum of a lecture hall as well as from the command post of a regiment, from an erotic or charitable relationship as well as from scholarly discussion or athletics."[14] Consequently, Weber distinguishes a special form of power—domination—which he divides into two general types: the indirect type refers to the power that a monopoly over economic resources can convey, and the direct type, germane to our discussion, refers to control over others. This latter form of domination is one that expresses an "authoritarian power of command" that will be obeyed.[15]

There are three types of direct domination that are determined according to the legitimacy claims made by the power holders and confirmed by the ruled. The legitimacy claims are the reasons why the ruler expects obedience, and they therefore provide the normative basis for the exercise of power. The three types are (1) rational-legal domination, based on formally constituted rules and laws that justify the ruler's claims to his position; (2) charismatic domination, based on extraordinary, but fortuitous or timely, qualities of the individual; (3) and traditional domination based on tradition or custom justifying, or even sanctifying, the position of the ruler.

The form taken by the legitimation of power has consequences for the manner in which the ruler can exercise that power. For the traditional ruler, power is administered in a patrimonial manner of which patriarchy is the basic form. Patriarchy is a form of domination characteristic of the household group or clan organized on kinship and economic terms. Patriarchialism means "the authority of the father, the husband, the senior of the house, the sib elder over the members of the household and sib . . ."[16] The "founding father" or some association in the distant past with a great or even divine connection or event that generates inviolable traditions usually provides the basis for the claim to power. If the past association is with a divinity, that divinity may be male or female, but it is the male line through which claim to power is made.

In his description of ideal type patriarchy, Weber indicates that the power of the patriarch is a personal prerogative. He is able to exercise power without restraint, "unencumbered by rules," at least to the extent that he is not "limited by tradition or by competing powers."[17] However, in reality, both tradition and competing powers often curb the absolute power of the patriarch. For the ideal type patriarch, however, his domination is absolute and is legitimized as well as constrained by traditional norms.

The sanctity of tradition provides the household members with some protection from any arbitrary actions or decisions made by the patriarch, although the possibility that the patriarch may interpret, revive, or even "discover" traditions can leave him a certain degree of freedom from such control by household members. Basically, however, the patriarch must be seen to exercise his power in the interests of all the members of the household, and in order to ensure that this is so, there "is a complete absence of a personal . . . staff."[18] The patriarch is therefore dependent upon the subordinates' willingness to obey in the absence of any means of enforcement.

If the actions of the patriarch repeatedly violate tradition then he will jeopardize his legitimacy and create opposition among household members. This opposition is directed at the *person*, not at the *form* of domination that the patriarch represents. Incompetent or wicked patriarchs may be overthrown, but they are usually replaced, according to traditional rules and customs, by another patriarch—often the next eligible male within the same patrilineal line. "The king is dead, long live the king" expresses the nature of such transitions.

The origin of pure patriarchy in the household has an important effect on sex relations. As Weber points out, the only "natural" relationship is that of the mother and child "because it is a biologically based household unit that lasts until the child is able to search for means of subsistence on his own."[19] The basic form of the family is therefore taken to be the mother and her children, although Weber continues with the observation that "it does not mean—indeed, it is unimaginable—that there ever were societies with maternal groupings only." Society is defined by the relationship of men as husbands and fathers to the basic unit of mother and child which, in turn, depends on the organization of economic activities that generates a household.

Separated from the household as a unit of economic maintenance, the sexually based relationship between husband and wife, and the physiologically determined relationship between father and children are wholly unstable and tenuous. The father relationship cannot exist without a stable economic household unit of father and mother; even where there is such a unit the father relationship may not always be of great import.[20]

Weber suggests that in societies in which the maternal grouping of mother and child constitutes the family form, there exist military and economic relationships among men, and economic and sexual relationships between men and women. The maternal group is therefore, in Weber's view, a secondary form that can be found where "men's everyday life is confined to the stable community of a 'men's house,' at first for military purposes, later on for other reasons."[21]

The basis of the household is economic and in its pure form is characterized by "solidarity in dealing with the outside and communism of property and consumption of everyday goods within (household communism).[22] That is, the household represents a "community of fate" in which commitment to the whole outweighs the needs and desires of individual members and the household confronts external society as a unified group. This "primeval household communism" characteristic of early groups is altered with the development of "exclusive sexual claims of the male over women subjected to their authority."[23] That women in the more primitive household are subject to male authority as a general group rather than being individually subject to any particular man is explained by the fact that the "authority" of the household is based on two attributes: superior strength and practical knowledge and experience. As a result, it is "the authority of men as against women and children; of the able-bodied as against those of lesser capability; of the adult as against the child; of the old against the young."[24]

The exclusive sexual claims of men to specific women means that women become individually, rather than collectively, an individual man's property. For the patriarch *all* women under his command are his subjects, such that the offspring of these female subjects can be considered "his" children, and this "holds whether the woman is a wife or a slave, regardless of the facts of paternity."[25]

In fact, the practice of selling children or of renting or mortgaging women and children is seen as evidence of the patriarch's authority, as well as being "the original form of adjusting manpower and labour demand among different households" resulting from the property rights held by the patriarch. The value of property lies in its utilization in the patriarch's interests. For the women of the household the value of their labour power also includes their sexuality and reproductive capacity. Consequently, a new patriarch will acquire, without qualification, the powers of the old master, including the "sexual disposition of his predecessor's women—possibly of his own father's."[26]

The basic family form of mother and children that Weber regards as the only natural relationship is altered by the exclusive sexual claims of males that make women their property. The natural family form is therefore subverted by the socially constructed authority of the patriarch. The problem remains, however, as to why the natural form lends itself to the process that makes women and their children the property of males when, in the last analysis, only maternity can be determined with any accuracy. Like many other theorists, Weber resorts to nature for an explanation for the transformation.

Within the patriarchal household the authority of the master is based on tradition, which includes the belief that the personal relations within the household are natural. Consequently, the arrangement of domination and subordination within the household follows from the fact that

> "the woman is dependent because of the normal superiority of the
> physical and intellectual energies of the male, and the child because
> of his objective helplessness, the grown-up because of habituation,
> the persistent influence of education and the effect of firmly rooted
> memories from childhood and adolescence, and the servant because
> from childhood on the facts of life have taught him that he lacks
> protection outside the master's sphere and that he must submit to
> him to gain that protection."[27]

For the patriarchal household, the differentiation among the members is through *nature* for women and children, but through *nurture* or socialization and experience for others.

Women and children, as well as slaves, are more tightly bound to the patriarchal household and the authority of the master than are adult males. In practice, not all adult men may be capable of becoming patriarchs of a household either because of simple economic reasons or because of more complex social prohibitions on such actions. In theory, as long as a male can lay claim to exclusive sexual access to a female and can "persuade" others to submit to his authority, then he may assume the position of patriarch. Whatever the social controls over the proliferation of patriarchal households, the submission of adult men to the authority of a patriarch is always more problematic than the submission of women and children, who can be conceptualized as "naturally" weaker and lacking power, or the submission of slaves, who, through fear and brute force, can be controlled.

Weber recognizes that some differentiation within the household may arise from the "oldest typical division of labour, the division between the sexes,"[28] and women may assume some household authority. However, the split between the "independent authority of the matron" is found next to the "normally superordinated authority" of the patriarch. The modification is usually the result of the exclusive food provisioning tasks of women, or because of the complete separation of male warriors from the household. The modification does not, however, give women comparable power to men, but only separates a particular sphere within which some women may exercise some authority under the general domination of the patriarch. Whatever the scope or importance of the domestic sphere as a locus of female power, such power is always secondary to that of the patriarch, and this becomes clear in Weber's discussion of the household as the fundamental social group.

Organized society begins with households. The ideal-type household is a collectivity that is marked off from others by the fact that the members present a solid, unified face to the rest of the world and practise "household communism." That is, there is a "communism of property and consumption of everyday goods" among all the members of the household. However, it becomes clear that the communal sharing of household goods does not mean that all are equal within the household. Weber indicates that one of the ways in which household communism is weakened is not through economic practices but through the "development of exclusive sexual claims of the male over *women subject to their authority.*"[29] In other words, at the outset of organized society, with the formation of households, women are already subject to men. The subjection of women to one male, and the regulation of sexual relations among the members of the household, are characteristics of an advanced patriarchal power relationship.

Weber continues his speculations regarding the progressive differentiation of society from the natural group of mother and child with the suggestion that the household is often of less importance to hunters and nomads and even groups with "technically well-advanced agriculture" than the kinship and neighbourhood group.[30] In the latter cases he observed that there occasionally "existed independent organizations of women with female chieftains alongside the men's organizations."[31] Such divisions are not indicative of shared or equal power, but are merely the result of a division of labour such that the "man's absence from the house for his military service led to a 'manless' household management by wives and mothers."[32] In addition, in his discussion of the neighbourhood or kinship as the basis of social organization, it is again clear that the basic organizing principle remains in the hands of males, so that, for example, the neighbourhood is described as "an unsentimental economic brotherhood."[33]

The household group is a pivotal concept in Weber's speculations on the early forms of social organization, and he insists that in such a group, even with communist property ownership, "any kind of communist sexual freedom is most thoroughly banished from a house" in the interests of "safeguarding solidarity and domestic peace in the face of jealousies."[34] The sexual closure within the household is followed soon after by incest prohibitions beyond the immediate household to include the kin group. This group is "not as 'natural' as the household or neighborhood" and is usually the result of an "artificial blood brotherhood."[35] The kin group may be organized in terms of matrilineal or patrilineal descent patterns, but matrilineal descent does not mean that women exercise authority. "In the case of matrilineal descent the child is protected and disciplined by the mother's brothers, apart from his father, and also receives his inheritance from them (*avunculate*); the mother exercises domestic authority only in rare cases subject to special conditions."[36]

Whether descent is reckoned through the maternal or paternal line, it is men who have the disposition of authority, and the "imprecise collective name of *matriarchy*" is a result of a misinterpretation of the way the male household head disposes of the female members of the household. Female children can play a special role in this regard as the household head "might offer them to his guests, just like his own wife, or he might permit sexual relations temporarily or permanently in exchange for goods and services."[37] It is this "prostitution" of the female members of the household that Weber sees as giving rise to the mistaken idea of matriarchy. In the circumstances described above, the women remain part of the original household, and their children therefore belong to the mother's household. But the head of her household is her father. In fact, the term matriarchy is restricted by Weber to the situation in which a woman can enter her husband's household, but the resulting offspring "belong to the mother's kin group . . . and are subject to the rules of blood revenge and inheritance of her group."[38] Even in the latter case, the power in the maternal kin group is the power of the mother's father or brother.

Patriarchy, according to Weber, describes the social organization of power between men as exercised over women, children and slaves. Although both men and women are subject to the power of the patriarch, adult free men have, at least potentially, a different position vis-à-vis the master than do their female counterparts. This difference is clarified by the observation that for ideal type patriarchy, the authority of the master is contained within the household. Outside the immediate household, the patriarch may exert influence only "by example, by advice, or by other non-compulsory means."[39] Outside the confines of the household, compliance, particularly on the part of other males, is problematic and requires a different organization that codifies the nature and extent of the power of the various patriarchs in their relationship with each other. Such power relations are exemplified in the ideal types of traditional, charismatic and rational-legal domination.

Weber's ideal type patriarchy must be recognized as a concept that has limited application as an historical entity. The authoritarian power of command exercised by the patriarch is confined to his immediate household, and the major factor in the nature of the patriarch's power is his regulation of the daily needs of the household. That is, the patriarch is "the 'natural leader' of the daily routine" with his power "rooted in the provisioning of recurrent and normal needs of the workday life."[40] When economic production is differentiated into domestic, household work and paid labour outside the household, then patriarchy as a form of domestic, household power alters significantly.

Although ideal type patriarchy may be limited empirically, Weber sees it as the foundation for traditional patrimonial power exercised on a society-wide basis. In fact, Weber suggests that when social relations are codified outside the immediate household, then the rule of the patriarch is inevitable. We have seen that Weber recognized the possibility of the maternal grouping rising above the military and economic grouping of the men's house, but he considered this a primitive and precarious arrangement, with no significance for more extensive social organization. As soon as effective and extensive territorial and political power come into play, the "patriarchal and agnatic structure of the household and kin group became usually predominant."[41] The great empires of the Far and Near East, of India and the Mediterranean, as well as northern Europe, all developed, in Weber's view, out of the framework exemplified by the patriarchal household. As a consequence, Weber suggests that there is no evidence that any other form of kinship relations existed before patrilineal descent "ever since kinship relations . . . had been regulated by law at all."[42] Matriarchy as a previous form of relations is rejected on the basis that it confuses the situation in which, under primitive conditions, the relations between parent and child are unregulated, and "the mother is indeed closer to the children whom she feeds and rears" with the very different situation of a culturally defined, *legal* arrangement that would be labeled matriarchy.

This particular analysis is interesting in the light of our earlier observation that sociological theory is not objective. Preconceptions do inform the questions asked and the presentation of the data. For Weber, the mother-child link that associates her with feeding and rearing her offspring is not a social relation. Mothers and their children form the basic "natural" family, but this is not sociologically significant. Only when the parent-child connection is legally established, is the natural relation socialized. For the parent-child connection, then, we must read father-child connection. The mother-child connection is "naturally" known, but it is fathers that civilize the relationship.

Like those of Durkheim, Marx and Engels, Weber's position on the question of matriarchy is partly a response to the nineteenth-century debate on the proposition that matriarchy preceded the historical evidence of patriarchy. In Weber's view the natural (biologically based) relation between mother and child may provide a basis for subsequent social relations but it cannot by itself be considered a social relation. Like other theorists, Weber did not distinguish between the biological capacity of women to reproduce and the social arrangements which surround that action and the subsequent care of the offspring.

There is one further point that is relevant to our discussion of Weber's dismissal of matriarchy. If matriarchy is regarded as the mirror image of patriarchy, according to the ideal type, then there is evidence from diverse cultural and historical sources of women assuming the direction and control of the domestic economy of large households in their own right.

The dismissal of matriarchy as a possibility is not, however, based on contrast with the ideal type patriarchy of the primitive household, but rather is related to the more general question of political power. That is, there is no female equivalent of the exercise of political power by men as a group over women as a group through the male monopoly of the means of coercion. There is no evidence of women systematically excluding men from the exercise of political power on the same basis and in the same manner as women have been excluded by men in many societies. Like many other theorists, Weber dismisses the question of matriarchal power by identifying "civilization" or "culture" with the male regulation of society, with the result that the seeming comparison between matriarchy and patriarchy is non-existent, since the basis for the conceptualizations of the two forms are not equivalent. At the same time, it must be recognized that ideal type patriarchy is not identical with, but only the foundation of, political domination.

The extension of patriarchy beyond the household results in patrimonial domination. This form of domination is a "special case of patriarchal domination—domestic authority decentralized through assignment of land and sometimes of equipment to sons of the house or other dependents."[43] Traditional domination exercised outside the household represents a modification to the "rule of the Father" that "pure" or "primitive" patriarchialism represents. Such modifications, although of benefit largely to men have, as we will see, also provided the means for the participation of women in the formal, public exercise of power.

TRADITIONAL DOMINATION

Patrimonialism

The patriarch has a limited sphere of power for two reasons. His power beyond the household is curtailed, and within the household, he has no formal administrative machinery to enforce his authority. The patriarch must rely upon the voluntary obedience of the household members, and this could produce situations of considerable tension in the relationship between the master and the subordinates.[44] The reliance upon the sanctity of tradition and the belief in the "natural" character of the relationship to ensure obedience is a tenuous foundation for the persistence of patriarchal power. The patrimonial ruler, although he represents a "special case of patriarchal domination,"[45] has greater resources to command obedience, namely an administrative apparatus and a military force personally indebted to himself. These groups will generally enforce the ruler's commands over the rest of the subjects in return for status and privileges.

The power of the patrimonial ruler may in practice be diluted by the administrative apparatus of his domain, but he remains an absolute ruler and can assert his absolute power whenever he wishes. The patrimonial ruler is the embodiment of the state, and his domain is administered like a large patriarchal household. His subjects render "compulsory labor and services, honorary gifts, regularly and irregularly levied taxes, formally according to the master's need and discretion, in fact according to established custom."[46]

The absolute power of the ruler is checked by custom and, more significantly, by his recognition of his "powerlessness in the face of the group."[47] This check on his power is exercised by the group that acts on behalf of the ruler in the enforcement of his authority, usually the military men. The ruler must keep these subjects happy if he wishes to continue to rule. The rewards accorded to these subjects, who are necessary for the protection and the administration of his domain, tend, over time, to become customary. The subjects closest to the ruler, who are the beneficiaries of the greater share of his largess, become a privileged group. As a privileged group, they are able to confront the ruler with their own interests and demands that will, in turn, limit the absolute power of the patrimonial ruler. Knowledge of common interests vis-à-vis the ruler will generate "the inclination and the ability to look after them, so that the subordinates may confront the ruler at first only occasionally, then regularly, as a closed, privileged stratum."[48]

It is in the dynamics of the relationship between the ruler and an entrenched, privileged group of subjects that the possibility of female power is found. In theory, all who fall under the jurisdiction of the patrimonial ruler are equally subject to his rule and therefore the ruler can play favourites—he can elevate or cast down any subject according to his pleasure. In fact, the ruler may attempt to curb the power of privileged status groups by elevating or favouring those whose lowly status or alien origins make them personally indebted to himself for their position and privileges. Such favourites are likely to be opposed by privileged status groups because of the threat they represent to the group's own continued enjoyment of privilege and status. It is under such conditions that women may benefit. An ambitious woman who could catch the eye of the ruler might translate her sexual attractions into political power, whatever her former status in life. For example, history records that the Empress Theodora, who shared in the exercise of power with the Emperor Justinian in sixth-century Byzantium, had been an actress and probably a prostitute before her marriage to the Emperor.

The acquisition of power by women under patrimonial domination is, however, unusual and short-lived. In addition, it does not establish any precedents for the *regular* participation of women in the exercise of power. For the majority of women under such domination there is little legitimate scope for them other than in their traditional roles of wife and mother, irrespective of the status of the man to whom they are attached. Where women did step beyond their traditional roles, usually as a consequence of their sexual attractiveness, it was often at the expense of other women, as the career of Fredegund illustrates.

> Fredegund, of humble birth and a maid to Queen Audovers, wife of King Chilperic, intrigued to have her mistress repudiated and dispatched to a convent, where Fredegund had her murdered. Then Fredegund married the king herself, the first step in a violent career which encompassed the murder of Chilperic's third wife, . . . the assassination of numerous political enemies, including Chilperic's brother Sigebert; the killing of Chilperic's sons by other wives and concubines; and assorted tortures and poisonings.[49]

Although Fredegund's career could compare in its violence and intrigue with many of her sixth-century male counterparts, it was a career dependent upon the "pleasure" of Chilperic. Patrimonial domination might offer scope for some form of female participation in the political public sphere, but the significance of such participation is tempered by the fact that the power base, in common with any male "favourite," is tied exclusively to the goodwill of the patrimonial ruler and is secure only to the extent that the ruler appreciates the individual's particular value to himself.

Patrimonial domination, as an extension of pure patriarchy,

involves some modification to the nature of power and its exercise. Although, in theory, the power of the patrimonial ruler is as absolute as that of the household patriarch, in fact the administrative needs of the territory over which he rules encroach upon that power. The tempering of the ruler's power is, however, confined to the activities of a select group of loyal subjects at the apex of the social structure who are necessary to the administration of the realm. Such a select group is normally composed of men. The rest of the population, the majority of women and other men, are merely subjects who can be coerced into obedience. Even the enjoyment of the ruler's pleasure by the select few can be short-lived because, for the patrimonial ruler, *all* are subjects.

Weber compares patrimonial domination with another form of traditional power, feudalism. Feudalism as a general type of domination was characteristic of western European society and other societies, such as medieval Japan. In our consideration of Weber's discussion of ideal type political power, we will pay particular attention to feudalism because it is precisely the characteristics of this form of domination that alter in significant ways the patriarchal basis of such domination, and hence the nature of power relations between the sexes.

Feudalism

Feudalism is differentiated from patrimonialism by the fact that the relationship between the ruler and his subordinates, or vassals, is reciprocal, involving rights and obligations on both sides. Although the relationship may have evolved out of the dependency of the patrimonial retainer, it is different because it is a contractual relationship and "thus it is presupposed that the vassal is a free man."[50] The hereditary form of the feudal relation retains its link with patriarchy in that the complex of rights, obligations and duties that binds the participants is supposedly transmitted through the male line.

The feudal relationship also emerges out of the military needs of the patrimonial ruler. Hereditary land grants are made by the ruler in exchange for military service. The relationship between the ruler and the feudal vassal is a fraternal relationship, despite the fact that it has a "legally unequal basis"—the ruler being both traditionally and legally superior to any vassal. The reciprocal obligations that bind ruler and vassal are maintained by a code of honour that outlines a particular lifestyle. It is therefore a relationship that produces, as a consequence of hereditary privilege and lifestyle demands, a privileged status group.[51]

Status groups are characterized by the claim to social esteem and to monopolies of privilege. As Weber indicates, status groups can develop first "by virtue of their own style of life, particularly the type of vocation": secondly, by "virtue of successful claims to higher-ranking descent": and finally through the monopoly over political or hicrocratic (priestly) powers.[52] The three claims to status are not mutually exclusive, as the example of the status group of feudal knights illustrates. The knights were able to claim status privileges and therefore social esteem and deference on the basis of their exclusive control over effective military power and equipment as well as through their hereditary or family connections. In addition, many members of the group were able to translate their privileged status into political or priestly power. Many of the princes of the church were younger sons, or even illegitimate offspring, of great feudal families, just as the abbesses and the prioresses of the nunneries were unmarried or unmarriageable daughters or other female kin of those same families.

Looking after family interests or, more accurately, the interests of the immediate kinship group is one of the significant features of feudal relationships, particularly among the privileged status group of the knights. What is important to the privileged group is that the hereditary rights and privileges that accrue to the kin are not altered by circumstance or, more likely, by the actions of more powerful feudal overlords. It is in the protection of such rights and privileges on behalf of the family and kin that women can assume a leadership position. In addition, the complications of vassalage that arise when all members of the privileged strata are tied to each other through feudal obligation often give women considerable scope for political action in their own right. The feudal relationship, however, retains the patriarchal basis in that the complex of rights and obligations that binds the participants is usually transmitted through the male line. Females are incorporated only in the absence of any immediate male heir. However, female inheritance and its ensuing complications in this complex system can provide women with unusual scope for action, as illustrated in the career of Eleanor of Aquitaine in twelfth-century Europe.

On the death of her father in 1137, Eleanor came into possession of two of the most desirable and politically important fiefs of the French King.

> The young duchess . . . was King Louis's vassal, his lawful marriage prize to be quickly gathered in, for by reason of the anarchy that reigned in her provinces, she was more than likely to be rapt away by some rebel baron of her own vassalage, who might thus make himself a formidable rival of the king.[53]

The king moved quickly to marry Eleanor to his own heir in order to expand and consolidate his power and that of his lineage. The right exercised by the ruler with regard to the disposition of his vassal's women when they were left "unprotected" by their own kin is characteristic of feudal society and is a reminder of the property status of women under patriarchy. However, it must also be recognized that Eleanor, as a rightful heir to the fief, could command her own extensive group of sub-vassals independently of her own feudal overlord. It was precisely the possible mobility aspirations of one of those sub-vassals, who might persuade or coerce Eleanor into marriage and so gain control of her land, that prompted King Louis's speed in the marriage arrangements.

Eleanor's subsequent career was also affected by the feudal system of rights and obligations. Eleanor was a somewhat problematic wife to the French prince, later King Louis VII, not the least because she seemed to be capable of producing only female children. On these grounds her marriage to the French king was annulled in 1152, and later in that same year she married the future king of England, Henry II. Unfortunately, her marriage was the signal for the resumption of war between Louis and Henry. This was in part because Henry's action, not Eleanor's, was regarded as a grave affront to Louis. Once Eleanor ceased to be Louis's wife, she reverted to her formal vassal status, and he therefore had the legal right to determine who she might marry. Eleanor had not, understandably, consulted Louis on her second marriage, and Henry had certainly made no request to Louis for her hand in marriage. On this count, it was Henry's action that disturbed, in formal terms, the relations between the two men.

Although historians indicate that Eleanor was by no means a passive counter in the marital moves indicated above, nevertheless, the political consequences of her moves primarily affected the power relations among men. Eleanor's relationship with Henry appears to have been somewhat stormy, especially in regard to her continued ownership of the fiefdoms of Poitou and the Aquitaine. In 1168, during a dispute with Henry over the eventual disposition of her two provinces among their sons, she retired to Poitou. As duchess of Poitou and Aquitaine, and therefore a vassal of the French king, she claimed his support and protection from the bellicose reactions of her own husband.

Eleanor's actions were made possible in large part by the feudal system of reciprocal obligation associated with hereditary land ownership, rather than being the consequence of any ideas about sex equality in the top ranks of feudal society. In theory, women remained subject to the control of males. A woman was subject first to her father, then to her husband. If her father died before her marriage, she became a ward of her father's lord and could be married according to his dictate. In fact, wardship was often a lucrative enterprise for many rulers, with wards and even ex-wives being "bought and sold like securities."

> In 1214 King John of England succeeded in dealing his first wife, Isabella of Gloucester, whose marriage to him had been annulled in 1200, to Geoffrey de Mandeville, Earl of Essex, for the huge sum of 20,000 marks . . . On a more modest scale, John's accounts of the year 1207 recorded payments of "100 marks and two palfreys" from one man for marriage with a widow, "with her inheritance, her marriage portion, and her dower," and "1200 marks and two palfreys" from another for an heiress.[54]

Some of the provisions of the Magna Carta (1215) included the agreement that the king no longer had the right to auction off widows, or to hold heirs ransom. Finally, if a woman remained single, there was only one course open to her, if she was a member of nobility, and that was the convent. An unmarried woman among the nobility was a social and financial embarrassment, and when no husband could be found, many women were sent, willingly or not, to the convent.

Many noble women were sent to the convent because families would "invest all their savings in a dowry for one of the daughters (usually the most beautiful), so as to marry into a family with appropriate status and assets. The remaining daughters were obliged to take the veil, a situation condemned by the preachers."[55] Admittedly, some of the nuns had productive and stimulating lives. For many women the convent was a refuge from the demands of the secular world that left little choice other than marriage, but it was a life supposedly cut off from the mainstream of events.[56] In addition, the women's orders had, theoretically, limited independence from the control of the male-dominated church hierarchy. In practice, abbesses often did wield considerable power, both religious and secular, but this power did nothing to reverse the basic misogynist teachings of the church.[57]

The subordinate "place" of women under feudalism is reinforced by the requirements of status honour, upon which the feudal system of reciprocal obligation rests. The basis for traditional domination, whether patrimonial or feudal, is its military origin. As Weber indicates,

> The feudal system produces men who can equip themselves and handle weapons professionally, who in war identify their own honor with that of the Lord, who see in the expansion of his power the chance to secure fiefs for their heirs and, above all, who find the only *basis for the legitimacy of their own fief* in the preservations of *his* personal authority.[58]

The behaviour associated with knighthood is based on personal bonds that transcend other divisions. These bonds are defined through special training in the ethos of knighthood, and thus in the characteristics of status honour. The training and the initiation into knighthood creates a bond between an elite group of men from which women are excluded. Shahar suggests that the only role women played in the ethical and aesthetic values of knighthood was in "one of its least vital aspects, the courtly culture, and even then as objects more than subjects."[59] However, it is precisely the requirements of the knightly lifestyle, so important to the preservation of status honour, that had the effect of making women prime economic managers of hereditary fiefdoms and often powerful actors on the feudal scene.

Weber's account of feudalism as an example of ideal type traditional domination takes no account of sex relationships other than women's general subordination and compliance with that status under the patriarchal origins of this form of power. Whereas the extension of patriarchy beyond the household has significant consequences for the nature and distribution of power among men, the same possibility for change regarding women is ignored by Weber. However, historical evidence suggests that the transformation of patriarchy, especially in the case of feudalism, does produce important modifications in sex relations. Generally, among privileged status groups, gender seems to be less significant than property and kin in the actual exercise of public power. In addition, the effects of "pure" patriarchy that might be supposed to have continuing significance among less privileged groups such as the peasantry are also modified significantly by the socio-economic consequences of the feudal rights and obligations of their "betters."

An examination of the ethos of knighthood and the significance of the kin group in feudal society illustrates the basis for modifications to patriarchal power. These two factors, combined with the rigid hierarchy of deference characteristic of status society, provide an explanation for the seemingly unusual actions and positions assumed by many women in western European feudal society. These factors also help to extend our understanding of the historical realities of traditional domination.

Ethos of Knighthood
The complex ties among all the members of feudal society arose initially from the military and fraternal connections of the ruler and his immediate vassals. Fiefs were originally granted in return for military service, but over time they also came to include administrative duties. In turn, the incumbent of the fief might duplicate the vassal relationship with a subordinate who would assist in the administration of the fief. There were limits, however, to the extension of the vassalage and therefore to knightly status. The most important restriction was the ability to supply horse and arms, since the "peculiarity of occidental, fully developed feudalism was largely determined by the fact that it constituted the basis of a cavalry."[60] The peasant's obligation to his superior overlord was therefore of a different order from the obligation of a minor lord who could equip himself and possibly a few retainers in the event of war.

The reciprocal obligations of loyalty that bound the privileged group of knights were clearly delimited. The obligations were upheld by a code of knightly status honour, which ideally transcended all other divisions, even nationality. Problems often arose, however, when kinship was complicated by nationality. The story of Eleanor and Simon de Montfort is illustrative. Simon was a French knight and Eleanor the sister of Henry III of England. In 1238 the two were secretly married, causing considerable alarm, given the relationship of the bride to the King of England and the nationality of the husband—despite his legitimate status as a high-ranking knight with possessions in England. As Geis and Geis point out, a foreign adventurer had "assured himself of the property, power, and status of a King's sister which properly belonged either to a native magnate . . . or to a royal suitor . . . the barons, jealous of their rights as royal counselors, had been hoodwinked."[61]

Ideally, the privileged group of military men formed a cohesive, fraternal association whose transcendence of the divisions of nationality was consolidated by the religious overtones of the chivalric code of behaviour. For example, the Church's frequent call for a crusade for the "return" of the Holy Land to Christian hands always involved an appeal to the participants to realize the true fraternal ideal of chivalry. In the beginning, crusades often united feudal overlords who had been bitter enemies in the past. The friendship might prove short-lived and often did not last long enough for the start of the crusade, but the initial endorsement of brotherhood was important in reinforcing the idea, if not the fact, of the status group solidarity of "true Christian Knights."[62]

In some cases, the announcement of a crusade, or the promise to undertake such a venture, was the means for the resolution of festering disputes among various knights who could renounce their enmity in the interest of the greater good of the crusade. The transnational nature of chivalry and the wearing of the crusader cross supposedly protected the knight in his journey across possibly hostile territory on his way to the Holy Land. Unfortunately, the political or territorial advantages to be gained by the detention of crusaders of rank were often too much to resist. However, fraternity and the code of chivalry were still supposed to apply, and the treatment of a prisoner of rank was considerably better than the rough justice any ordinary, non-knightly followers would receive. Waley records that the division between the knight and the ordinary foot soldier was so great that "it was felt by some nobles to be unfitting that a knight should be killed by an infantryman; indeed the duke of Julliers hanged one of his foot soldiers who was so rash as to claim responsibility for the death of the duke's enemy the count of St. Pol."[63]

The central tenets of the knightly ethos were military prowess, loyalty to the feudal overlord and courtesy and consideration towards other knights. The chivalric code united the knights as a class, and the demonstration of the legitimacy of one's knightly status was through personal conduct. As Weber points out, all relationships were permeated with personal bonds, which had the "effect of centering the feeling of knightly dignity on the cult of the personal."[64] This personalization of the status was demonstrated in both the training and the performance of military skill. The military training of the knight was designed to perfect individual skill. The "typical feudal army is an army of knights, and that means individual heroic combat, not the discipline of a mass army."[65] This meant that the knight had to maintain his skill and prowess, and it was in this regard that the tournament played a vital role. Although minor and major wars seem, in many of the traditional historical accounts, to have been a permanent feature of medieval Europe, in fact, there were significant stretches of peace when the knight needed some way of maintaining combat readiness. In addition, feudal overlords and heads of families needed to find legitimate outlets for the energies of many young, ambitious, but poor second sons of the nobility whose lineage made it impossible to consider anything other than the lifestyle of the noble.[66] The tournament was the solution, and although comparable to modern war games, it could be as bloody and lethal as actual warfare. Like their modern counterparts, tournaments were not cheap affairs, although killing an opponent could, in some cases, be remunerative if the winner gained the horse, armour and trappings of the defeated knight.

The training of the knight and the maintenance of his military prowess either in actual war or on the tournament circuit entailed much expense. In addition, the demands of hospitality by travellers and the need to demonstrate to subordinates as well as to visitors one's legitimate claim to status meant that a certain minimum expenditure was necessary on the domestic front. Such exigencies could be problematic when the not uncommon situation of bad harvest and/or the wartime pillage of the land resulted in decreased goods, services and taxes from the peasantry. It is not surprising that the usurer played so important a role in the daily lives of the feudal nobility. In general, as Weber indicates, luxury, splendour and ostentation were essential components of the knight's lifestyle. Luxury is "for the dominant feudal strata nothing superfluous: it is a means of social self-assertion."[67]

An adequate degree of consumption and display required good management of resources, but this behaviour was precisely what was forbidden the "true" knight. The knight's very existence was theoretically sufficient explanation for his purpose in life. As Weber points out, the "positively privileged feudal strata do not view their existence functionally."[68] In fact, the ethos of the knight was contrary to rational economic behaviour. In feudal conduct could be seen "that nonchalance in business affairs which has been typical of all feudal strata, not only in contrast to the bourgeois, but also to the peasants' proverbial shrewdness."[69] Since the knight could not compromise his status and style by a concern with mundane affairs, the management of those affairs, so critical to the demonstration and maintenance of his lifestyle, was often in the hands of his wife.

Thus women of feudal nobility were often required to manage the estates and possessions of their husbands. This frequently meant that it was the wife rather than the husband who dealt with the various claims and obligations surrounding the day-to-day administration of the household, which is to say, the economy. For example, the English Paston and the Lisle letters document the running of large estates by women on behalf of, although largely in the absence of, their husbands. Margaret Paston negotiated with the peasants, leased land, collected rents, sold crops and made purchases necessary for the household and estates. She also appeared as her husband's representative before the law and repelled an attack by another lord who claimed some of the Paston lands.[70]

Lady Lisle not only undertook daily management of the extensive Lisle holdings in the absence of her husband, but also conducted a complex defence of the Lisle interests in a dispute with the king's representative, Thomas Cromwell. The dispute concerned Lord Lisle's annuity for his activities on behalf of the king.[71] Both Margaret Paston and Lady Lisle found themselves financially embarrassed on more than one occasion as a consequence of their husband's status needs. Indeed, Lady Lisle's negotiations with Cromwell, which terminated in her selling part of her own land to Cromwell in order to gain a resolution of the dispute, was occasioned by the fact that Lord Lisle was in debt. Although the financial problems of the Lisle family were not entirely the result of Lord Lisle's personal extravagance, many other wives found themselves in difficulties as a result of the cavalier attitude of their husbands towards finances. For example,

In the letter in which Jean de Montreuil lists the grievances of his friend Gontier Col's wife against her husband, he mentions her complaints against Gontier's profligacy and supports her claim that if it were not for the fact that she managed their financial affairs with care and responsibility, their situation would be atrocious.[72]

For the feudal nobility their possessions were the household writ large, but it was often their wives who were expected to take care of those possessions and undertake the major administrative tasks, leaving the knight free to undertake his military duties or simply roam around the tournament circuit. Charlemagne conferred on his queen the power to run his estates: that is, to take care of "finances and domestic affairs of the realm—in order to leave the king free for what were considered more important duties," such as war and diplomacy.[73] The division of labour among the nobility worked to the advantage of many women in that their control over the source of the knights' wealth and status provided them with the means to influence the structure of power. Consequently, the ethos of knighthood that gave rise to an exclusive male status group often resulted in bringing women, as important players, into the structure of power relations. This situation was compounded when hereditary claims on behalf of powerful lineages were protected by female heirs in the absence of any suitable male.

The nature of the feudal economy and the status claims of the knight meant that over time the protection of the patrimony could be undertaken by women themselves, as heiresses. As several historians have pointed out, from about the ninth to the thirteenth centuries, many women inherited and administered fiefdoms and generally exercised considerable political power.[74] Part of the explanation for this seeming anomaly, given the patriarchal basis of traditional feudal power, has to do with the importance of the kin unit and its need to conserve land. This need arose when the purely military significance of the fief was complicated by administrative duties. Property and kin became, therefore, the important factors in the distribution of power in traditional feudal society and enabled many women to assume significant social and political power.

Property and Kin

The gradual conversion of fiefdoms into hereditary possessions and the entrenchment of the power of the great feudal overlords in medieval Europe meant that personal kin relations became very significant. As a result, in the top ranks of society, the maintenance of family status and power could be protected through female

inheritance in the absence of a legitimate male heir. To prevent
land from passing out of the immediate family line in the absence
of a legitimate son, daughters could and did inherit. A woman who
inherited a fief and exercised the rights it entailed violated the
formal political/legal definitions of the position. However, this
contradiction, while recognized, did not prevent many women
from performing the administrative and even the military requirements of the inheritance.

> Sometimes one clause of a legal code cites the physical weakness and
> mental limitations of women to justify depriving them of authority,
> while the following clause specifies ways in which the oath of fealty
> should be rendered by a woman who inherits a fief entailing ruling
> powers, and the best way in which lords *and ladies* can rule their
> vassals.[75]

In accordance with the patriarchal basis of the system, the rights
of sons generally took precedence over those of daughters, and the
rule of primogeniture generally applied. However, the chances of
daughters inheriting were fairly good because of the high death
rates among men of the knightly status group. Huizinga refers to
the "violent tenor of life"[76] during the Middle Ages, particularly
among the nobility. The basic reason for the knight's existence was
his military prowess, and as our discussion of the ethos of the
knight has indicated, the pursuit of perfection as a fighting
machine was the major task for a knight. Shahar points out that the
average life expectancy of the men of ducal families in England
between 1300 and 1475 was 24 years. In contrast, women's life
expectancy from birth for this group was 32.9 years. As many as 46
percent of all men died violently after their fifteenth year.[77] When
not engaged in warfare or a crusade, the feudal knight competed in
tournaments, which could be as hazardous as the battles they
simulated.

The high death rates of the knights made female inheritance a
probability, enhanced by the association of land and status and the
marriage practices of the feudal nobility. The retention of privileged status that rested on land as a form of wealth meant that the
division of such a patrimony must inevitably result in the diminu-
tion of the status of the next generation. Families wished to retain,
if not increase, their status and their power, and the knights were no
exception in this desire. As a consequence, over time the practice
developed that the inheritance of the major portion went to the

eldest male, and the marriages of other siblings were restricted. As Duby remarks, marriage, designed to safeguard the unity of the inheritance, meant that the "eldest son would exercise control over the common property handed down from his forebears, as a guarantee that the family might maintain its ascendancy."[78] To limit the possibility of having to split up the inheritance on behalf of other sons, only the eldest, or at most two, of the sons would marry. The rest would be found positions in the Church or become part of those bands of roving youths on the lookout for a tournament to obtain some wealth or, better still, a rich heiress to marry and enable them to appropriately maintain their knightly status.

Rich heiresses were available because (1) the superiority of direct descendants over collateral branches of the family was preferred for inheritance purposes; and (2) the effects of restricted marriages "frequently resulted in a daughter who had no brothers inheriting her father's possessions, even though she had uncles and cousins living."[79] The preference for direct descendants, combined with the mortality rates of young males of the privileged status group, meant that many women held and administered fiefs in their own right as heiresses.

Related to the death rates of the knights and the restricted marriage practices was another important feature of feudal society—widow power. Although classed by the Church as a *miserabilis persona*, the widow generally enjoyed greater freedom of action than other women in medieval society. A widow was free to choose either to remain single or to remarry, and she was guaranteed dower rights that could be up to a third to one half of her husband's assets. A noble widow's dower rights could include control over fiefs that would revert back to the heir only on her death. Noble widows could therefore exercise considerable power through their control over land.

The advantages of the status of widow extended to all women in medieval society. Among the peasantry and the merchant and trader groups, the widow was often a more desirable marriage partner than the never-married woman. Widows could, through their inheritance, provide propertyless males with the resources to establish themselves in a comfortable manner. The apprentice who married the boss's daughter was a less likely occurrence than the apprentice who married the boss's widow.[80] Even peasant widows, if they had control over such things as rights to common pasture, or if they ran a small "bye" industry, such as brewing, were more desirable marriage partners than young single women.

Whether feudal lord or peasant, the maintenance of the connection between land and family was often of greater significance than exclusive male inheritance. As Hilton points out, historians have tended to minimize the hereditary rights that peasants felt they had in their land, but the evidence suggests that a "primary feature of the peasant outlook was a deeply rooted sense of family property rights in the peasant holding, and the various appurtenances which made it a viable economic unit—such as claims for common pasture and other customary usages."[81] This protection of a family's interest in the land is exemplified by the practice of men taking a woman's family name.[82] The man who married a widow, like the husband of an heiress, was often "regarded as a kind of custodian, who could keep the land for life if the marriage produced an heir, but after whose death the holding reverted to the original bloodline."[83]

In general, "widow power" is one of the more significant aspects of relations between the sexes in feudal society. Single women and married women were legally under the control of a male. Although they may have had considerable freedom of action through their indispensable economic contributions, they nevertheless were ultimately constrained by the *de jure* power of men. Widows, in contrast, could often exercise considerable power as a result of their control over property. "Widows often profited from marriage contracts that, in place of the traditional widow's third, gave them far more of their husbands' land, even, on occasion, all of it."[84] As Geis and Geis point out, some widows took the opportunity provided by their inheritance to marry a younger man. Others, "more materialistic or less romantic, used remarriage to increase their wealth. Still others remained widows, often keeping property from the ultimate heirs, male or female, for decades."[85]

The ethos of knighthood and the importance of family and kin enabled many women to play decisive roles in feudal society, especially women of the nobility. Such women appeared as "judges, castellans, controllers of property," and even as military leaders. For example, in the eleventh century, Matilda, countess of Tuscany, personally led her troops against the German emperor in her support of a beleaguered Pope. The supposedly exclusive military role of the knight was, in practice, assumed by women when it came to the defence of their inheritance or, in the frequent absence of their husbands, in defence of the fiefdom. Such women may not have taken to the field as did Matilda. But their command over an armed force and the fact that such actions were not unusual, and were even expected, modifies our conceptualization of gender relations under feudalism.

The ethos of knighthood and the importance of lineage to the retention of property, combined with the rigid hierarchy of a status society, meant that the patriarchal ideal was considerably modified in practice.

Status Society

Weber claimed that the "essence of feudalism is status conscious-ness,"[86] and the maintenance of status divisions was of critical importance for the continued enjoyment of privileges and benefits by high status groups. The ideological universe of feudal western Europe was described in terms of a three-part division of those who prayed, those who fought and those who worked—worshippers, warriors and workers. This was a limited description of reality, since it took no account of the merchants, traders and other urban dwellers who did not fit into the model. However, this was the model endorsed by the Church and regarded as divinely ordained and therefore unchangeable through human agency. Within the model it was those who fought and those who prayed who benefited from the status divisions, and neither group had any interest in changes that might threaten their privileged positions.

The Church espoused an ideology that benefited the clergy and the warriors and one that associated the status divisions with an evaluation of the spiritual worth of the incumbents. The knight protected the land and those who worked the land; at the same time he was supported by the land through the work of the peasants. This was only appropriate, since working the land was associated with servility, which, in turn, verged on bestiality and was furthest removed from spirituality.[87]

The justification of the status divisions was part of the legitimacy claim which the privileged group could advance. In fact, Weber's ideal type traditional domination rests on the assumption that all other groups in the society concur with the legitimacy claims of the privileged. In reality, the latter were more likely to ensure the compliance of the lower orders through force. Compliance would therefore be assured by fear and the weight of custom. In the last resort, it was the monopoly of military hardware on the part of the knights that allowed stability even if, as Parkin suggests, "the many who shouldered the burden of production did *not* accept the legitimacy of the few who lived off the surplus."[88]

The acquiescence of the lower orders was always potentially in question, as the history of peasant revolts and the turbulence of urban workers indicate. Such disruptions were, however, fairly easily contained through physical as well as ideological coercion. Laslett suggests that when subordination and the exercise of power are based on tradition, then "critical examination of the reasons why some men are better placed than others was unlikely to come about." The "submissive cast of mind" in such a society is nearly universal, and "once a man in the traditional world got himself into a position where he could catch a glimpse of his society as a whole, he immediately felt that degree, order, was its essential feature. Without degree, unquestioning subordination, and some men being privileged while all others obeyed, anarchy and destruction were inevitable."[89]

The fear that any disruption to the hierarchy of status would produce revolutionary consequences accounts, in part, for the various sumptuary laws that were constantly proclaimed in various medieval societies. The sumptuary laws were attempts to regulate dress and appearance so that the proper distance between social levels was visibly maintained. What was particularly noticeable was that such laws were often directed explicitly at the urban merchants and their wives who did not "fit" the tri-part order of society. Many medieval commentators expressed indignation that some of the merchant's wives were better dressed, better housed and possessed more finery and jewels than their noble "betters." The imitation of the dress of the nobles by the lesser orders was a direct and observable affront to the *status quo* and one that had to be resisted firmly if social order was to be maintained. As a result, elaborate codes were devised in the attempt to regulate the dress and expenditures of the various social strata.

> Proclaimed by criers in the country courts and public assemblies, exact gradations of fabric, color, fur trimming, ornaments, and jewels were laid down for every rank and income level . . . In France territorial lords and their ladies with incomes of 6,000 livres or more could order four costumes a year; knights and bannerets with incomes of 3,000 could have three a year, one of which had to be for

summer. Boys could have only one a year, and no *demoiselle* who was not the *chatelaine* of a castle or did not have an income of 2,000 livres could order more than one costume a year.[90]

In any status society the observance of "proper" status honour and deference is critical to the maintenance of the status hierarchy. The person who claims status honour or to whom deference is accorded is of less importance than the appropriateness of the claim. Consequently, gender takes second place to appropriate status relations in the regulation of behaviour. In feudal society, therefore, women in general could have been, in the eyes of the Church and society, problematic beings too prone to the lures of the devil, but individual women of rank still had to be accorded due deference by men of lesser rank and status. For example, for female heirs the military requirements of the fief could, theoretically, have eliminated their enjoyment of its power and privileges. But, this requirement was overcome by the assumption that their husbands would undertake this obligation. In addition, many women demonstrated their own competence in organizing the defence of their property, even taking to the field themselves and, on those occasions they were obeyed out of status deference that overrode their inappropriate sex.

Women were theoretically excluded from power in feudal society, but that exclusion was subject to many exceptions in practice. The very characteristics of the power structure—the complex of vassalage, lineage and the ethos of the knight—had the contradictory effect of making sex a secondary consideration in the actual exercise of power.

It should also be observed that modifications to the patriarchal ideal—largely the result of the nature of economic relations—were apparent at all status levels of feudal society. The circumstances of daily living invariably meant the modification of ideal type patriarchy. Tuchman suggests that in daily life, "women of the noble as well as the non-noble class found equality of function, if not of status, thrust upon them by circumstance."[91] The household was the economy. "The richest families of the manor and those squatting on the scrubbiest commons ate most of what they grew and grew most of what they ate, made most of what they used and used most of what they made."[92] The circumstances of peasant existence especially made mutual dependency, rather than patriarchal domination, a more realistic description of the peasant couple's relationship. In general, the peasant woman shared in the daily work of her husband, "sowing, reaping, gleaning, binding, threshing, raking, winnowing, thatching," as well as producing the food and clothing for the family.[93] Likewise, the wives of craftsmen and merchants played indispensable roles in the businesses, and some guilds allowed widows to continue their husband's trade.

Taking into account the various modifications to ideal type patriarchy and traditional domination as exemplified by feudalism, we must now assess the utility of Weber's ideal types. The questions to be addressed are first, to what extent do the types provide more or less adequate understanding of power relations between the sexes and, secondly, can ideal type patriarchy be extended to account for sex relations outside the confines of the household?

THE TYPES RECONSIDERED

Ideal types are, according to Weber, indispensable as a methodological tool for the social sciences. As he points out, as soon as the investigator wants to explain the *significance* of an event, then the investigator *"must* use concepts which are precisely and unambiguously definable only in the form of ideal types."[94] The use of ideal type methodology is necessary because social science data are never fully conceptually "fixed." That is, "all knowledge of cultural reality . . . is always knowledge from particular points of view,"[95] and the intellectual basis from which that reality is approached changes according to the "evaluative ideas which dominate the investigator and his age."[96]

Sociological knowledge is generated out of the interests of the researcher, and the "intellectual contexts from which it is viewed and scientifically analyzed shift."[97] Weber's major interest is in the structure and process of power. His definition of the effective exercise of power as the probability of the actor exercising "his own will despite resistance" is sex neutral and could apply to the drawing room as well as to an army command post. However, when he applies his general definition of power to forms of domination, it is clear that these more realistic forms of the "authoritarian power of command" are not sex neutral. In fact, this is clear in the use of ideal type patriarchy as the basic form of *all* structures of domination.

Ideal type patriarchy assumes that the domination of women is a "natural" phenomenon. But the closest empirical, historical approximation of this form of domination is found in relatively isolated and self-sufficient household groups in which the members accept without question the sanctity of tradition that supports the patriarch and regulates the subordinates' lives. Beyond the household, the power of the patriarch is considerably modified because that power must be negotiated with many other males.

Ideal type patriarchy is a blueprint for a relatively primitive collectivity maintained by a subsistence economy, occasionally supplemented by the spoils of brigandage. Stone has suggested that, in the European context, the utility of ideal type patriarchy as a tool to analyze the structure and relations of an historical society was limited to the eastern and southern shores of the Mediterranean, and was present only in modified form elsewhere in Europe. He suggests that the observable characteristics of the Weberian ideal type are as follows:

> In terms of power relations, the man rides to work on a donkey or a mule—if he goes to work at all—while the wife follows behind on foot with the heavy tools. The husband is legally and morally free to beat his wife, although not to the point of maiming or murder. A wife has no right whatever to dispose of her own property, and all she owns passes to her husband on marriage. A wife serves the husband and the eldest son at the table, but rarely sits down with them. In terms of sex, male adultery is a venial sin, female adultery an unpardonable crime. Female premarital chastity is a matter of family honor, unmarried girls are always chaperoned, and seducers are killed. Marriages are arranged by the fathers without consulting the wishes of the bride or groom. A wife provides the sexual services demanded by her husband, but is not herself expected to achieve orgasm in sexual intercourse."[98]

Stone's description brings into focus the basis and perspective of the conceptualization of ideal type patriarchy. First, social power as the possibility of exercising legitimate domination is seen to be essentially and even naturally a male prerogative. Secondly, the type assumes that the subordination of women, children and slaves will not produce any of the complications that the presence of free adult males in the household might generate. The discussion of household obedience is therefore about relations among men. The patriarch commands the household but the experience of that command and the differential nature of obedience in terms of sex are left unexplored. Finally, it is assumed that women have no interest in and no resources of power within the patriarchal household. In fact, even the submissive wife of the Stone example might have resources at her disposal that mitigate, even if they do not entirely eliminate, the negative consequences of her subordination.[99]

The nature of relations between men and women is, however, a secondary concern for Weber in light of the fact that patriarchy is about relations among men. Modifications to the power of the patriarch are seen as significant only when they involve adjusting relations among men, especially with regard to valued goods and services. Weber suggests that "because of the very predominance of patriarchy, property law develops in the great empires in the direction of steadily *weakening* unlimited patriarchal power."[100] For example, women are one of the objects of negotiation among men, as they can "be legitimately acquired from another household only through exchange or purchase."[101] The absolute power of patriarchs over women "from their own circle" is checked to some extent when fathers, for example, begin to protect the interests of their daughters and the children of those daughters in terms of the father's interests as opposed to those of the daughters' husbands.

Weber's ideal type patriarchy is useful in understanding the process and structure of domination among men as patriarchial heads of households. However, to understand the nature of sex relations under patriarchy, an examination of compliance or obedience is necessary. Without this component patriarchy remains conceptualized as the generalized power of men over women. As the basis for a historical analysis of traditional domination, the concept is limited when it is clear that some women exercise domination, and that a uniform, hierarchical division of labour between the sexes is absent from some societies.

Patriarchy's extension beyond the household is, according to Weber, the result of the need to formalize relations among adult, free men—particularly sons of the patriarch. Patrimonialism retains the closest structural affinity to patriarchy both in terms of the ruler's relationship with his close, personal retainers as well as in terms of gender relations. Feudalism, in contrast, introduces important modifications to the relations of power and domination between the ruler and his vassals as well as with regard to privileged women. The anomaly of women's exercise of power can best be addressed when the nature of obedience and compliance is taken into account. Feudal society as status society demands the clear separation of status groups and the recognition and practice of deference due the privileged group. Status groups are marked by the members' recognition of their collective identity and their solidarity so that it is the interests of the whole that take precedence over the interests of the individual. Consequently, women of the nobility identify their interests with the men of their strata and may command and expect obedience from both men and women of the lower orders.

Reassessment of traditional domination as exemplified by feudalism does not, however, reverse the understanding basic to ideal type patriarchy. Power remains a male prerogative. Whatever the actions of women of the nobility and despite the fact that women at all levels played vital productive roles in feudal society, men, irrespective of status, had rights that were denied women and that gave men real advantages. Women of the nobility might inherit and exercise the ruling powers of a fief, but they did so on behalf of the lineage that still maintained agnatic descent patterns. Such women were "stand in" males.[102] Similarly, although wives of tradesmen and craftsmen were often part of the business, and many urban women were business women in their own right, they were always subject to some restrictions that were not applied to men engaged in similar activities.[103] For the peasantry there was little division of labour by sex, and women participated along with their men in nearly all aspects of agricultural labour. Yet even those peasant women who engaged in wage labour were paid only a fraction of the male wage for the same work.[104]

In examining gender relations under feudalism, it becomes clear that it is not necessarily the division of labour in a society that accounts for sex inequality. Women's complementary roles and the interdependence of the sexes in feudal life did not alter women's inferiority. Women as a collective group, irrespective of their individual status, were set apart and subject to different expectations than men. Whatever their status affiliation, women did not have rights equal to those of men, so that women as a group were subject to "a negative common denominator"[105]—their subordination to the collectivity of men.

We can conclude that it is not patriarchy as a structure of power negotiated among men that is the root cause of women's subordination in the household under traditional forms of domination. The structure of power is based on a fundamental proposition that women are somehow less than men. Patriarchy takes this proposition for granted, and the various structures of domination, whether traditional, rational-legal or even charismatic, are hierarchical arrangements of men that also enable men, in varying degrees, to have power over women. As Hartmann suggests, "Though patriarchy is hierarchical and men of different classes, races, or ethnic groups have different places in the patriarchy, they are also united in their shared relationship of dominance over their women; they are dependent on each other to maintain that domination."[106] In those cases, illustrated in this chapter, where women exercised power over other men and women, they did so on behalf of their men or their kin group, but not as legitimate participants as *females* in structures of power and domination.

Examining Weber's ideal types has yielded two important insights for our investigations. First, the ideal types provide a useful conceptual starting point for analysis but tend to obscure the nature and implications of power in sex relations. In this sense, ideal type patriarchy and ideal type traditional power reinforce the idea that these forms have a natural, historical inevitability regarding relations between the sexes within such structures of power. Secondly, our examination of ideal type patriarchy alerts us to the basic form within which patriarchal relations are thought to develop, that is, the household group with its division of labour organized in terms of sex. As our discussion of Marx and the question of social class will indicate, the sexual division of labour within the family and household group is a basic issue in the relationship between patriarchy and capitalism.

CHAPTER 4

Marx and Engels: Social Class and the "Woman Question"

In his essay "Private Property and Communism," Marx suggested that the character of female-male relationships in any society is an indication of "man's whole level of development" from animal to a human essence.[1] Only if men and women are equal can there be fully human relations. As a formal tenet of Marxist thought and practice, the equality of the sexes has been an essential component of an egalitarian, socialist society. However, in Marx's practical strategies for change and in his analysis of class society, feminism, or a concern with the "woman question," tended to take, at best, a second place to the furtherance of the proletarian revolution. Hartmann has suggested that the "marriage" of Marxism and feminism has been "like the marriage of husband and wife in English common law: Marxism and feminism are one, and that one is Marxism."[2]

For Marx, class rather than gender is the important issue, especially with regard to supporting the revolutionary potential of the working class. Guettel maintains that "historical materialism holds that in a society founded on private property the class struggle is primary; racial, national, and sex contradictions are secondary."[3] The issue that Guettel's statement defends has been the subject of radical rethinking by many feminists, who have taken the concept of social class and the position of women in relation to the family as the critical points of departure in formulating alternative explanations for sex relations. Nearly all the alternatives have sought to preserve some transformatory possibility in the reap-praisal of relations between the sexes, so that feminism, rather than Marxism, is, in some cases, regarded as the more revolutionary stance.[4]

Before considering the nature of the recent feminist critiques, we will first examine the work of Marx and Engels. Although Marx and Engels foresaw women's equality with men as critical to socialist society, how women's experience under capitalism differed from that of men was not directly addressed in their work. For example, Engels's analysis of the family is an evolutionary account of the transformation of relations between the sexes in the interests of the preservation of private property. The "woman question" is ultimately resolved in the assumption that women's increased participation in paid labour would be the means for greater equality.

Like the work of Freud, that of Marx and Engels has been "claimed" by sociology. It represents a less direct theoretical heritage than the work of Durkheim and Weber, although both Durkheim and Weber referred to Marxism in their own writing and both expressed reservations about the economic determinism that dominated Marxist analysis to the exclusion of other factors.

We will begin our discussion with an outline of Marx's theory of social class and social change. The relationship of Marx's theory to sex relations will then be examined using Engels's work *The Origin of the Family, Private Property and the State*, which expands on the theme first developed in *The German Ideology*: that the first division of labour is the "natural" division of labour "between man and woman for child-breeding."[5] The recent femi-nist critiques of Marxist theory will then be presented, with particular emphasis on the relationship of patriarchy to capitalism.

SOCIAL CLASS

As McLellan remarks, the only systematic analysis of social class in Marx's work occurs in an unfinished form in volume 3 of *Capital*.[6] In this short passage, Marx indicates that in a capitalist society there are three classes; "wage labourers, capitalists and landlords, form the three great classes of modern society resting upon the capitalist mode of production."[7] In other works, Marx described other social groups as classes, but in the *Communist Manifesto* he used a two-class model—proletariat and bourgeoisie. The variabil-

ity of Marx's use of "class" is problematic because of the importance of the concept to his theory of social change: it was the
conflict between social classes that constituted the basis for social
change. As the *Manifesto* proclaims, "The history of all hitherto
existing societies is the history of class struggle."[8]

Although the use of "class" is problematic in Marx's work,
Marxist scholars generally agree that three distinct but related ideas
regarding social class can be found in Marx's work. A social class
can be identified according to: (1) its relationship to the means of
production; (2) a consciousness of a common exploited position in
the productive process; and (3) political organization on the part of
the disposed to take action on their own behalf against the
exploiting class. These three ideas are connected by Marx's view of
the nature of social relationships and social change as being
"materialist" or grounded in the real activities of human beings in
producing their livelihood.

> Men can be distinguished from animals by consciousness, by reli-
> gion or anything else you like. They themselves begin to distinguish
> themselves from animals as soon as they begin to *produce* their
> means of subsistence, a step which is conditioned by their physical
> organization. By producing their means of subsistence men are
> indirectly producing their actual material life.[9]

Being human is therefore being productive; it is being active in
creating one's life. "As individuals express their life, so they are.
What they are, therefore, coincides with their production, both
with *what* they produce and with *how* they produce."[10]

When the productive techniques of social groups expand beyond
the provision of mere subsistence, then inequality develops as some
individuals are able to accumulate surplus wealth. In *The German
Ideology* it is the extension of a division of labour beyond the
family group that is seen to generate surplus wealth and the
subsequent private, rather than communal, ownership of economic
resources. When this occurs, the division between the owners and
non-owners of the surplus marks the beginnings of class division.
Such divisions generate conflict throughout history. As Marx and
Engels wrote in the *Manifesto*, "Freeman and slave, patrician and
plebian, lord and serf, guild-master and journeyman, in a word,
oppressor and oppressed, stood in constant opposition to one
another, carried on an uninterrupted, now hidden, now open fight,
a fight that each time ended, either in a revolutionary re-constitu-

tion of society at large, or in the common ruin of the contending classes."[11]

Social class presumes conflict, and social change is the product of such class conflict. The mechanism of conflict and change is the contradiction between different productive methods and the replacement of the old dominant group by a new group that is able to establish a new and better mode of production. As Marx pointed out, "The economic structure of capitalistic society has grown out of the economic structure of feudal society. The dissolution of the latter set free the elements of the former."[12] The new technical, instrumental and organizational forces of production result in change in the relations of production that sees the replacement of one class of owners, such as feudal lords, with another class, in this case, capitalists.

The transition to capitalism is critically important to Marx and Engels, since they see this stage as containing the potential for a truly revolutionary transformation of social relationships from the inequality and antagonisms of classes to the equal, cooperative relations of a communist society.[13] Whereas all societies are characterized by various rankings and gradations, capitalist society gradually eliminates the intermediate groups and makes the basic class antagonism starkly evident. "Society as a whole is more and more splitting up into two great hostile camps, into great classes directly facing each other: Bourgeoisie and Proletariat."[14]

The bourgeoisie or the capitalists own the means of production, which includes capital and land, as well as the labour of the workers. It is from the labour of the proletariat or the worker that the capitalist's profit or surplus value is extracted. The proletariat are forced to sell their labour for their continued subsistence. However, the return obtained for their labour is always less than its worth, the extra being the surplus that the capitalist retains. For example, Marx asks us to suppose that six hours of average labour is sufficient to produce a wage of three shillings that will enable the labourer to live. But if he works for six hours and receives that wage, then there is no profit for the capitalist. Consequently, for profit to result, the labourer is forced to work twelve hours for the profit of the capitalist. *"Over and above* the six hours required to replace his wage, or the value of his labouring power, he will, therefore, have to work *six other hours,* which I shall call hours of *surplus labour,* which surplus labour will realize itself in a *surplus value* and a *surplus produce.*"[15]

The difference between the value of the workers' labour and the surplus value produced by that labour represents a contradiction that Marx believed would eventually provide the basis for the transformation of capitalist society to a socialist, and eventually a communist, society. As the workers attempt to improve their wages and working conditions, they would begin to recognize their common, disadvantaged position in the relations of production and organize as a class to oppose the capitalist class. The first condition, a common relationship to the means of production, gives rise to the second and third conditions for the formation of social class. That is, the objective criterion of class is supplemented by a subjective understanding and hostility towards the exploiting class and this, in conjunction with political organization on the part of the proletariat, is the basis for the revolutionary transformation of society.

It is social classes that are the actors in social historical change, and classes are defined in terms of productive activity. That is, the basis for class is tied to labour that has *exchange value,* since this is what generates *surplus value.* When an object is produced for others and is offered as a commodity, then it has exchange value in contrast to the *use value* of a product when it is simply for the use of the producer.

> Whoever directly satisfies his wants with the produce of his own labour, creates, indeed, use-values, but not commodities. In order to produce the latter, he must not only produce use-values, but use-values for others, social use-values . . . To become a commodity a product must be transferred to another whom it will serve as a use-value, by means of an exchange.[16]

This distinction is important when considering the different relationship of women to the productive process, compared with men. As we will see in the domestic labour debates, the unpaid labour of women in the home is an example of the production of use-value in contrast to the exchange value produced by paid labour. Since it is a position in the production of surplus that provides the basis for class identification, then women with no direct relationship to paid labour cannot have a class position other than through association with someone in paid labour. It is this issue, among others, that generates considerable difficulty for feminist analysis when confronted with Marxist analysis.

For many feminist scholars, the dynamic struggle between

proletariat and capitalist is really the struggle between the male proletariat and the male capitalist. In Delphy's view, the proletariat described by Marx as " 'theoretically asexual' is well and truly sexed . . . . It is concerned entirely with only the male part of the working class. All the concepts used by Marx, and then by the others, take as a structural and theoretical definition of the worker's condition the lot of the male worker."[17] More particularly, women are invisible, either as paid labourers or as domestic workers, in much Marxist analysis. It appears that in the class struggle, women, somewhat like the tail of a kite, simply tag along with their men and, if they are associated with proletariat men, they will be the beneficiaries of the utopian future their men will organize.

A considerable part of the problem with the Marxist account as it concerns women is connected with the assumption of "natural" biological differences that place women in the family. Once women are located in this manner, they are forgotten, since the family then becomes the unit of analysis. An examination of Engels's work on the family illustrates the manner in which real issues surrounding the "woman question" become submerged in the analysis of the abstract "family."

MARX AND ENGELS ON THE FAMILY

In general, relations between men and women in Marx's and Engels's works were subsumed under the family. In *The German Ideology* it was the family that was seen as the basis for antagonistic relations that culminated in extra-familial class conflict. The original division of labour was seen to be in the sexual act, a division that developed "spontaneously or naturally" by virtue of "natural predisposition (e.g. physical strength), needs, accidents, etc., etc."[18] The division of labour within the family and the "separation of society into individual families opposed to one another," as a result of their differential relationship to property, produced the "nucleus" of class divisions, "the first form of which lies in the family, where the wife and children are the slaves of the husband."[19] The power of the husband-father over the labour of the wife and children represents, in Marx's view, the first form of private property. The State developed in response to the need to regulate and protect private property, which included the possession of other human beings such as the wife and children in the institution of marriage.

The relationship of the family, the state and private property was more fully examined in Engels's work *The Origin of the Family, Private Property, and the State*. The book was, in Engels's words, the "fulfillment of a bequest."[20] Marx had read and made notes on Lewis Morgan's *Ancient Society*,[21] which both Marx and Engels saw as a materialist account of primitive, prehistorical social relations that complemented Marx's materialist account of written historical social relations. Marx did not produce the work that would have related Morgan's findings to his own investigations, and so Engels, using Marx's notes, undertook the task.

In Morgan's account the evolution of social relations occurred throughout three broad periods: savagery, barbarism and civilization. Savagery represented a period of "primitive communism" in which unequal class and sexual divisions were absent. It was in the period of barbarism that transformations occurred, laying the foundations for class and sexual inequalities, and the evolution of the family structure played a critical part in these changes.

Engels indicated that the "oldest, most primitive form of the family," on Morgan's evidence, was group marriage.[22] This form gradually changed with the introduction of various prohibitions regarding appropriate sexual partners during barbarism. The first prohibitions were thought to have been those between adult generations, then between parents and children and subsequently those between brother and sister.

> The evolution of the family in prehistoric times consisted in the continual narrowing of the circle—originally embracing the whole tribe—within which marital community between the two sexes prevailed. By the successive exclusion, first of closer, then of ever remoter relatives, and finally even of those merely related by marriage, every kind of group marriage was ultimately rendered practically impossible, and in the end there remained only the one—still loosely united couple, the molecule, with the dissolution of which marriage itself completely ceases.[23]

The marital pair was at first only a weak connection that did not, according to Engels, eliminate the "communistic household" in which women were supreme.

The supremacy of women in this early period of barbarism was thought to be a consequence of the fact that fatherhood was impossible to determine with any certainty. Since descent could be traced only through the mother, there was "high esteem for the women, that is, for the mothers."[24] This pre-eminence of women prevailed throughout the savage and barbarian stages. Descent through the female line provided the "material foundation of that predominancy of women which generally obtained in primitive times,"[25] and constituted a primitive matriarchy.

The development of new economic resources and relationships of production were the critical factors in the development of the paired family and monogamy. In Engels's view it was women who pushed for monogamous sexual relations. With the "undermining of the old Communism and the growing density of population," the more the old sexual relations appeared to be "degrading and oppressive . . . to the women; the more fervently must they have longed for the right to chastity, to temporary or permanent marriage with one man only, as a deliverance."[26] This advance, Engels insisted, "could not have originated from the men, if only for the reason that they have never—not even to the present day— dreamed of renouncing the pleasures of actual group marriage."[27] Women's introduction of the marital pair, however, enabled men to introduce strict monogamy "for the women only, of course."

With the introduction of monogamy, the transition from matrilineal to patrilineal descent was made possible. The transition became relevant only, however, when the wealth to be passed to descendants increased. Engels suggested that when wealth was of the simplest kind, then no change from matrilineal to patrilineal kinship structures was likely to develop. But with the domestication of animals and the development of agriculture, new sources of wealth were created and new social relationships developed. The monogamous pair introduced the authenticated father along with the mother, and this, in combination with the father's possession of the new forms of wealth, resulted in the transformation of gender relations.

The possession of significant wealth fell to the men according to Engels, because of the natural division of labour between the sexes. "According to the division of labour then prevailing in the family, the procuring of food and the implements necessary thereto, and therefore, also, the ownership of the latter, fell to the man; he took them with him in the case of separation just as the woman retained the household goods."[28] When the man's task was expanded with the domestication of animals and the development of better agricultural implements and techniques, his wealth increased, giving him "a more important status in the family than the woman," and prompting him to want his own children to inherit.[29]

Changes in the family were enhanced by the introduction of slavery that accompanied the new sources of wealth. The slave was of little use to the barbarian, because "human labour power at this stage yielded no noticeable surplus as yet over the cost of its maintenance."[30] With cattle breeding, field cultivation and metal-working, however, more people than could be produced in the family were needed to undertake all the necessary tasks. As Engels states, "The family did not increase as rapidly as the cattle."[31] War captives came in handy as slaves and they, along with the cattle and other possessions, became the *private*, rather than communal, possession of families; more precisely, they became the possessions of men. "[S]lavery, side by side with monogamy . . . slaves who belong to the *man* . . . from the very beginning stamped on monogamy its specific character as monogamy *only for the woman*, but not for the man."[32] The increased wealth and status of the man enabled him to "overthrow the traditional order of inheritance in favour of his own children." When this occurred, patriarchy was established, and "the *world-historic defeat of the female sex*[33] resulted.

With this transition, the monogamous marital relationship became based on economic factors, not on "individual sex love." Monogamy at this stage meant the subjection of women to men. Engels thus concludes: "The first class antagonism which appears in history coincides with the development of the antagonism between man and woman in the monogamian marriage, and the first class oppression with that of the female sex by the male."[34] Consequently, the nature of particular marital relations and sexual arrangements might vary over time and place, but in all cases the general relationship is seen to hold that women are subject to men in and out of marriage. In the modern family, Engels suggested, the husband is "the bourgeois; the wife represents the proletariat."[35]

A number of questions arise in connection with Engels's account of the development of monogamy and private property. They revolve around a number of assumptions implicit in the account. The first has to do with the "natural" biological differences Engels assumes for the sexes. These differences contribute to the second assumption regarding the manner in which women can be incorporated into class analysis and, consequently, into the revolutionary practice of the proletariat. An examination of these two points

will demonstrate the problem with Engels's optimistic conclusion
that "the first premise for the emancipation of women is the
reintroduction of the entire female sex into public industry."[36]

Biology and the Composition of the Family

In the preface to the first edition of *The Origin of the Family,
Private Property and the State*, Engels states that the determining
factor in a materialist conception of history is the "production and
reproduction of immediate life." This conception represents two
processes. "On the one hand, the production of the means of
subsistence, of food, clothing and shelter and the tools requisite
therefore; on the other, the production of human beings themselves,
the propagation of the species."[37] The two processes of production
are found in the historically variable social relations of labour and
the family. In early primitive societies, the social order was constructed in terms of the biological link of mother and child, and
this link comprised the family. It was only with the development of
greater labour productivity that "the old society based on sex
groups bursts asunder in the collision of the newly developed social
classes . . . and a society develops in which the family system is
"entirely dominated by the property system."[38]

In Engels's account, then, the biological fact that women have
children was used first as the explanation for matrilineality and for
the pre-eminence of women in early societies. This biological fact
became a liability, however, when ownership of property increased.
Increased property and the wealth it brought resulted in some sort
of psychological change in the men that made them want to pass
their possessions on to "their" children. Engels does not explain
why men had this sudden change of heart, although he quotes a
comment made by Marx that the change to father right "appears
altogether to be the most natural transition."[39] The transition was
simple, involving only a renaming process, and the immediate
effect was the formation of the patriarchal family in which monogamy, or the sexual fidelity of women, was enforced in order to
ensure legitimate offspring for the father.[40] Engels suggested that
women did not, in fact could not, protest at the loss of their former
status. "The 'savage' warrior and hunter had been content to
occupy second place in the house and give precedence to the
woman. The 'gentler' shepherd, presuming upon his wealth,
pushed forward to the first place and forced the woman into second
place. And she could not complain."[41]

The reason women could not complain related to the assumption made about the "natural" division of labour between the sexes. Marx had suggested that in the family, "there springs up naturally a division of labour, caused by differences of sex and age, a division that is consequently based on a purely *physiological* foundation."[42] Engels added that the division of labour between men and women, which is a "pure and simple outgrowth of nature," meant that "the men went to war, hunted, fished, provided the raw material for food and the tools necessary for these pursuits. The women cared for the house, and prepared food and clothing; they cooked, weaved and sewed."[43] Man the hunter and woman the domestic nest-builder were elementary "natural" roles, whose meaning was transformed when the nature of the productive process changed. Because it was men who supposedly had the more important means of production when property increased, "it now put the former domestic relationship topsy-turvy simply because the division of labour outside the family had changed . . . the woman's housework lost its significance compared with the man's work in obtaining a livelihood."[44] Consequently, the women could not complain.

The assumption made about "natural," that is, physiologically determined, sex roles was related to the idea of the relative strength of the sexes. Both Marx and Engels assumed that the greater strength of males meant that they hunt, fish and fight, whereas the weakness of women, compounded by their reproductive role, confined them to the home. There are two problems with this assumption. First, anthropological data as well as evidence from our own society indicate that physical strength has never been a major determinant of the division of labour. In peasant societies women work along with their men and often do more work than the men.[45] As Mitchell has pointed out, "Physical deficiency is not now, any more than in the past, a sufficient explanation of women's relegation to inferior status."[46]

The second problem with the assumption of physiologically determined sex roles is the idea that reproduction confines women to the domestic sphere and that this invariably means their subordination. Anthropological and historical evidence suggests, however, that separating the domestic from the public sphere is often an arbitrary exercise and, secondly, that the tasks usually undertaken by women "confined" to the domestic sphere are not necessarily regarded as secondary or of lesser value to the society."[47] Furthermore, emphasizing the reproductive capacity of women as the only or most important determinant of their behaviour suggests that the process by which it is accommodated is a natural, and therefore fixed, attribute of human nature. Consequently, any radical tampering with the social order that supposedly accommodates this fixed, natural attribute will be regarded as dangerous, if not anarchic.[48]

For Marx and Engels the physiological basis of their analysis was not seen as problematic. Reproduction was a natural and therefore taken-for-granted activity unmediated by any social forms. This is demonstrably not the case, however, since, for example, birthing procedures vary considerably over time and place. However, the difficulties involved in their assumption were not regarded as significant by Marx and Engels; their only concern over physiological sex differences related to the possibility that capitalist technology increasingly made brute strength superfluous and therefore more women could be drawn into the workforce. Incorporating women into productive labour would then promote their emancipation.

> In so far as machinery dispenses with muscular power, it becomes a means of employing labourers of slight muscular strength, and those whose bodily development is incomplete, but whose limbs are all the more supple. The labour of women and children was, therefore, the first thing sought for by capitalists who used machinery.[49]

It was the fact that women were excluded from productive labour, in part by their relative physical weakness compared to men, that maintained their subordination. When women were allowed to enter paid labour, then their emancipation would be imminent.

> The emancipation of women and their equality with men are impossible and must remain so as long as women are excluded from socially productive work and are restricted to housework, which is private. The emancipation of women becomes possible only when women are enabled to take part in production on a large, social scale, and when domestic duties require their attention only to a minor degree.[50]

It was this analysis that enabled classical Marxism to regard the "woman question" as an important but secondary concern, and to ignore the significance of reproduction other than to acknowledge its importance to capital's need for an adequate supply of workers. The family became the place in which future workers were produced and in which present workers were serviced in order to continue their productive role. The fact that women reproduce and are responsible for domestic, unpaid labour was seen to have no significant effects on the analysis of class relations. Part of the neglect, as we will see, has to do with the fact that Marx's theories regarding the value of labour power cannot accommodate the sexual divisions characteristic of paid and domestic labour.

The Family and Class

Women's entry into paid labour was to be women's entry into class relations, and this would, eventually, eliminate the basis for her subordination. It was because women did not enter into exchange relations, because they did not have control over property but were themselves property, that accounted for their subordination in the family. When property was absent, however, and when husband and wife were both involved in exchanging their labour power for subsistence, there was no basis for unequal, antagonistic relations.

> Full freedom in marriage can become generally operative only when the abolition of capitalist production, and of the property relations created by it, has removed all those secondary economic considerations which still exert so powerful an influence on the choice of a partner. Then, no other motive remains than mutual affection.[51]

In fact, in Engels's view, true "sex love" based on mutual affection was possible only among the proletariat, because property, "for the safeguarding and inheritance of which monogamy and male domination were established," was absent and there was therefore "no stimulus whatever here to assert male domination."[52] However, it was male domination, not monogamy, that was to be altered by the elimination of the property relation. Monogamy was to be strengthened by the fact that "sex love" would become exclusive, and "marriage based on sex love is by its very nature monogamy."[53]

The idyllic conception of marital relations freed from the negative consequences of property, however, fails to take account of the critical significance of reproduction. The "production and reproduction of immediate life" form the basis for social organization, and changes in productive relations must be matched by changes in the social construction of reproductive relations if equality between the sexes is to result. But in Engels's account, changes in reproductive relations are left out, because they are regarded as "natural," despite the fact that reproduction produced the first basic division of labour and was, according to Engels, the basis for inequality between the sexes.

Reproduction gives rise to the first division of labour and represents the first class antagonism. But class is defined primarily in terms of a relationship to the productive process, so that the only antagonism between husband and wife in terms of reproduction must be related to the father's socially recognized possession of the offspring. In other words, biology provides the first division. But it is a division that can be understood only as a class division in terms of a social construction of inequality, not as a natural biological fact. The contradiction in Engels's account is based on the fact that different criteria are used for class membership inside and outside the family. "Engels does not use the categories of male as bourgeoisie and female as proletariat *outside* of the family. There, people are assigned class position according to their relations to the means of production, not their sex."[54]

Within the family, all women represent the proletariat class; outside the family, women, as well as men, are part of a class in terms of a relationship to the productive process. Therefore, it might be assumed that if women were drawn out of the family and into production, they would participate along with their men in the future transformation of society. In this context the in-family class position of women would be transcended and proletarian workers of either sex would triumph over the bourgeois of either sex.

The problem with this analysis becomes clear when it is recognized that bourgeois women can only be categorized as such by virtue of their marital/family connection. Whereas it may be possible to understand the common exploited position of women and men in paid labour, the commonality of bourgeois men and women has, in general, no connection to the productive process. Most bourgeois women do not have access to the means of production in common with their men; moreover, for most of these women it is *only* their marital/family connection that places them in the bourgeois class. Furthermore, women, whether proletariat or bourgeois, can be said to form a separate "class" by virtue of their sharing in common both childrearing and domestic labour. Women, therefore, have a separate and different relationship to the productive process than men. The subordination of women cannot simply be attributed to the nature of capitalist relations, and theorized as alleviated by women's entry into paid labour, and in the end overcome by the abolition of property relations. The social construction of reproduction upsets this equation.

The contradictions that emerge in the Marxist account of gender relations can be partly explained by its economic explanation of class formation. It is the productive exchange relationship that determines class position, and this relationship is, theoretically, an individual one. That is, the surplus value extracted by the capitalist can be produced by men, women or children. Capital is interested only in surplus; the sex, age or even race of the labourer is, theoretically, immaterial. What counts is the provision of labour power that the capitalist can exploit. Yet the particular characteristics of the labourer, such as sex or race, are significant in "placing" the individual both within and outside the capitalist mode of production. Women, in particular, have a special place in being responsible for domestic labour as well as in being more exploitable than men in paid labour.[55]

In most Marxist accounts, the problem that the abstract, individual conceptualization of labour entails when the sex qualification is introduced is often "solved" by using the family as the major unit of analysis. In this manner, women "disappear" into the family. Consequently, Guettel, for example, can suggest that:

> Breadwinners are the units in the family which tie family to the exchange economy under capitalism . . . Capitalism must reproduce and maintain labour power; therefore, the maintenance of the worker's family is included in the wages bill . . . The woman's domestic work is itself without value.[56]

The family becomes a cohesive unit of analysis, and the "sexual and familial bond is thought to override class distinctions; it constitutes men and women as an economic unit in spite of the fact that the imagery used to describe this unit is one of the slave master and his slaves."[57] The antagonism of the marital relations disappears when class relations are discussed as relations among undifferentiated family units. Antagonisms form between proletarian families and bourgeois families to the extent that all members of such families can claim the class position of the male head of the family. Coward points out that "what begins to be apparent is that there is a hierarchy by which certain social divisions are designated antagonistic and others are not. Antagonistic divisions arise, it appears, exclusively from the production, distribution and control of surplus."[58]

What emerges from Marx and Engels is the understanding that women do not have a direct relationship to the class structure except as the personal dependants of men. Giddens suggests that even when women are in paid labour, this does not provide for a direct relation to the class structure. "Given that women still have to await their liberation from the family it remains the case in capitalist societies that female workers are largely peripheral to the class system, or expressed differently, women are in a sense the "underclass" of the white collar sector."[59]

It was the need to account for the class position of women that generated a rethinking of the orthodox Marxist approach. Initially, the rethinking concentrated on women's relationship to the productive process and took account of the fact that women have primary responsibility for housework and childcare. An examination of the domestic labour debate, as this initial rethinking was usually called, serves as the beginning of the feminist critique of Marx and Engels and of the theoretical reformulations of sexual relations that emerged out of this critique.

THE DOMESTIC LABOUR DEBATE

The ownership of the means of production includes the labour power of the worker. "The maintenance and reproduction of the working-class is, and must ever be, a necessary condition to the reproduction of capital."[60] Marx suggested that capital provided the basic means for the maintenance and reproduction of the worker, but *how* the worker proceeded to maintain and reproduce himself was seen as immaterial to capital and could be left "to the labourer's instincts of self-preservation and of propagation."[61] Subsequent accounts of the reproduction and maintenance of labour power, including domestic female labour, were also devoid of details of how this was to be done.

The feminist resurgence of the 1960s took the previously unexamined details of domestic labour as an indication of the problems with the Marxist analysis of gender and class. The first reformulations attempted to find some means of incorporating women's domestic production into an unmodified Marxist account.

One of the problems with domestic labour from the Marxist perspective was seen to be the fact that it produced use values, as opposed to the exchange values produced by paid labour. It was only the latter form of work that was directly related to capital. "Capitalist production is not merely the production of commodities, it is essentially the production of surplus-value . . . That labourer alone is productive, who produces surplus-value for the capitalist, and thus works for the self-expansion of capital."[62]

The above definition makes it clear that the housewife has no *direct* relationship to capital, since she is unpaid and does not produce surplus value. According to Benston, however, it is precisely the association of women with domestic labour that sets women apart from men and enables the conceptualization of housework as a separate mode of production. Women are defined by their domestic roles "as that group of people who are responsible for the production of simple use-values in those activities associated with the home and the family. Since men carry no responsibility for such production, the difference between the two groups lies here."[63] The household under capitalism could then be seen as a preindustrial unit in which women performed private labour for their family, and it was this type of labour that accounted for their inferior position. Dalla Costa took the analysis a step further with her insistence that housework was productive labour, as it reproduced labour power. Women's domestic labour prepared the male worker for another day's work as well as reproducing and rearing the next generation of workers. As such, in Dalla Costa's view, domestic labour represented the *"hidden source of surplus labour."*[64] The family is seen as the "very pillar of the capitalist organization of work," and unless this is recognized, housewives will continue to be thought of as "external to the working class."[65] In other words, Dalla Costa was at pains to demonstrate that housewives are also directly exploited by capital, and the recognition of this situation by women could produce a revolutionary consciousness to match that of proletarian paid labourers.

The attempt to incorporate domestic labour directly into class analysis has been rejected by other participants in the domestic labour debate.[66] It has been pointed out that Marx was quite specific about what constituted productive labour—wage labour that produced a surplus. As Seccombe indicated, domestic labour does not produce surplus value and is not therefore, in the strict Marxist sense, productive labour.[67] Domestic labour, he pointed out, had an indirect relation to the productive sphere of paid labour through the husband's wage. The husband's wage, although represented as

an individual wage for the labour of the husband, in fact, represented a family wage; ". . . the wage in reality pays for an entirely
different labour—the labour that reproduces the labour power of
the entire family."[68] The domestic labour of the wife was therefore
part of the labour power that the husband was able to sell to the
capitalist in return for the wage. This led to the conclusion that the
value of the wife's domestic labour could therefore be measured by
the amount of money she got from her husband for her maintenance.

Seccombe's analysis leads to "empirically ridiculous conclusions," according to Gardiner.[69] For example, it suggests that "the
less a wife receives from her husband's wage packet the less she
contributes to the creation of value." Gardiner argued that it is
impossible to regard domestic labour as creating value in strict
Marxist terms, but that domestic labour does contribute to surplus
value by decreasing the value of the husband's labour to a level
lower than his actual subsistence. "For example, it could be argued
that it is cheaper for capital to pay a male worker a wage sufficient
to maintain, at least partially, a wife who prepares meals for him,
than to pay him a wage on which he could afford to eat regularly in
restaurants."[70] More generally, Gardiner indicated that Seccombe's
analysis presumed that the exchange between husband and wife
was an equal exchange, "the value of the wife's services is equal to
the value she receives from her husband's wage packet."[71] Seccombe
failed to take into account the unequal power relations in the
family resulting from the wife's economic dependence on the
husband.

The need to put a value label on women's domestic labour was
seen to be important in accommodating early feminist criticisms of
Marxist theory. Attaching a value label to domestic labour was not
only necessary in determining the objective—that is, the correct—
class position of women, it was also important in determining their
role in the class struggle. Because of the privatized, pre-capitalist
nature of domestic work, women were regarded as potentially a
brake on the move towards socialism. Seccombe suggested that the
housewife was politically backward in that she could only protest
her individual oppression. The housewife therefore operates "to the
detriment of her husband and children and her actions do not
contest the relations of capital directly."[72] In fact, in Seccombe's
view, the role of the housewife was logically limited, since "revolutionary transformation is only possible because the proletariat is

engaged directly in socialized labor and therefore bears as a class the pre-requisites of a socialist mode of production."[73] In the process of labelling, however, the significant aspects of the issue tended to disappear. Hamilton observed that "by closing off discussion that does not fit into preconceived formulations, the debate has provided some Marxists with a neat and tidy way to suppose that they are dealing with 'the woman question' even as they studiously avoid such an encounter."[74]

The poor, benighted housewife was not left to the abstract categorization and condemnation of Marxist orthodoxy for long. Feminist theorists began to focus on the actual experiences of women in domestic and paid labour. Their attempts to understand the relations between women and men involved a broader understanding of women's labour and included reproduction and sexuality as integral parts of the analysis. In many cases what emerged was an understanding that the Marxist concept of social class was limited and did not accurately represent reality even within capitalist societies.

Below, we will examine recent feminist theory that has focused on those dimensions of women's reality—domestic and paid labour, reproduction and sexuality—and that has contributed to a reassessment of the concept of social class.

Women's Labour: Housework

> The thing about food and meals, about cooking you know, is that it is endless. Just as you get one meal done with, it's time to start the next.[75]

> It's never ending. You've no sooner done one lot of washing up than you've got another lot, and that's how it goes all day.[76]

The two comments above come from a Canadian and an English housewife, respectively, and they point to a dimension of the day-to-day labour of housewives that was concealed in the abstract domestic labour debate. Oakley's study of English housewives was one of the first to examine the daily realities of women's domestic work and the reactions women had to such work. Although she found differences in the attitudes of working-class and middle-class housewives regarding their status as house*wives,* she found that both groups were likely to express dissatisfaction with house*work.*

In addition, in their work activity the experiences of both groups were similar.

In examining the tasks of the housewife as houseworker, Oakley found that monotony, fragmentation and excessive pace, which have been linked to the dissatisfaction and alienation of (male) assembly line workers, also characterized housework. In general, she found that "dissatisfaction with housework predominates," and housework was the "most disliked aspect of 'being a housewife'."[77] In contrast, autonomy, or being one's own boss, was often expressed as a positive part of the experience, a compensation for the unpleasant aspects of the work. However, Oakley found that the autonomy was often compromised by the imposition of rules and standards by the women themselves. These had the effect of controlling some of the fragmentation of tasks and establishing for her a psychological reward in her adherence to and achievement of her personal standards. When this happens, the standards become externalized; they become "external obligations to which she feels a deep need to conform." Such "objectification effectively robs the housewife of her much-prized autonomy."[78]

Luxton, in her study of housewives in Flin Flon, Manitoba, also found that housework resembled assembly line work and was often a source of dissatisfaction. Like Oakley, she also found that technological aids made a difference to the manner in which the work was done and the satisfaction derived from it. Her study, covering three generations of housewives, examined the technology of housework from an historical perspective. In general, technological changes such as dishwashers for the present generation and, for earlier generations, automatic stoves and streamlined kitchens, made housework easier. At the same time, however, they also changed the experience and status of the housewife. Luxton suggested that the work becomes "despecialized" as well as "dull and repetitive," thus contributing to "the low esteem that many people have for domestic labour and, consequently, for the women who do it."[79] That is, the nature of the work process reflects upon the status of the housewife.

Oakley also noted the distinction between the work of housework and the status of housewife. "[T]he concept of women's *orientation to the housewife role* describes the relationship between the notion of 'being a housewife' and the psychological identity of women."[80] Oakley suggested that the distinction related to the association in our society of femininity with the role of the housewife. Consequently, feelings about housework and housewifery overlapped, and when women identified positively with the role of house*wife*, then they tended to have high standards for their house*work*. Such women also believed in "natural" female domesticity and subscribed to the idea of clearly demarcated sex roles. As a result, housework could be seen as a means to demonstrate a commitment to the housewife role or, by extension, a commitment to the perceived "normal" female role in our society.

The commitment to the role is, however, significantly affected by the economic organization of the society, as many of the housewives in the two studies realized. Luxton found that the commitment was often frustrated by the inadequate means available for the performance of the role. The frustration was most often linked to the husband's wage, which was insufficient to meet her own standards in the performance of her housewife/houseworker role. "Every payday I sit there holding the money and I think—this is it. I know what we need. I know what everyone likes. And I have to get what we need and as much as I can what they want and this (money) is all I got to do it with. I should be a magician."[81] Most Flin Flon husbands regarded their wage as a sufficient contribution to the household. It was the wife's task to manage what her husband gave her, and she should not complain if this was insufficient. Some women went to work. As one woman remarked to Luxton, "The best part about working is having my own money. I don't have to ask for everything. I feel more like my own person."[82]

Generally, the major part of housework and childcare is regarded as the woman's responsibility. This division of labour is little altered by women's participation in paid labour, even when women must work because the husband's wage is insufficient for the household needs.[83] As we have noted, Marx and Engels assumed that women's entry into paid labour was the initial step towards their emancipation from the oppression of the domestic sphere. In fact, women's paid labour in both socialist and capitalist economies has simply meant that women carry a double work load so that their oppression is magnified. Women in paid labour remain responsible for the household and for childcare, and little domestic work is contributed by their husbands. Cross-cultural time-budget studies have indicated that women's time spent in household tasks has not significantly decreased in recent decades, and that paid labour, whether full or part-time, simply adds to the total work load of women and reduces their leisure time.[84]

That paid labour extracts costs for women, most evident of which is a greatly increased work load, has been demonstrated in numerous studies. For example, Meissner's study of Vancouver households indicated that,

> When there are young children, and women contribute to an otherwise inadequate income, the greater requirements to which the household has to respond are being met almost entirely by women. Men do not respond to the demands made on their households by their wives' job, and they make only token additional contributions to meet the requirements deriving from young children.[85]

Not only did the husbands in the Vancouver study make minimal adjustments to their wives' paid labour, it was found that for both husband and wife leisure time decreased, except in the case of entertainment such as watching television or reading: "the effect of household requirements on men's 'entertainment' activities is positive—they watch *more* television as life gets to be more difficult for their wives."[86]

Meissner suggests that to speak of leisure for women may be superfluous. Woman's role as housewife means that "she is legitimately on call at any time and for any demands or requests. In the language of a labour contract, that state of affairs would make for a 24-hours a day, 7-days a week requirement to be available for work."[87] In addition, the association of work and leisure gives rise to an asymmetry for men and women in paid labour.

> Men's ideal is "leisure", and they regard work as most ideal if it approaches the characteristics of a state of leisure, namely, of being free from obligation, done for its own sake, and without practical usefulness. However, the necessities of obligations, purposefulness, and usefulness remain, and the more men succeed in approaching the ideal state of leisure in their work and their free time, the greater the cost to others, that is, women and other social inferiors.[88]

Not only does women's housework support the "leisure" of their husbands, but the great proportion of women's paid labour supports the more preferable, "leisurely" work of men.

Women in paid labour occupy a different position from those of men, and the difference is accounted for by their sex. That is, sex differences determine the appropriate occupations for women, which are often extensions of the domestic tasks that are regarded as particularly appropriate to women's capabilities. Consequently, the provision of a woman's personal services to the household spills over into the work she might do in paid labour. The unequal relationship that characterizes marriage, in which women do the routine work that maintains the husband and children, is paralleled in the organization of paid labour. Smith (1979) points out that most women associated with managerial and professional activities perform the concrete, routine tasks that enable the male professional/manager to perform his more "leisure-like" conceptual tasks.

> They do the clerical work, giving material form to the words or thoughts of the boss. They do the routine computer work, the interviewing for the survey, the nursing, the secretarial work. At almost every point women mediate for men the relation between the conceptual mode of action and the actual concrete forms on which it depends.[89]

At the same time that the work done by women serves to connect and anchor the abstract to the real world, it also conceals from men producing the abstractions the manner in which the anchoring is done. Women's work is therefore easily devalued by men because they have no comprehension of its character or significance. This applies to both paid labour and domestic labour.

Domestic labour cannot be accommodated within orthodox Marxist categories of "labour power" and "surplus value," although it is, in reality, connected both materially and ideologically. Materially, the work women do, either domestically or in paid labour, is related to the paid labour of their men as well as to the structural arrangement of men in the paid labour market. Ideologically, women's labour has a different, lower value than that of men. The private, personal labour performed by women for their husband and children is seen as "valueless" in labour market terms at the same time that it reinforces the lesser value attached to women's paid labour.

Delphy has suggested that the marriage contract is, in fact, a work contract in which the husband is entitled to the work of the wife (and later his children) in return for their keep. The relationship becomes clear when women are also in paid labour but remain responsible for domestic work. In such a situation, it would appear that not all women's labour is appropriated by their husband, since they can divert some of it into paid work. However, "since they earn wages they provide their own upkeep."[90] If the marriage contract is one in which women exchange their labour for their maintenance, then their entry into paid labour should eliminate the contractual condition of providing domestic labour. Since it does not, then "it is clear . . . that their domestic work is given for nothing."[91] What results is a paradox that illustrates the relationship between women's labour, paid and unpaid, and the productive world of men.

> On the one hand marriage is the (institutional) situation where women are exploited; and on the other hand, precisely because of this, the potential market situation for women's labour (which is that of all women, not just those who are actually married . . .) is such that marriage still offers them the best career, economically speaking.[92]

The problems women confront in paid and unpaid labour are often "explained" by the fact that it is women who bear children. In the preceding discussion, the fact that women are largely responsible for the care and socialization of children as part of their domestic, unpaid labour was not addressed directly. The childcare functions performed by women do have, however, a critical bearing on their relationship to "productive" labour as well as their position within the household. Biological reproduction can be considered work and as being of productive value for society. However, it is the treatment of women's reproductive capacity as an ahistoric, pre-social (in the sense of "natural") fact in sociological theory—including, as we have indicated, the work of Marx and Engels—that we set it apart for consideration as women's work in this chapter.

Women's Labour: Reproduction and Socialization

> The societies in which these available males undertake the harder labours, and so, relieving the female from undue physical tax, enable them to produce more and better offspring, will, other things equal, gain in the struggle for existence with societies in which the women are not thus relieved.[93]

Spencer's remarks, above, reflect a particular sociological perspective in late-nineteenth-century and early-twentieth-century works that adapted the Darwinian biological theory of evolution to theories of social evolution. In these works it was assumed that the nature of sexual relations provided the clue to the nature of social relations. That is, since women appeared to be universally excluded from the political governing sphere of societies, then the cause of this social arrangement was sought in the different biological capacities of the sexes. Women's reproductive capacity was seen to provide the basic answer to their common position cross-culturally and throughout history. From this it was assumed that the domination of the "stronger" sex over the "weaker" sex was a natural, unalterable—except at society's peril—situation. In the quotation above, Spencer was contrasting societies with a pronounced division of labour between the sexes with those in which greater equality was evident, and suggested that it was the former that represented the higher, more civilized form of society.

As Coward has demonstrated, the nineteenth-century debates took sexual relations as a focal point, because they were regarded as "existing on the border between 'nature' and 'society'." That is,

> On the one hand, sexual behaviour was taken as belonging to the individual; on the other hand, sexual regulation, such as marriage and the family, was seen as a social institution. Sexual relations therefore become the point of contestation as to the relation between nature and culture.[94]

The work of Morgan and Engels was a part of this debate. Their examination of sexual and social relations challenged the view that patriarchy was a preordained social form. Theories of matrilineaty and of some original pre-social matriarchy were based on the assumption that women's reproductive capacity at first gave them an advantage in the organization of social groups. This formulation was problematic, however, when it came to the question of property, and, by extension, political rights. If matriarchy was the original form, how then did patriarchy develop? As we have seen, Engels's answer was basically psychological: the desire of fathers to possess their children in order to pass on their property. His conclusion assumed that women did not protest their forced inferiority and that they could not use their command over the household or the reproductive process to resist the men. Although Engels offered a properly materialist explanation as to why women did not resist, or "complain," this explanation rested ultimately on assumptions made about the natural, biologically given nature of men and women. The realm of production was theoretically sex-blind, but the realm of reproduction was not and could not be blind in the Marxist account because the mother-child connection was regarded as a natural, pre-social connection.

We have already seen that the association of women with their biological capacity as a natural and therefore pre-social factor has been a persistent theme in the classic sociological and anthropological accounts. Most recently, feminist theory has attempted to sort out the multitude of issues subsumed under this general, superficial assumption that "biology is destiny." Feminist theory has attempted to find a means of incorporating the analysis of women's position in productive *and reproductive* relations in the light of the social and cultural assumptions regarding biological differences. As Simone de Beauvoir pointed out, "the facts of biology take on values that the existent bestows upon them."[95]

The consequences of the social construction of reproductive relations are found in women's situation in the family. Mitchell[96] pointed out that it was in the family that the particular oppression of women was to be found. "However inegalitarian her situation at work (and it is invariably so) it is within the development of her feminine psyche and her ideological and socio-economic role as mother and housekeeper that woman finds the oppression that is hers alone."[97] The particular nature of women's oppression was to be found in the structures of reproduction, sexuality and the socialization of children, in addition to their oppression in the extra-familial productive realm of paid labour. It was the relationship between these four structures that formed the basic framework of Mitchell's examination of gender relations. Women are submerged in the family, which is enclosed by the male world of production. "The contemporary family can be seen as a triptych of sexual, reproductive and socializatory functions (the woman's world) embraced by production (the man's world)."[98] The male world of production is, however, the determining realm that maintains the ideological construction that constrains women and prevents the understanding of their true position in society.

The ideological construction that defines and supports the oppressive structures surrounding reproduction, sexuality and the socialization of children is the universal "law of the father"—the patriarchy—which is the "symbolic law of order" that "defines society and determines the fate of every small human animal born into it."[99] In Mitchell's account, patriarchy is a persistent feature of all historical societies, although its manifestations may vary according to the prevailing mode of production.

It seems that the values of the present-day family are appropriate to peasant production. But it is the function of the ideology precisely to give this sense of continuity in progress. The dominant ideological formation is not separable from the dominant economic one, but, while linked, it does have a certain degree of autonomy and its own laws. Thus the ideology of the family can remain: individualism, freedom and equality; (at home you're 'yourself'), while the social and economic reality can be very much at odds with such a concept.[100]

Mitchell's analysis was important in demonstrating the significance of women's reality as defining and supporting their subordination. But in her account the actual labour of reproduction, sexuality and the socialization of children remains something other than real productive work. The structures take on the status of ideological abstractions that support the economic realm, and the material consequences of the ideology are left out of the account. Hartmann pointed out that for Mitchell, "only market work is identified as production; the other spheres (loosely aggregated as the family) in which women work are identified as ideological. Patriarchy, which largely organizes reproduction, sexuality, and childrearing, has no material base for Mitchell."[101]

Although patriarchy has taken a front seat in the recent feminist critique, Weber's work on the subject has been overlooked. In general, feminist analysis has taken the form of attempting to reconcile the phenomenon of male control over women irrespective of class with the Marxist analysis of class and social change. As we have seen, Weber's discussion of patriarchy was concerned with men's power over women as a generalized phenomenon as well as, and more importantly for him, the nature of the hierarchical relations among men in systems of domination. In recent feminist work, the latter issue of male hierarchy, in relation to male-female hierarchy, has not been significant. An examination of the recent work in this regard demonstrates this point.

CAPITALISM, PATRIARCHY AND SOCIAL CLASS

Although Marxist analysis has been the most important basis for the most recent feminist thought and practice, the reflections of Hartmann on the "unhappy marriage" of Marxism and feminism indicate that the association has not been idyllic. In fact, on a practical, personal level the current women's movement emerged in large part from the disillusionment women experienced in the new left and civil rights movements of the 1960s and early 1970s.

Women discovered that "in groups dedicated to human liberation, they were second-class members—useful at the typewriter, in the kitchen, and in bed, but expected to leave policy making to the men."[102] The trivialization of women's issues by revolutionary men was summed up in the Stokely Carmichael statement: "The only position for women in SNCC is prone."[103] But, as Mitchell demonstrated, the "position" of women was more complex and potentially more radical in implication than this facile and chauvinist dismissal of the question by male revolutionaries.

Revolutionary Marxist theory sought explanations for exploitation and oppression in economic relationships. Although the economy as a determining factor cannot be ignored, feminist analysis introduced patriarchy as a continuing and supportive component of economic exploitation and oppression. In her analysis of western society, Eisenstein suggested that, although patriarchy preceded capitalism, patriarchy combined with and reinforced the capitalist economic structure such that it makes more sense today to talk about a system of capitalist patriarchy rather than simply a capitalist system. Feminism, therefore, is concerned with both economic power relations as well as the power relations of sexual and racial oppression. The latter two forms of oppression are not equivalent to economic exploitation. Eisenstein points out that,

> Exploitation speaks to the economic reality of capitalist class relations for men and women, whereas oppression refers to women and minorities defined within patriarchal, racist, and capitalist relations. Exploitation is what happens to men and women workers in the labor force; woman's oppression occurs from her exploitation as a wage-laborer but also occurs from the relations that define her existence in the patriarchal sexual hierarchy—as mother, domestic laborer, and consumer. Racial oppression locates her within the racist division of society alongside her exploitation and sexual oppression.[104]

In the organization of patriarchy, it is the control that men exert over women's sexuality and reproduction that defines patriarchy. Society is ordered or structured in terms of sex differences assumed to be "natural" biologically given differences. What this illustrates, in Eisenstein's view, is that men have simply "chosen to interpret and politically use"[105] throughout history the fact that women reproduce humanity.

The nature of patriarchy as the general control exerted by men over women is seen as a historical constant, although the particular forms such control might take are seen to vary. Eisenstein suggests that the variation is ultimately related to changes in the economic system but the relationship between patriarchy and the material, economic base is not unidirectional. Capitalism is shaped by the patriarchal order as much as the actual manifestations of patriarchy are affected by capitalist economic relations. For example, in capital's continuing search for cheap labour, more and more women enter paid labour, and when this occurs "some of the control of patriarchal familial relations seems to be undermined—the double day becomes more obvious. But the ghettoization of women within the labor force at the same time maintains a system of hierarchical control of women, both sexually and economically, which leaves the sexual hierarchy of the society intact."[106]

Eisenstein's conclusion is that a dual Marxist-feminist analysis is necessary in order to formulate and rejuvenate Marxist analysis. She points out that "what we must do is begin to understand what class means for women. We must not just reexamine the way women have been fit into class categories. We must redefine the categories themselves."[107] The redefinition must take account of the cross-class commonalities among women of reproduction, childrearing, sexuality, consumption, and maintenance of the home.

Eisenstein's analysis sets the stage for the problem that introduced this discussion—the nature of the relationship between Marxist and feminist analysis. Hartmann suggested that the relationship between the theoretical frameworks has been characterized by the pre-eminence of Marxist class analysis and, as a result, strategic action has been taken on this front at the expense of feminism.

> The woman question has never been the 'feminist question'. The feminist question is directed at the cause of sexual inequality between women and men, of male dominance over women. Most Marxist analyses of women's position take as their question the relationship of women to the economic system, rather than that of women to men, apparently assuming the latter will be explained in their discussion of the former.[108]

Hartmann pointed out that patriarchy, like class oppression, has a material basis that is evident in the present as well as the past.

Like Eisenstein, Hartmann sees patriarchy as pre-existing capitalism. Consequently, the techniques used under capitalism to maintain control over the labour of women and children are variations on earlier forms and persist because the patriarchal system has taught men "the techniques of hierarchical organization and control."[109] Hartmann points out that capitalism introduced the idea of a "free" market in labour. A free market should make all labourers equal in the marketplace.[110] Therefore, as Marx pointed out, such arbitrary factors as sex or age should be immaterial in capital's exploitation of labour power. But such a labour market would threaten the power of individual patriarchs over "their" women and children. The male response to such a threat was, according to Hartmann, to ensure that women's inferiority was also part of their labour market position. The primary means by which patriarchal control was maintained under a system that seemed, at least theoretically, to undermine such control, was through job segregation by sex and the maintenance of wage differentials. The labour market techniques that maintained women's subordination had a spillover effect into their domestic situation. Women's market disadvantage maintained their dependency on men by encouraging them to marry. The result is, as we have indicated earlier, men benefiting from both high wages and women's domestic labour, just as women's domestic labour undermines her position in the labour market and, by extension, reinforces her domestic subservience.

In the economic and political structures of society, individuals are ranked hierarchically. Men are therefore ranked against other men and occasionally against some women. But, irrespective of the relatively high occupational position that a minority of women might achieve, their sex is never entirely discounted. Consequently, men may be ranked hierarchically with other men, but all men are superior *as men* to all women. Patriarchal hierarchy therefore ensures that "all men, whatever their rank in the patriarchy, are bought off by being able to control at least some women."[111] Patriarchy and the mode of production, whatever form the latter may take, reinforce each other in the maintenance of male dominance.

The "empty places" that the Marxist analysis of capitalism proposed are, in fact, filled by the information that patriarchal (as well as racial) hierarchies provide. Consequently, Hartmann points out,

Capitalist development creates the place for a hierarchy of workers, but traditional Marxist categories cannot tell us who will fill which places. Gender and racial hierarchies determine who fills the empty places. *Patriarchy is not simply hierarchical organization*, but hierarchy in which *particular* people fill *particular* places.[112]

The identification of the material basis of patriarchy and the acknowledgement that all women have a common position under patriarchy produces a problem for class analysis, both theoretically as well as in any possible transformatory practice. Hartmann advises that "women should not trust men to liberate them after the revolution, in part, because there is no reason to think they would know how; in part, because there is no necessity for them to do so. In fact their immediate self-interest lies in our continued oppression."[113] Hartmann suggests that women must develop their own power bases and organize as women. At the same time, women should form an alliance with the revolutionary group of men to raise men's consciousness with regard to what men must struggle for. Whereas women's subordination has enabled them to "understand what human interdependence and needs are," this understanding has been closed to men because of their positions under capitalism and patriarchy. Women understand the positive values of nurturance, sharing and growth because these have been part of their reality and experience. These are, in Hartmann's view, the values men must come to share. "While men have long struggled *against* capital, women know what to struggle *for*."[114] Despite this observation Hartmann remains pessimistic in her conclusion that "even if we raise their consciousness, men might assess the potential gains against the potential losses and choose the status quo. Men have more to lose than their chains."[115]

The definition of patriarchy in the sense of control exerted by men over women, effected primarily through the interpretation of the meaning of biological differences, is an important qualification to Marxist analysis. However, the discussion of patriarchy and its relation to an economic system does little more than point to and illustrate the mutual accommodations between the two systems. The practical issue of revolutionary change that is fundamental to Marxist class analysis has not been addressed by a dual systems theory. The dual systems theory that examines patriarchy in relation to, in opposition to, or as reinforcing, exploitive relations in the economic system effectively maintains the divide between domestic power relations and the "abstract" power relations of a mode of production—the divide between Marxism and feminism. Iris Young has suggested that

> the dual systems theory allows traditional Marxism to maintain its theory of productive relations, historical change, and analysis of the structure of capitalism in a basically unchanged form. That theory, as Hartmann points out, is completely gender-blind. The dual systems theory thus accepts this gender-blind analysis of the relations of production, wishing only to add onto it a separate conception of the relations of gender hierarchy.[116]

In Marx's definition of social class, the world of paid labour under capitalism is critical to the location, definition and understanding of social class position. We have already seen that the private, familial exploitation of women that persists under capitalism in both proletariat and bourgeois households nullifies the assumption of a unified class consciousness among men and women. Both in the domestic and the public modes of production, women's real social and economic positions are different from those of their husbands or their male co-workers. Engels's observation that within the family the woman represents the proletariat and the man the bourgeoisie could, in an analogous sense, be extended to the world of paid labour. Consequently, Balbus observes that patriarchy penetrates the world of paid labour, so that

> if there is a domination-subjection relationship based on sexual identity, then there is a structural basis for hostility, rather than solidarity within the working class. If the male worker views his wife as inferior, he cannot see her as a "comrade"; indeed he is probably more likely to vent his rage on her than on his capitalist boss. On the other hand, since the woman is oppressed by her husband, she has good reason to view him as an "oppressor", as part of the problem rather than part of the solution.[117]

Recognizing the dilemma, Ehrlich has suggested that it is simply not possible to "marry" Marxism and feminism without Marxism taking the dominant position.[118] Harding concluded that in any union of Marxism and feminism, there will "be no independently recognizable Marxism," and since all men have an interest in the preservation of some aspects of power relations as they relate to women, then the transformatory group in our society is not the male proletariat but women.[119]

SUMMARY

Marxist analysis has been identified as problematic in approaching the "woman question" and most specifically with regard to class analysis. A three-part interrelated definition of social class was identified from the work of Marx and Engels. Class position was determined by (1) a relationship to the means of production, (2) a consciousness of a common position in the productive process, and (3) the organization of the exploited group to take action on their own behalf against their exploiters. In examining these three characteristics of social class in Marx's and Engels's work, it is clear that they represent an inadequate means of understanding women as class actresses. Taking the three characteristics separately, we find that:

1. Women, whether they are paid labourers or domestic workers, do not have a common position with men in the productive process. To the extent that the majority of women in paid labour, especially in industrialized countries, are in segregated occupations, then their class position is different from and incomparable to those of males. Domestic labour, since it cannot be accommodated within the labour theory of value, means that if women are to have a class position, they must be classed with their men, although it is women's domestic labour that accounts for the different position women have in paid labour as compared to men.

2. The consciousness of belonging to a class is determined by the understanding of a common position in relation to the means of production. More specifically, for Marx and Engels, it was the close association generated by the factory system and urban living that would facilitate the realization of the common exploited position of the proletarian workforce. Since women are located in a different space, then the possibility of their class consciousness can be deduced as remote, if they are solely domestic workers and somewhat isolated in their homes, unless it is assumed that by a process of osmosis they absorb the consciousness of "their" men. Alternatively, it can be assumed that their consciousness is acquired in the same manner as men when they are in paid labour, but takes a different form because of their different relationship to the paid productive process. Therefore, their consciousness is not necessarily consistent in aims and tactics with that of proletarian men.

3. Revolutionary action is dependent upon a common relationship to the means of production, which then produces a common consciousness of exploitation and generates organization to combat that exploitation. The revolutionary organization was seen as being facilitated by the proximity of workers under the factory system. Women, as domestic workers, do not enter into such a situation. They are therefore either "non-combatants" or hanging onto the coat-tails of their men. In either case, it might make sense to place the "woman question" as secondary to the major battle. However, even when women are paid labourers, there is no guarantee that their revolutionary consciousness will coincide with that of their men; in fact, there is every reason to suppose that it will conflict. Women's consciousness generated by their paid labour must reflect the inequities of pay, status and working conditions they experience, in contrast to those experienced by most men, as well as their exploitation as domestic workers.

In order to demonstrate how women could be part of the transformation of society, that is, part of the class struggle, it was necessary for orthodox Marxism to demonstrate how capital exploited women. However, as we have seen, the explanations advanced simply cannot accommodate women as class actresses because patriarchal structures and relations confound the situation. The conclusion reached by some feminist theorists in the light of these problems has been to look to feminism either exclusively or as the major determinant of revolutionary theory and practice. Harding suggests that "women must take the lead not only in the struggle against patriarchy, but also in the struggle against the underlying interests men have in controlling both patriarchy and capital and in perpetuating dominating relations through various kinds of oppressive relations with others."[120] Harding concludes that "women are now the revolutionary group in history," and it is women who must address the "man question" in transforming and surmounting the resistance of men to feminist theory and practice.

The "man question" is basically a question of power. As Weber's discussion of patriarchy, and by extension, of traditional domination, indicates, patriarchy is about the hierarchical ranking of men with other men on the basis of their control and subordination of women. For Marxism, social classes are contending male groups in the struggle for power over productive resources on the basis of the undifferentiated domestic labour of women. Whatever the nature of power relations, then, sexual inequality is a common factor. It is the status of male or female that provides the basis for the social construction of domination and subordination. That is, it is the biological difference between the sexes that has been interpreted as the "natural" foundation for the inequality. The "great moving power of all historic events," according to Firestone, is to be found in the "division of society into two distinct biological classes with one another; in the changes in the modes of marriage, reproduction and childcare created by these struggles."[121] Consequently, the question raised is how and why biology has been the basis for the creation and maintenance of inequality?

In the following chapter we will examine some of the recent discussions on biological differences and the nature of power. The key issue is the nature of exploitation that biological differences are seen to condone. The generalized concept of patriarchy as the rule of men or of the father is grounded more firmly in historical and cross-cultural situations when the biological accounts are examined.

CHAPTER 5

Ideology, Biology and Freud

In Durkheim's work, a key issue was the stability and the harmony of the society in the face of the developing complexity of the modern industrial world. For Durkheim, as well as for Weber, Marx and Engels, a significant factor in conceptualizing the state of society and the possibilities for change was the natural dichotomy between the sexes. Moreover, the biological difference between the sexes, as expressed in sexuality and reproduction, was what distinguished nature from culture. The debates on this issue during the nineteenth and early twentieth centuries were fueled by anthropology's discoveries of radically different cross-cultural sexual arrangements. Sociology, as we have seen in the work of the previous theorists, was vitally interested in the anthropological findings and what they meant for social organization, past and present.

The debate over matriarchy was one of the issues that developed out of anthropological research. As Coward points out, the debate over matriarchy/patriarchy was really about the nature of social and political power—its origins and its current manifestations. Sexual relations were of critical importance, since "the real subject was the contest over how to theorize the relationship between instinctual and culturally determined behaviour."[1] For the social sciences,

> The study of sexual regulation increasingly looked like the study of the regulation of sexual reproduction by social exigencies. As a result, the old problem of philosophy, that of nature versus culture, begins to be viewed in a distinctive way . . . Marriage relations begin to be theorised as the critical moment between nature and culture.[2]

125

As we have seen in the preceding chapters, all of the theorists make a distinction between the natural and the social. Durkheim sees the social as progressively "taming" the natural, the latter implicitly including women. For Weber the mother-child bond was a biological given and could not be regarded as a proper social relationship. For Engels, the origins of social order exemplified by patriarchy rested upon the regulation of the "natural" relation of mothers and children. Monogamy was the sign of civilized society. And for Marx, the "natural" family based on love was the social relation that provided the foundation for civil society. For all the theorists, "nature" was tamed by "nurture."

In the nature/nurture debate, the work of Freud has been used as a twentieth-century legitimation, especially in the western world, to reinforce traditional gender roles. Instead of regarding sexuality as a natural phenomenon, as something "given," Freud insisted that it required explanation. The Freudian theory of psycho-sexual development has been an important component of sociological theorizing, but a problem for current feminist theory. Many feminist debates have been critical of Freud.

In this chapter we will first examine the Freudian theory of psycho-sexual development, looking at the Oedipus complex and the myth of the murdered father. This will be followed by an outline of some of the early feminist dissenters and by a discussion of current feminist thought that acknowledges Freud but seeks to go beyond him in the analysis of sexuality, reproduction and motherhood.

SIGMUND FREUD, BIOLOGY AND SEX DIFFERENCES

For Freud, understanding the nature and development of sexuality was part of understanding the nature of human culture. He explored how individuals, with what he believed were originally bisexual dispositions, became males and females. Freud addressed this issue in his theory of the Oedipus complex, the critical phase in the socialization of the child when the cultural prescriptions for male or female roles are internalized by the child. It is at this stage that children find their appropriate places in the social order, but since that order is patriarchal, the places are marked by gender inequality.

The Oedipus complex affects not only the shaping of social roles but also sexual impulses and objects. Initially, human infants experience pleasure in diffuse ways. Their sexuality is not gender-specific either in its object or its source; that is, both girls and boys enjoy the same pleasures, such as being given the breast or being fondled and caressed. The source of sexual pleasure proceeds through various stages that generally comprise the oral, anal, phallic and, lastly, the genital stage. It is at the phallic stage, when both girls and boys take interest in the penis, that "culture," in the sense of the formation of appropriate sex-specific gender roles, intervenes through the Oedipus complex.[3]

The Oedipus complex socializes the sexes by (1) instructing them in their culturally appropriate masculine and feminine roles, and (2) providing both sexes with the moral precepts of the culture that will guide their behaviours. The Oedipus complex, when resolved normally, develops a censor, the superego, that controls the progress of the individual ego in real life as well as the repressed instinctual desires of the id found in the unconscious. For example, if the "devil made you do it," then the superego was not in control of the wicked (i.e., socially unacceptable) impulses of the id that produced the ego's behaviour.

The Oedipus complex derives from Sophocles' play *Oedipus Rex*. In the play Oedipus's father, Laius, is told by an oracle that his son will kill him. Consequently, Laius sends Oedipus away to be killed. But he is not killed and does indeed return when older and slays his father. However, he does not know that the man he has slain is his father, or that his father's widow, whom he marries, is his mother. When he discovers what he has done he blinds himself. Oedipus's crime was twofold: murder of the father and incest with the mother. Freud regarded the instinctual desire that Oedipus consummated as basic to *all* infants in the early stages of their development when the mother is a primary love object for both girls and boys. In the phallic stage and maturing of the penis, however, the desire for the mother takes on a different meaning for each sex.

For boys, in the phallic stage, the sexual desire for the mother brings the fear of castration, because to desire the mother is to challenge the rights and power of the father. The boy's fear of castration as punishment for desiring the mother is resolved by identifying with the father and renouncing his desire for the mother. Once identification with the father has occurred, the boy enters the social-cultural realm, that of the patriarchy. The realm of the patriarchy is the realm of order, control and justice—the realm of the superego.

In the boy the Oedipus complex, in which he desires his mother and would like to get rid of his father as being a rival, develops naturally from the phase of his phallic sexuality. The threat of castration compels him, however, to give up that attitude. Under the impression of the danger of losing his penis, the Oedipus complex is abandoned, repressed and, in the most normal cases, entirely destroyed and a severe superego is set up as its heir.[4]

For girls the process is different and begins with their discovery of their lack of a penis. Girls not only notice the physical difference, they also recognize the significance of the difference. They "feel seriously wronged, often declare that they want to 'have something like it too' and fall victim to 'envy for the penis'."[5] Initially, the girl assumes that the error will be remedied with time and that, as she gets older, a penis will grow. When it becomes clear to her that she will never have a penis she assumes that she has been castrated. The girl blames her mother for the castration and begins to hate the mother for sending her out into the world so ill-equipped. "[G]irls hold their mother responsible for their lack of a penis and do not forgive her for their being thus put at a disadvantage."[6] Mother is abandoned as a love object, and the envy the girl feels for the male's penis and her wish to possess the same are translated into the desire for a child. Initially, she desires her father's child as she takes him for her love object; later the desire is focused on other males.

> The wish with which the girl turns to her father is no doubt originally the wish for the penis which her mother has refused her and which she now expects from her father. The feminine situation is only established, however, if the wish for a penis is replaced by one for a baby, if, that is, a baby takes the place of a penis in accordance with an ancient symbolic equivalence.[7]

Girls never really sever their association with their mother, however, because accepting their castration is accepting their likeness to their mother. At the same time, because girls blame their mother for their lack of a penis, in Freud's view, this accounts for the devaluation of women by other women just as boys and men also devalue females.

When the girl transfers the wish for a "penis-baby" onto her father she enters the Oedipal stage. Unlike the boy, however, she lacks that critical component that fully resolves the Oedipus complex—the castration fear.

The castration complex prepares for the Oedipus complex instead of destroying it; the girl is driven out of her attachment to her mother through the influence of her envy for the penis and she enters the Oedipus situation as though into a haven of refuge. In the absence of fear of castration the chief motive is lacking which leads boys to surmount the Oedipus complex. Girls remain in it for an indeterminate length of time; they demolish it late and, even so, incompletely.[8]

Freud concluded that the different experience of the Oedipal situation on the part of the sexes results in differences in the formation of the superego.

I cannot evade the notion (though I hesitate to give it expression) that for women the level of what is ethically normal is different from what it is in men. Their superego is never so inexorable, so impersonal, so independent of its emotional origins as we require it to be in men. Character traits which critics of every epoch have brought up against women—that they show less sense of justice than men, that they are less ready to submit to the great exigencies of life, that they are more often influenced in their judgements by feelings of affection or hostility—all these would be amply accounted for by the modification in the formation of the superego . . .[9]

As for Aristotle and others, so for Freud, women remain partially socialized, less divorced from the instinctual "natural" desires than men. It is the man's superego that will be, in the normal course of affairs, fully attuned to the moral and ethical precepts of society.

Freud attempted to qualify the conclusions he expressed in the above quotation with the observation that he was describing a general phenomenon. In fact, many men also failed to live up to "the masculine ideal," and "all human individuals, as a result of their bisexual disposition and of cross-inheritance, combine in themselves both masculine and feminine characteristics, so that pure masculinity and femininity remain theoretical constructions of uncertain content."[10] This qualification is less than satisfactory to the extent that if it is the superego that is the repository of culture, and if the superego can be developed only through the resolution of the Oedipus complex, then women will "normally" be less civilized because their complex is never fully resolved. The idea of bisexual disposition cannot alter Freud's claim of the basically different processes of psycho-sexual development that modify the original bisexuality and the resulting association of the ideals of the superego with the masculine principle.

Freud's investigations into the sexual development of individuals was governed by the question of why originally polymorphic sexuality could become heterosexuality. He concluded that it was the Oedipus complex that normally channelled the sexes into their heterosexual roles. This formulation fits the patriarchal structure of male dominance characteristic of western societies quite well, so that theoretically, it would appear that a cultural explanation could be fitted into the psychoanalytic explanation. But Freud could not accept such a position, as it would restrict his observations to a particular cultural context. This would then call into question his discovery of the unconscious and the fact of a psychological reality set apart from material and cultural reality. According to Freud, the Oedipus complex was a universal experience, not an experience common only to members of a specific culture or society. The question then becomes, how is such a common psychic experience transmitted if it is not based on real events and is not the result of some fantasy spontaneously produced by all individuals? The answer, according to Freud, lies in the memory of a common mythic past. The initial explanation of the nature of that past that accounted for the origins of the Oedipus complex and the establishment of patriarchy is found in Freud's work *Totem and Taboo*.[11]

Freud pointed out that one of the characteristics of primitive tribes was the worship of a totem. The totem, often personified by a sacred animal or bird, was usually accompanied by two taboos: first, the totem animal should not be eaten, and, secondly, women belonging to the same totem group, or clan, were out-of-bounds sexually. Freud suggested that the origins of both the totem and the taboos lay in the myth of the murder of the primeval father. This myth was found in anthropological accounts of primitive peoples as well as the Oedipus saga, and had been confirmed in Darwin's reconstruction of human development.

Darwin had speculated that pre-cultural, pre-historical humans had formed groups or hordes under the dominance of one strong male. Darwin's scientific account, combined with the anthropological evidence of the veneration of the totem among diverse primitive peoples, suggested to Freud the nature of the origins of religion and social organization. Freud's reconstruction of those origins was as follows:

In the pre-cultural horde one strong male had sexual access to all the women of the horde and resisted the attempts of any other men to usurp this right. As a result, the younger males— the "sons"— united to murder the father in an attempt to obtain the women for themselves.

> One day the expelled brothers joined forces, slew and ate the father, and thus put an end to the father horde . . . Now they accomplished their identification with him by devouring him and each acquired a part of his strength. The totem feast, which is mankind's first celebration, would be the repetition and the commemoration of this memorable criminal act with which so many things began, social organization, moral restrictions and religion.[12]

But the murder did not initially liberate the sons, as each was the "other's rival" for the women.

> Each one wanted to have them all to himself like the father, and in the fight of each against the other the new organization would have perished . . . Thus there was nothing left for the brothers, if they wanted to live together, but to erect the incest prohibition . . . through which they all equally renounced the women whom they desired, and on account of whom they had removed the father in the first place.[13]

The commemoration of the murder of the father was to be found in the celebration of the totem among primitive peoples. The totem represents the dead father, and its celebration represents the remorse of the sons for their action. Freud suggested that:

> They hated the father who stood so powerfully in the way of their sexual demands and their desire for power, but they also loved and admired him. After they had satisfied their hate by his removal and had carried out their wish for identification with him, the suppressed tender impulses had to assert themselves . . . a sense of guilt was formed which coincided here with the remorse generally felt . . . What the father's presence had formally prevented they themselves now prohibited in the psychic situation of "subsequent obedience" which we know so well from psychoanalysis.[14]

The sons consequently renounced their sexual access to the women and "undid their deed by declaring that the killing of the father substitute, the totem, was not allowed."[15]

Freud did suggest that the immediate aftermath of the murder of the father probably produced a short-lived matriarchy because of the initial conflict among the brothers for the women. This probability would then account for the maternal deities that Freud found to have always preceded the paternal deities, as well as accounting for "the germ of the institution of mother right discovered by Bachofen."[16] The power of the women was broken, however, when paternity was discovered, and the brothers were able to agree on the incest taboo. As a result, any power exercised by women was pre-cultural, pre-Oedipal. As we have seen, Engels and others also postulated that a matriarchy, if it ever existed, could have done so only before the beginning of civilization.

If the totem is the symbol for the father, then the thesis presented in *Totem and Taboo* parallels the Oedipus complex. The two taboos of totemism are Oedipus's two crimes—killing (or supplanting) the father and marrying the mother. The myth of the murdered father provided Freud with the basis for his claim that the Oedipus complex was a cultural universal. The absence of any common childhood experiences or events was of less importance than the collective memory of the original event that provided the structure of the common Oedipal experience. Each individual, then, becomes subject to a common phylogenetic inheritance. Freud sought to demonstrate this common inheritance from the evidence of the behaviour of neurotics.

> When we study the reactions to early traumas, we are quite often surprised to find that they are not strictly limited to what the subject himself has really experienced but diverge from it in a way which fits in much better with the mode of a phylogenetic event and, in general, can only be explained by such an influence. The behaviour of neurotic children towards their parents in the Oedipus and castration complex abounds in such reactions, which seems unjustified in the individual case and only becomes intelligible phylogenetically—by their connection with the experience of earlier generations.[17]

With the position taken in *Totem and Taboo* regarding the origins of the Oedipus complex and civilization in general, the psycho-sexual development of the sexes would appear to be locked into a patriarchal power structure from which it is somewhat difficult to envisage any possibility of change. In fact, Freud's account is problematic in that the origins of patriarchy are explained in terms of primeval patriarchy. That is, he theorized that the original horde was under the rule of one strong male. The removal of this one patriarch was accomplished to ensure the eventual rule of many patriarchs. The problem is largely the result of Freud's insistence on the reality of the events of the distant past and its consequences for the structure of the unconscious. But it was only by insisting on the "reality" of the events that Freud could maintain the universal characteristic of the Oedipal complex.

Early criticisms of the Freudian account, as well as those by current feminist theorists, have attempted to confront both the assumption of some universal mental structure that exists independently of the cultural location and Freud's conclusion of the effects of the Oedipus complex for women. In general, his reliance on biological explanations for feminine behaviour was one of the reasons for the initial rejection of Freud. The feminist opposition insisted that anatomy was *not* destiny, and this position often led to a total rejection of Freud. Freud's observations, such as the one that follows, suggesting a biological basis for the problematic feminine personality, seemed to strengthen the conviction of such rejection.

> I cannot help mentioning an impression that we are constantly receiving during analytic practice. A man of about thirty strikes us as a youthful, somewhat unformed individual, whom we expect to make powerful use of the possibilities for development opened up to him by analysis. A woman of the same age, however, often frightens us by her psychical rigidity and unchangeability. Her libido has taken up final positions and seems incapable of exchanging them for others. There are no paths open to further development . . . as though, indeed, the difficult development of femininity had exhausted the possibilities of the person concerned.[18]

This comment is indicative of the cultural myopia that Freud seemed to exhibit in his observations of women in late nineteenth-century and early twentieth-century Europe. It might be that the psychical rigidity that so frightened psychoanalysts was simply the recognition by women who consulted psychoanalysts of the futility of their attempts to break out of the confining social and cultural expectations that left few paths open to them other than being wife and mother. The next two sections will examine some of the early criticisms of Freud.

SOME EARLY DISSENTERS

There was considerable criticism from the outset of Freud's work both from within the ranks of psychoanalysis as well as from other disciplines, such as sociology and anthropology. Two general issues can be distinguished in the debates among the early critics. First, the biological basis of much of Freud's work on femininity was questioned. Secondly, the assumption of the universality of the patriarchal nuclear family that formed the basis of the universality claim for the Oedipus complex was challenged by anthropology.

An early critic from within psychoanalytic ranks was Karen Horney. Horney maintained that psychoanalytic theories of femininity were tainted by male biases. For example, the assumption that women feel their genitals are inferior to those of a male is questionable. Freud had stated that

> envy and jealousy play an even greater part in the mental life of women than of men. It is not that I think these characteristics are absent in men or that I think they have no other roots in women than envy for the penis; but I am inclined to attribute their greater amount in women to this latter influence.[19]

In response, Horney suggested that penis envy should be treated as an hypothesis; proof was required that healthy women, as well as women from other cultures, experienced penis envy before it could be accepted as fact. Horney herself did not rule out the possibility of penis envy, but she suggested that a more viable explanation of the existing evidence was cultural. She pointed out that in a culture that devalues women and stresses, from birth, the inferiority of the female, it was hardly surprising to find envy of the male, as represented by the penis.

Horney's criticisms suggested that elaborate psychoanalytic explanations for women's responses were unnecessary, since most women, in the majority of societies, quickly learn that to be male is to be privileged. As a result, many of the problems Freud associated with the female constitution and female psychological development were amenable to cultural explanations. For example, the greater degree of narcissism and masochism attributed by Freud to women could be explained, in Horney's view, by the ideological assumptions and social-structural arrangements that stressed women's weakness, dependence, emotionality and inferiority. Freud had indicated that "the suppression of women's aggressiveness which is prescribed for them constitutionally and imposed on them socially favours the development of powerful masochistic impulses."[20] Horney pointed out that masochism was not simply a sexual problem of obtaining pleasure from pain; nor was it a specifically female problem. It was not biology but culture that produced masochistic tendencies. As Horney pointed out, the "dynamics of masochism" entail

> the attempt to gain safety and satisfaction in life through inconspicuousness and dependency . . . this fundamental attitude toward life determines the way in which individual problems are dealt with; it leads, for instance, to gaining control over others through weakness and suffering, to expressing hostility through suffering, to seeking in illness an alibi for failure.[21]

She concluded that, in this respect, "there are indeed cultural factors fostering masochistic attitudes in women."

Horney agreed with Freud that different sexual functions and constitutions influenced the individual's mental life. However,

> it seems unconstructive to speculate on the exact nature of this influence. The American woman is different from the German woman; both are different from certain Pueblo Indian women. The New York society woman is different from the farmer's wife in Idaho. The way specific cultural conditions engender specific qualities and faculties in women as in men—this is what we may hope to understand.[22]

Horney concluded that the importance of cultural factors is overlooked by Freud, because "he has a primarily biological orientation . . . and on the basis of his premises cannot see the whole significance of these factors."[23]

The critique advanced by Karen Horney received support from Alfred Adler. He rejected Freud's views that instinctual sexual drives were the root causes of adult behaviour. For Adler, individual social interests motivated behaviour, and these were generated by the interaction of the creative self, fictional goals, inferiority feelings and superiority strivings.

In contrast to Freud, Adler believed that the only biological fact of significance was the initial helplessness of the human infant. From this fact developed feelings of inferiority common to both males and females, which in turn generated strivings for superiority. Normally, individuals did not aim for a powerful position in society but for the completion of self, the actualization of self. Such strivings entailed taking the more general social interests into account, since it is "in the world" that the actualization of self occurs. From this general theory of personality development, Adler indicated that in a society such as ours, the feminine personality was at a disadvantage. The first universal inferiority feelings shared by all mankind were compounded for women by the addition of socially ascribed inferiority. Women are constantly confronted with social impediments to their striving for superiority *because they are women,* and it is therefore not surprising that women exhibit a considerable degree of mental disorder. "The whole history of civilization . . . shows us that the pressure exerted on women, and the inhibitions to which she must submit today, are not to be borne by any human being; they always give rise to revolt."[24]

The negative characteristics of the feminine personality denoted by Freud could be accounted for, according to Adler, by the fact that everything in our society has been "determined and maintained by privileged males for the glory of male domination."[25] The negative consequences of cultural arrangements are not confined only to women. Men are also adversely affected by the fact that they are forced into dominant behaviour and the denigration of the female sex.

Freud, although attempting to balance the two perspectives with his emphasis on the initial bisexual and polymorphic disposition of the human infant, nevertheless, in his discussions on femininity, "falls" on the side of nature rather than nurture as the predominant factor. For example, the libido, or the sexual impulse, is theoretically asexual. But Freud speculated that

> it is our impression that more constraint has been applied to the libido when it is pressed into the service of the feminine function, and that—to speak teleologically—Nature takes less careful account of its (that function's) demands than in the case of masculinity. And the reason for this may lie—thinking once again teleologically—in the fact that the accomplishment of the aim of biology has been entrusted to the aggressiveness of men and has been made to some extent independent of women's consent.[26]

Consequently, sexual frigidity in women may occasionally be psychogenic, but it is hypothesized that in most cases it is "constitutionally determined and even . . . a contributory anatomical factor."[27] Horney and Adler proposed that in the nature/nurture dichotomy, Freud was wrong and that nurture rather than nature was the more significant factor in the development of sexual identity.

The second challenge to Freud involved the Oedipus complex

and the myth of the murdered father. The insistence upon the murder as a real event in some far distant past, for which Freud believed he had found evidence in totem feasts and religious practices, was challenged as ethnocentric in its attribution of different degrees of primitiveness to various societies and different family structures, and problematic in the suggestion of a unilinear evolutionary development. Anthropologists found that the idea of a universal patriarchal family structure consisting of biological parents was contradicted by alternative structures in other cultures. For example, anthropologists pointed out that many societies traced their descent through the maternal line, and maternal uncles rather than biological fathers were the significant authority figures for children. Malinowski, in his description of Trobriand society, observed that this pattern, in conjunction with an incest taboo between brother and sister rather than between parents and children, seemed to indicate the need to modify the theory of the Oedipus complex.[28] Other variations in family forms noted by anthropologists also called into question the universality of the nuclear patriarchal family structure.

Malinowski's argument of cultural relativism was more significant initially than the critique of Freud's views on femininity. For, if the universality of the Oedipus complex proved questionable, as the evidence of alternative family structures implied, then the idea of the murder of the primal father as the origin of the complex was also doubtful. If the totem myth were proved wrong, then the idea that patriarchy represents the universal foundation for culture and civilization must also be questioned. But, as Coward states, the issues of "cultural relativism and the universality of psycho-sexual complexes"[29] that emerged from the anthropological and psychoanalytic confrontations went unresolved.

The lack of resolution was partly due to the ambiguity in Freud's work about the real as opposed to a mythical status of the murder of the father. Orthodox psychoanalysis exemplified in the work of Ernst Jones came down on the side of the real, which then posed a problem for anthropology and sociology. Jones insisted that psychoanalysis had discovered the nature of the unconscious and the universality of the Oedipus complex. This, in turn, meant that he had to insist on the universality of the patriarchal nuclear family. As a result, it was not surprising that

> Malinowski and functionalist anthropology should chide psycho-
> analysis for its ignorance of the variety of form and function of the

family. No wonder a wedge should have been driven between psychoanalysis and those branches of anthropology seeking to provide an account of human relations which did not assume those human relations a priori, but looked at them in the context of the other social relations in which they occurred.[30]

The problems anthropology encountered with the Freudian account were not entirely paralleled in sociology. In the structural-functional tradition of much North American sociology, the nuclear family and the dichotomized roles of males and females in family and social life took much of the Freudian account for granted and, in some cases, transformed the separation of roles into normative prescriptions. As a result, women tended to appear in sociology in discussions of marriage, the family and socialization of children in their "proper," "functional" and "un-neurotic" roles of wife and mother.[31] As in the Freudian account, men were the norm against which women were measured—and often found wanting.

A feminist reappraisal of Freud and the normative assumption that the male was the yardstick of culture and civilization is found in Simone de Beauvoir's *The Second Sex*. This book, first published in 1949, has become a classic feminist text, despite the fact that de Beauvoir believed, at the time of writing, that "quarreling over feminism"[32] was for all practical purposes finished. De Beauvoir addressed the issues raised by Freud and psychoanalysis and explored the realities of women's existence under patriarchy. We will examine the basic premise of her book in the next section.

SIMONE DE BEAUVOIR AND *THE SECOND SEX*

De Beauvoir began her book with the question, "What is a woman?" and this question suggested a preliminary answer. "The fact that I ask it is in itself significant. A man would never get the notion of writing a book on the peculiar situation of the human male."[33]

Women appear to men as sexual beings; for them "she is sex—absolute sex, no less. She is defined and differentiated with reference to man, not he with reference to her."[34] Woman is the second sex to his first place. "He is the Subject, he is the Absolute—she is the Other."[35] As de Beauvoir indicates, the duality of Self and Other is a primordial ordering of the world, found in primitive as well as more advanced societies. However, the duality was not originally attached to a division of the sexes. All groups set themselves up as "the One" at the same time that they set up "the Other" in contrast to, or in conflict with, the One. But those designated as Other set up reciprocal claims to being regarded as the One. This reciprocity, de Beauvoir points out, is demonstrated in wars, festivals or trade between groups or individuals. However, such reciprocity is not found between the sexes. Women generally do not set themselves up as the One to the male Other.

De Beauvoir asks, "Why is it that women do not dispute male sovereignty?"[36] Why are women submissive enough to accept their status as Other, as second, to men? The answer is seen to lie in the assumption that the condition is a natural one. When it is regarded in this light then it can be seen as "beyond the possibility of change."[37] The condition is seen to lack "the contingent or incidental nature of historical facts" that would make the possibility of change a legitimate idea and goal. Women do not dispute their Otherness, and this accounts for the seeming unchanging nature of gender relations.

> To decline to be the Other, to refuse to be a party to the deal—this would be for women to renounce all the advantages conferred on them by their alliance with the superior caste. Man-the-sovereign will provide woman-the-liege with material protection and will undertake the moral justification of her existence; thus she can evade at once both economic risk and the metaphysical risk of a liberty in which ends and aims must be contrived without assistance.[38]

It should be noted that the advantages supposedly guaranteed by men are often not supplied, but the point stands that the majority of women often subscribe to a belief that there are advantages to be gained from their submission.[39] Like Engels and Freud, de Beauvoir asks, "How did all this begin?"[40] How does the human infant become male or female? Because one is "not born, but rather becomes, a woman."[41] She points out that it is not biology, psychology or economics that determines the nature of the female, but "it is civilization as a whole that produces this creature, intermediate between male and eunuch, which is described as feminine."[42]

In pursuing her question, de Beauvoir examines the biological arguments advanced to explain the relationship of the sexes. Whereas the biological differences are acknowledged as important, they are not regarded by de Beauvoir as determining.

> The body being the instrument of our grasp upon the world, the
> world is bound to seem a very different thing when apprehended in
> one manner or another . . . biological facts . . . are one of the keys to
> the understanding of women. But I deny that they establish for her a
> fixed and inevitable destiny. They are insufficient for setting up a
> hierarchy of the sexes; they fail to explain why woman is the Other;
> they do not condemn her to remain in this subordinate role forever.[43]

She points out that physiological facts take on meaning only in the
context of cultural values and ends. Consequently, the reproductive
function is socially determined rather than biologically regulated.
"The bondage of women to the species is more or less rigorous
according to the number of births demanded by society and the
degree of hygenic care provided for pregnancy and childbirth."[44]
De Beauvoir concludes that humans are not natural species but
rather an historical idea, and the task is to discover "what humanity
has made of the human female."[45] As part of that investigation, de
Beauvoir examines Freud and psychoanalysis, as well as Engels's
account of the nature of the female.

In examining Engels's *The Origin of the Family, Private Property, and the State*, de Beauvoir points to a number of problems.
First, she suggests it is not "clear that the institution of private
property must necessarily have involved the enslavement of
women."[46] In fact, the division of labour between the sexes "could
have meant a friendly association."[47] Moreover, it was not private
property as such that resulted in the oppression of women, but
rather the previous designation of women as Other in opposition
to, or in contrast to, the activity and autonomy of Man. In addition,
women cannot be understood as a class because most are connected
to men through marriage. The separation between social classes is
economic, not biological, and, by extension, "woman cannot in
good faith be regarded simply as a worker; for her reproductive
function is as important as her productive capacity, no less in the
social economy than in the individual life."[48] For this reason
simple solutions such as the abolition of the family do not
necessarily emancipate women. The insights of historical materialism are not totally rejected by de Beauvoir, but their limitations in
explaining gender relations are seen to be the result of a one-sided
perspective that regards men and women as no more than economic
units.

Just as the sexes cannot be regarded simply as economic units, so they cannot be considered as merely sexually driven beings. De Beauvoir points out that the Freudian assumption that females come to feel that they are mutilated men because they lack a penis is problematic. The idea "implies comparison and evaluation" . . . "Many psychoanalysts . . . admit that the young girl may regret not having a penis without believing, however, that it has been removed from her body; and even this regret is not general."[49] On the contrary, woman's supposed envy of the penis, and the female's denigration of her own sex can more plausibly be explained by the total social situation of women. In de Beauvoir's view, "if the little girl feels penis envy it is only as the symbol of privileges enjoyed by boys. The place the father holds in the family, the universal predominance of males, her own education—everything confirms her in her belief in masculine superiority."[50] The phallus is celebrated because it is the symbol of male dominance in the culture and, de Beauvoir suggests, "If woman should succeed in establishing herself as subject, she would invent equivalents of the phallus."[51]

The psychoanalytic account is problematic also in the denial of any choice or liberty for the human subject. De Beauvoir posits woman as having "the power to choose between the assertion of her transcendence and her alienation as object; she is not the plaything of contradictory drives; she devises solutions of diverse ranking in the ethical scale."[52] The problem with psychoanalysis is that the psychoanalytic concept of the "normal" becomes the standard by which all are measured irrespective of any special or simply different social and personal situations.

> Replacing value with authority, choice with drive, psychoanalysis offers an *Ersatz*, a substitute, for morality—the concept of normality . . . If the subject does not show in his totality the development considered as normal, it will be said that this development has been arrested, and this arrest will be interpreted as a lack, a negation, but never as a positive decision.[53]

In her examination of the historical and current situation of women, de Beauvoir rejects both the "sexual monism of Freud and the economic monism of Engels."[54] She attempts to take the total situation of women into account, including the biological factors that are, along with the economic, psychological and social factors, essential components of women's reality. The conclusion she reaches is that it is women's social situation, not "a mysterious essence" that accounts for women's position. In fact, the duality of male and female that implies, and indeed results in, the opposition and hostility between the sexes is an historical and cultural invention and has no instinctual or physiological basis. De Beauvoir's prescription for the future is a society that would enable both males and females to achieve self-realization—"transcendence"— instead of the current situation in which male transcendence is acquired at the expense of the subjection of women as Other. A future society of autonomous individuals would not, however, mean the denial of sexual difference. "To emancipate woman is to refuse to confine her to the relations she bears to men, not to deny them to her; let her have her independent existence and she will continue none the less to exist for him *also*: mutually recognizing each other as subject, each will remain for the other an *other*."[55]

The Second Sex was an important text for many of the women who, in the late 1960s, revitalized the women's movement. Sheila Rowbotham, in charting her personal progress towards socialism and feminism in her book *Woman's Consciousness, Man's World*, acknowledged her debt to de Beauvoir: "I had been picking up and putting down *The Second Sex* since I'd been at university. But I found the ideas very inaccessible at first . . . I couldn't relate them to myself. But in fact Simone de Beauvoir must have been seeping through my way of seeing everything."[56]

In the more recent feminist theorizing on the questions of sexuality and reproduction, de Beauvoir has also been significant. Firestone acknowledges *The Second Sex* as the "most comprehensive and far-reaching" theory that has "attempted to ground feminism in its historical base."[57] More specifically, it has been de Beauvoir's attempt to incorporate the reality of biological difference into her account of the relationship between the sexes, especially her comments with regard to sexuality and motherhood, that have lately become of interest to feminist scholars. The following section will examine some of the current theorizing on the nature of sexuality, reproduction and the socialization of children.

RECENT FEMINIST REFORMULATIONS

Negotiating the nature/nurture terrain has always been difficult for feminists, largely because women nearly always lost in the comparison. *The Second Sex* was significant in that it did not shy away from a confrontation with the facts of biology that have been used to place women on the "nature" side of the equation, accompanied by the assumption of their inherent inferiority.

In her examination of the making of a second sex, de Beauvoir looked at the social, cultural and biological interactions of various life stages—childhood, adolescence, marriage, motherhood and old age, as well as other life patterns such as lesbianism and prostitution—and in each case attempted to understand the different nature of women's sexuality and the experience of her body in the light of her social situation. She pointed out that feminine sexuality has "a structure of its own, and it is therefore absurd to speak of superiority or inferiority in connection with the male and female libidos."[58] In fact, lesbian preferences are not abnormal, but "if nature is to be invoked, one can say that all women are naturally homosexual."[59] But the sexuality of women is contained by the social assumption of the normality of heterosexuality. In addition, women's expression of sexual desire is muted by the assumption of their passivity and controlled by the belief in the natural aggression of the male. Consequently, the sexual nature of women (as well as men) is conditioned both by their physiological differences as well as by cultural precepts. Similarly, motherhood may be the fulfilment of a woman's physiological destiny, but this natural "calling" is "never abandoned wholly to nature."[60]

How a society deals with biology, and especially women's biological potential, and how feminism can articulate the relationship between nature/nurture have been central issues for many feminists, some of whom took their cue from de Beauvoir. In our examination of some of the recent accounts we will look at the work of Shulamith Firestone, Sherry Ortner, Dorothy Dinnerstein, Nancy Chodorow and Mary O'Brien.

Shulamith Firestone: Rewriting Freud and Marx

Shulamith Firestone, in her book *The Dialectic of Sex*, attempted to expand the dialectical materialist explanation offered by Marx and Engels to include the sexual politics of sexual relations. Dialectical materialism was grounded in reality, but Firestone regarded it as a partial reality: "There is a whole sexual substratum of the historical dialectic that Engels at times dimly perceives, but because he can see sexuality only through an economic filter . . . he is unable to evaluate (it) in its own right."[61] Similarly, Firestone compliments de Beauvoir on her observation of the duality that makes woman the Other, but suggests that instead of the *a priori* Hegelian categories of thought and existence that "Otherness" and "transcendence" embody, there is a "much simpler and more likely possibility that this fundamental dualism sprang from the sexual division itself."[62] Gender inequality is therefore located in biology. "Procreation . . . is at the origin of the dualism. . . . Unlike economic class, sex class sprang directly from a biological reality: men and women were created different, and not equally privileged . . . . The biological family is an inherently unequal power distribution."[63]

In developing her argument, Firestone suggests an extension of the dialectic in a reworking of Engels's definition of historical materialism to include the biological division of the sexes in reproduction.

> Historical materialism is that view of the course of history which seeks the ultimate cause and the great moving power of all historic events in the dialectic of sex; the division of society into two distinct biological classes for procreative reproduction, and the struggles of these classes with one another; in the changes in the modes of marriage, reproduction and childcare created by these struggles; in the connected development of other physically-differentiated classes (castes); and in the first division of labor based on sex which developed into the (economic-cultural) class system.[64]

The fact that the sex class system has its origins in biology does not justify its continuation, because to be "human" is to "outgrow nature." Consequently, "we can no longer justify the maintenance of a discriminatory sex class system on the grounds of its origin in Nature."[65] The abolition of the system will not be easy, however, because although man is able to free himself from the "biological conditions that created his tyranny over women and children, he has little reason to want to give this tyranny up."[66]

Just as the end of economic class exploitation can result only from the revolt of the "underclass (the proletariat) and, in a temporary dictatorship" through the seizure of the means of production, so the abolition of sexual classes requires the revolt of women as the underclass and "the seizure of control of *reproduction*."[67] The control of reproduction is to involve not simply women's control over their own bodies but also women's control, albeit temporary, of all human fertility. The goal of the movement is not just the elimination of male privileges, but of "the sex distinction itself; genital differences between human beings would no longer matter culturally."[68]

This latter proposal is based on Freud's observations of sexuality as a "prime life force," and the suggestion that the only way in which human beings could adjust to civilization was through the repression of that sexuality. However, Firestone asserts that the Oedipus complex is really about power, that is, the power of men over women. The channeling of sexuality into heterosexual desires and the imposition of the incest taboo that underpins the Oedipus complex are a result of cultural power arrangements. Consequently, Firestone suggests that the prime life force can be reconstituted

> if we grant that the sexual drive is at birth diffuse and undifferentiated from the total personality (Freud's "polymorphous perversity") and, as we have seen, becomes differentiated only in response to the incest taboo; and that, furthermore, the incest taboo is now necessary only in order to preserve the family; then if we did away with the family we would in effect be doing away with the repressions that mold sexuality into specific formations.[69]

Firestone would not simply eliminate the family, but more importantly she would eliminate that which is responsible for women's oppression within the family—reproduction. Her solution is artificial reproduction. The freedom women would then gain from that biological "tyranny" would undermine the whole social structure that is based precisely on that tyranny. Although women are reluctant to approve such a program for fear of appearing unnatural, Firestone insists that most women would secretly agree that "pregnancy is barbaric" and that "childbirth *hurts*. And it isn't good for you."[70] Along with artificial reproduction, Firestone would promote the expansion of cybernation, that is, the "takeover of work functions by increasingly complex machines."[71] Cybernation and artificial reproduction become the keys to a "qualitative change" in productive and reproductive relationships. In production, machines would do the work, thus eradicating the basis of class society and the breadwinner role. Artificial reproduction, which would also allow for population control, would end the "oppression of the biological family" and liberate the sexuality of all members of society, including children. "The double curse that man should till the soil by the sweat of his brow and that woman should bear in pain and travail would be lifted through technology to make humane living for the first time a possibility."[72] According to Firestone, it is the task of the feminist movement to make this vision possible if the human race is to survive.

Firestone's work has generated both debate and criticism. The major criticism has been directed at the technological utopia she envisages and the potential danger of further oppression such as a future could entail. Hamilton points out that although Firestone's view, that the natural is not of necessity a human value, is correct, "she extends this to its perhaps logical but alarming conclusion that 'humanity has begun to outgrow nature'."[73] In the light of current uses and consequences of technology that "wreak havoc with nature," such a conclusion, Hamilton suggests, should "make feminists more cautious in assuming that radical changes to nature will necessarily bring liberation."[74] Hamilton's caution is well taken considering that Firestone proposes that it be an elite group of cybernetic engineers who direct the future society. Given the relationship of women to the engineering profession to date, there is no guarantee that women might be part of the new elite, or that the profession would necessarily be "humanized" by its new powers.

Mitchell criticizes Firestone's account from the perspective of its theoretical adequacy as a dialectical analysis of sex. Mitchell suggests that the simple incorporation of the division of the sexes does not make the analysis either historical or dialectical. On the contrary, the division "returns us to the type of dualistic concept that preceded the discovery of dialectical materialism."[75] In addition, the revolution Firestone envisages as transcending and harmonizing "the biological and cultural dualities—male/female—in no sense makes that a dialectical moment. Dialectical materialism posits a complex (not dualist) structure in which all elements are in contradiction to each other."[76] The dualism and the future revolution are also criticized by Elshtain. Firestone saw the revolution as the fusion of masculine and feminine modes that would result in the abolition of those very categories: "a mutual cancellation—a matter-antimatter explosion, ending with a poof! culture itself."[77] This apocalyptic vision suggests to Elshtain a yearning for a "totalistic solution of all human woes,"[78] which she finds politically regressive in its suggestion of a total community that would brook no dissent.

Firestone's account is significant for recognizing the fact that women have always borne the greater burden of the reproduction of humanity. However, her analysis of the meaning of that biological fact is ahistorical as well as persistently negative in its assumption that reproduction is hazardous and has no redeeming features. In her view, women recognize these facts about reproduction, at least secretly, and react by opting out of the situation whenever the opportunity arises. In fact, psychoanalysis as well as the social sciences were recruited, according to Firestone, to stem the early twentieth-century feminist movement and to send women back into the family to play their appropriate wife and mother roles.

> Masses of searching women studied psychology with a passion in the hope of finding a solution to their "hangups". But women who had grown interested in psychology because its raw material touched them where they lived soon were spouting jargon about marital adjustment and sex-role responsibility. Psychology departments became halfway houses to send women scurrying back "adjusted" to their traditional roles as wives and mothers.[79]

Other theorists have not been so dismissive of the psychoanalytic tradition or of the reproductive role of women. Although they recognize, like Firestone, the need to deal with the central difference between the sexes embodied in women's reproduction, their approach has been to understand male domination in the light of women's own collusion with their fate. As we indicated in the discussion of Weber and power, domination for any length of time presupposes some compliance or willingness on the part of the dominated to obey. Brute force, in the long term, does not suffice. Ideological formulations that persuade the dominated of the legitimacy of the ruler's claim can assist in ensuring obedience, but the onus is on the subordinates to believe. It is suggested that Freudianism, especially as embodied in psychoanalytic theory and practice, has been one of the means through which women's obedience has been sought and obtained. As Rubin has pointed out, "One could read Freud's essays on femininity as descriptions of how a group is prepared psychologically, at a tender age, to live with its oppression."[80] Psychoanalytic clinical practice has "often seen its mission as the repair of individuals who somehow have become derailed enroute to their "biological aims."[81]

A critical question that must be addressed, therefore, is why did women not protest, rebel, refuse to take second place, especially when the ideological justifications were understood by women as excuses, rationalizations, myth or simple lies?[82] De Beauvoir and Firestone have pointed out that neither the Freudian nor the Marxian accounts are sufficient to explain this collusion. Ortner, Chodorow and Dinnerstein are three authors who begin to address this issue.

Sherry Ortner, Nancy Chodorow and Dorothy Dinnerstein: Reconsidering Motherhood

Sherry Ortner observed that the secondary, subordinate status of women is one of "the true universals, a pan-cultural fact. Yet within that universal fact, the specific cultural conceptions and symbolizations of women are extraordinarily diverse and even mutually contradictory."[83] In her article "Is Female to Male as Nature Is to Culture?" Ortner is concerned with explaining the universal, culturally attributed secondary status of women. She suggests that this status has to do with the fact that women are "identified with—or, if you will, seem to be a symbol of— something that every culture devalues, something that every culture defines as being of a lower order of existence than itself."[84] That something is nature, which, in a generalized sense, is contrasted with culture or with the technology and ideas "by means of which humanity attempts to assert control over nature."[85]

Culture is separate from and superior to nature because it has the ability "to transform—to 'socialize' and 'culturalize'—nature."[86] Women's secondary status can therefore be accounted for by the identification or symbolic association with nature.

> Women are seen "merely" as being *closer* to nature than men. That is, culture (still equated relatively unambiguously with men) recog- nizes that women are active participants in its special processes, but at the same time sees them as being more rooted in, or having more direct affinity with, nature.[87]

Ortner argues that women's association with nature emerges out of their biological attributes. The argument is presented in three general stages.

First, women's procreative role suggests that women's bodily functions are "more involved more of the time with 'species life'," and this links her to nature, unlike a male's physiology "which frees him more completely to take up the projects of culture."[88]

Secondly, women's physiological functions place her in particularistic "private" roles that are also of a lower status than men's universalistic "public" roles.

> The family (and hence woman) represents lower-level, socially fragmenting, particularistic sorts of concerns, as opposed to interfamilial relations representing higher-level, integrative, universalistic sorts of concerns. Since men lack a "natural" basis (nursing, generalized to child care) for a familial orientation, their sphere of activity is defined at the level of interfamilial relations. And hence, so the cultural reasoning seems to go, men are the "natural" proprietors of religion, ritual, politics, and other realms of cultural thought and action in which universalistic statements of spiritual and social synthesis are made.[89]

Finally, "woman's traditional social roles, imposed because of her body and its functions, in turn give her a different *psychic structure.*"[90] That is, women are more concrete and subjective psychically compared to the abstraction and objectivity of the male psyche.

Ortner's argument demonstrates the cultural construction of the nature/nurture debate. But other than the observation that the dichotomy is not a "natural" one and can therefore be changed by developing a different cultural viewpoint, the issue of women's compliance in the arrangements is not directly addressed. Ortner quotes de Beauvoir to point out that women also "buy" the cultural argument, and that "woman's consciousness—her membership . . . in culture—is evidenced in part by the very fact that she accepts her own devaluation and takes culture's point of view."[91] Women, therefore, become cultural beings only by accepting their inferiority, but the question still remains, why should women accept nature and themselves as secondary? Ortner suggests that the answer lies in the nearly universal feature of family arrangements—women do the mothering. The mechanisms and consequences of this universal fact have been extensively examined by both Chodorow and Dinnerstein.

Chodorow suggests that the fact that women "mother" has to do with social convenience rather than biological necessity: "we find universally that men with full adult status do not routinely care for small children, especially for infants. Women care for infants and children, and when they receive help, it is from children and old people."[92] While there are cross-cultural and historical variations in family and kinship structures and in parental practices, "it is important to keep in mind their common status as variations *within* a sexual and familial division of labor in which women mother."[93] Rejecting the biological implications of the Freudian account, Chodorow suggests that it is the "social-relational experiences" of early infancy, which may not even be intended by the parents, that affect personality developments. The fact that women mother produces certain assymetrical personality characteristics in males and females. Specifically, women's mothering produces mothers, that is, women who want to mother.

> Whether or not men in particular or society at large—through media, income distribution, welfare policies, and schools—enforce women's mothering, and expect or require a woman to care for her child, they cannot require or force her to provide adequate parenting unless she, to some degree and on some unconscious or conscious level, has the capacity and sense of self as maternal to do so.[94]

Initially, both males and females identify with the mother and "experience a sense of oneness with her."[95] The fact that in most cases the mother is the natural mother is probably due to the convenient fact that women lactate. The social convenience of extending the major responsibility for childcare to women beyond the immediate needs of the small infant "extends and intensifies her/his period of primary identification with her."[96] The first years for both sexes, during which the child is concerned with separation and individuation issues, are characterized by the need to break the primary identification with the mother. But the actual experience of children in this pre-Oedipal stage differs according to sex. The mother is "more likely to identify with a daughter than with a son, to experience her daughter . . . as herself."[97] At the Oedipal stage, when the development of sex identity is accomplished, male and female development becomes markedly distinct.

The boy must transfer his identification from the mother to the father, and since the father is generally more remote, less involved in childcare, then that identification is likely to be in terms of abstract ideas as opposed to personal identification. One of the consequences, which affects the male's subsequent devaluation of females, is that the masculine identification is often defined negatively as "that which is not feminine or involved with women."[98] In general, then, the boy rejects feminine traits by "repressing whatever he takes to be feminine inside himself, and, importantly, by denigrating and devaluing whatever he considers feminine in the outside world."[99] Four processes characterize the formation of masculine identity:

1. defining masculinity as that which is not female;
2. denial of attachment, especially dependence on another and differentiation from another;
3. repression and devaluation of femininity on both psychological and cultural levels;
4. identification with father in attempts to internalize and learn components of a not immediately apprehensible role.[100]

The development of a girl's gender identity is different, because female roles are immediately visible in her daily life. The girl is able to identify personally with the general character and behaviour of that first significant other, the mother.

> A girl, then, can develop a personal identification with her mother, because she has a real relationship with her that grows out of their early primary tie. She learns what it is to be womanlike in the context of this personal identification with her mother and often with other female models (kin, teachers, mother's friends, mothers of friends). Feminine identification, then, can be based on the gradual learning of a way of being familiar in everyday life, exemplified by the relationship with the person with whom a girl has been most involved.[101]

Freud indicated that a critical part of the development of femininity was the transference of love from the mother to the father if adult heterosexuality was to be achieved. But the girl does not completely reject the mother, and Chodorow suggests that the Freudian psychoanalytic concern with "constitutionally based libidinal development, and with a normative male model of development" obscured the fact that a "girl's internalized and external object-relations become and remain more complex, and at the same time more defining of her, than those of a boy."[102] More specifically, the female retains closer primary ties with her mother and with other women as well as with her own daughter(s), than does the male in any of his relationships. Mother-monopolized childrearing produces women who are able to *and will want to mother* in their turn. This situation contrasts with males who have a separate sense of self and who lack the capacity or the desire to nurture others. In fact, it is in the Oedipal struggle of the male to free himself from mother dependency and affirm his masculinity that the fear of women and the compensatory desire to dominate women develop. "Thus, women's mothering creates ideological and psychological modes which reproduce orientation to, and structures of, male dominance in individual men and builds an assertion of male superiority into the very definition of masculinity."[103]

The development of personality and adult sex roles are not biologically determined; nor are they simply taught. In Chodorow's view it is the nature of the social structure—particularly the structure of mothering—as well as cultural beliefs and values that are "internalized through the family and the child's early social object-relationships," which are located largely in the unconscious, that determine the development of the sexes.[104] Chodorow concludes that the "reorganization of parenting" is therefore the "central political goal" for feminists,[105] if sexual equality is to be achieved.

Dinnerstein's analysis of the significance of mothering parallels Chodorow's in many important respects. Dinnerstein also examines the consequences of mother-monopolized child-rearing for sexual power relations. Like Chodorow, Dinnerstein points out that the mother is the one on whom all infants initially depend, and it is she who both satisfies as well as frustrates the infant. For example, she both gives and takes away that source of pleasure and comfort, the breast. Mother, like nature, is "both nourishing and disappointing, both alluring and threatening, both comforting and unreliable."[106] The frustration of the child's demands is, however, a critical part of promoting independence from the mother. That independence is vital to the infant's progress towards selfhood. In other words, progress towards the formation of identity is a painful one, dependent upon repeated frustrations delivered by the primary love object. The resulting love/hate relationship with the mother, or the primary love object, is common to both sexes but takes a different form in the development of females and males.

Like Chodorow, Dinnerstein sees the girl's Oedipal separation from the mother as less clear-cut than is ever the case for the boy. Both sexes turn to the father, who is seen to represent a "more mature human world." But the father is for the girl "over-idealized." Whereas the boy uses the Oedipal period "to *consolidate* his tie with his own sex by establishing a principled independence, a more or less derogatory stance, from women," the girl uses the period to "*loosen* her tie with her own sex by establishing a worshipful, dependence stance toward men."[107] This situation supports the subsequent asymmetry of power between the sexes, as well as encouraging the heterosexual union of a dominant male and submissive female.

Both sexes feel the "terror of sinking back wholly into the helplessness of infancy,"[108] and this feeling is what enables male domination and female compliance with their own subordination. In fact, to "mother-raised humans, male authority is bound to look like a reasonable refuge from female authority."[109] But the girl is never completely divorced from the mother, because she will eventually come to identify with her mother when she concentrates her energies on mothering her own child. Because Freud regarded women as inferior to males, he was unable to account for the near universal fear and hatred of women under patriarchy. Dinnerstein suggests that this fear and hatred are the logical result of mother-monopolized child-rearing. In addition, it produces the male need to control women and women's more-or-less willing submission.

Examining the consequences of women's monopoly on child-rearing enables Dinnerstein to understand the persistence of male domination irrespective of the particular mode of production. Since women's monopoly over child-rearing is a cultural universal, the need to separate self from the dominant mother is also a universal. Consequently, the subordination of women under quite different social, economic and political conditions is understandable. The solution, according to Dinnerstein, is one that Chodorow also advanced: change the nature of parenting to include both sexes. When this occurs the transformation in both child-rearing and power relations between the sexes will be remarkable.

> When woman's lone dominion over the early flesh is abolished, she will no longer be peculiarly available as a dirty goddess, a scape-goat idol, a quasi-human being toward whom we have no obligation to make the painful effort to see her steadily and see her whole. Once we give up this easy way out . . . Woman and man will start at last stably to share the credit and stably to share the blame, for spawning mortal flesh.[110]

Dinnerstein also suggests that the ecologically problematic domination of nature can be located in the consequences of mother-monopolized child-rearing. The adult who symbolizes the natural world is the first adult with whom the child has contact, the mother. "Because the early mother's boundaries are so indistinct, the non-human surround with which she merges takes on some of her quasi-personal quality. In our failure to distinguish clearly between her and nature, we assign properties that belong to the other."[111] Consequently, just as the infant has ambivalent feelings towards the mother so those feelings are projected onto "mother nature." Nature, like mother, is that dangerous Other that must be tamed and controlled so that it not destroy the individual. The need to dominate nature is part of the unconscious of both sexes, but the female's need is tempered by her closer identification, as an adult, with the mother. Nature is therefore more likely to evoke solicitation than attack from females.

> It seems to me possible that this component of the girl's reparative feeling extends to nature as well as to other women. What has kept women outside the nature-assaulting parts of history—what has made them (with striking exceptions, to be sure) less avid than men as hunters and killers, as penetrators of Mother nature's secrets, plunderers of her treasure, outwitters of her constraints—may well be not only the practical procreative burden that they have carried, but this special compunction too.[112]

Dinnerstein suggests, then, that if men could also identify more closely with the mother, "as they will if time permits us to make the necessary change in our child-care arrangements—we would not now be so close to the irrevocable murder of nature."[113]

For both Chodorow and Dinnerstein the basic proposition is a psychoanalytic one: that the earliest learning is what remains in the unconscious and is the most difficult to change. The object relations approach that they take, in contrast to Freud, enables them to see the mother, rather than the father, as the pivotal model in the early socialization of the child. Given the fact that women almost universally mother, the unconscious relationship with the mother is the most significant determining relationship in the development of adult sex status.

The accounts described in this section have not been received uncritically. For example, Sayers points out that in the last analysis both Chodorow and Dinnerstein see the possibility of shared parenting as an "act of will,"[114] and men will simply have to be persuaded to participate equally in parenting. Chodorow suggests that women are already dissatisfied with the results of their exclusive mothering role, but only sometimes do men express dissatisfaction. But it is not entirely clear, in either account, why men might be persuaded to participate equally in parenting, except for Dinnerstein's optimism that men will come to realize that their domination of nature is now life-threatening. It is assumed that this realization will somehow translate into the correct conclusion that it is all the result, at bottom, of mother-monopolized child-rearing. Perhaps the "correct" conclusion can be reached by men if women have already been persuaded of its validity. However, since women, according to Dinnerstein, to some extent support men in maintaining male domination and the nature/nurture split, then it is not clear how the universal incentive for women to persuade men of the evil of their ways could develop.

If, however, both men and women participated in childcare, then the child's primary identification would be bisexual and this could, in turn, challenge heterosexuality as a norm. The result would, ideally, eliminate the dichotomy in which men are associated with the abstract cultural role and women with the dependent, emotional, nurture role. From this the elimination of the domination of one over the other, especially sexual domination and exploitation, might also follow. But the utopian "humanness" that might emerge from shared parenting leaves a critical issue unresolved. Does the sharing mean a sharing of the social-cultural roles of both sexes, and if so, will women remain as unexploitive towards nature as they are assumed to be at present? Is it just men who will shed the exploitation and assault on nature because they no longer need to control female potency? Chodorow suggests that both sexes would benefit, each gaining the positive features of the other and rejecting the negative.

> Anyone who has good primary relationships has the foundation for
> nurturance and love, and women would retain these even as men
> would gain them. Men would be able to retain the autonomy which
> comes from differentiation without that differentiation being rigid
> and reactive, and women would have the opportunity to gain it.[115]

But, even if the parenting is shared, there is still a need for the individual to separate self from primary identification in order to achieve self-actualization. The ambivalent feelings would be directed at both parents instead of at only one, and it is not clear that this would necessarily produce a less conflict-ridden offspring or a more equitable society.

Finally, the proposition that women should work with men to change child-rearing practices assumes that men will be able to see women as credible participants in making cultural changes. This is a shaky proposition, given the deeply embedded notion of gender inequality in the psychic structures of both sexes. However, the problem does not arise because, in order to incorporate both sexes into the process, we must assume that men have already altered their perception of women and themselves, and so, by coming full circle, we are still at a loss to explain the tactics for the change proposed by these authors. The circularity is summed up, inadvertently, in Ortner's conclusion.

> Efforts directed solely at changing the social institutions . . . cannot have far-reaching effects if cultural language and imagery continue to purvey a relatively devalued view of women. But at the same time efforts directed solely at changing cultural assumptions . . . cannot be successful unless the institutional base of the society is changed to support and reinforce the changed cultural view.[116]

Despite the criticisms above, it could be conceded that equal parenting might well produce a more humane society. But O'Brien's work on reproduction as a fundamental divisive feature of sex relations makes this conclusion seem overly optimistic.

Mary O'Brien: Reconceptualizing Reproduction

O'Brien points out that according to traditional political theory, women are consistently relegated to the natural realm in the dualistic thinking that has characterized male thought. Women have been associated with nature because of their reproductive function and, as a result, that function has been largely ignored in political theory. Even for Marx and Engels, as we have seen, incorporating reproduction into historical materialism was problematic. In the preface to the first edition of *The Origin of the Family, Private Property and the State*, Engels pointed out that,

> According to the materialistic conception, the determining factor in history is, in the last resort, the production and reproduction of immediate life. But this itself is of a twofold character. On the one hand, the production of the means of subsistence, of food, clothing and shelter and the tools requisite therefore; on the other, the production of human beings themselves, the propagation of the species. The social institutions under which men of a definite historical epoch and of a definite country live are conditioned by both kinds of production.

Despite this observation, for Marx and Engels, "birth is not an object of philosophy—Marxist man, impressively human as he is, somehow never gets born,"[118] as O'Brien points out.

O'Brien sees reproductive labour as akin to productive labour, but suggests that the real nature of reproduction has been obscured in the past by male ideology as exemplified in the "male-stream thought" of social and political theory. For example, she regards the dualisms of traditional social and political theory as arising from the reproductive experience.

> The opposition of individual and community is an *a priori* of the dualist view of reality which patriarchy has nourished for centuries . . . What I have argued is that dualism is neither a primordial nor a sensory nor a theological perception in an *a priori* sense, but is in fact a specifically masculine reality rooted in the material realities of reproductive process.[119]

By the same token, the method of analysis, the dialectical method used by Hegel and Marx, is similarly limited, although useful when modified appropriately by feminist analysis. For example, in the Hegelian and Marxist accounts of the dialectical process, history is achieved from the contradiction between the natural and social worlds through the active intervention of "Man." O'Brien points out that this understanding of history is flawed by the fact that Man is not a real "universal," encompassing all humanity. In the nature/culture dichotomy, women fall on the side of nature, and the relations between the sexes are "ahistorical, outside history and therefore outside of dialectical process."[120] However, O'Brien insists that all human understanding is dialectical in nature, though rooted in "the primordial biological experience of our live bodies, in that both digestive process and reproductive process are dialectical structures: they are instances of separation, unification and transformation."[121]

O'Brien points out that because reproduction has been seen as "brute, dumb, and intransigent," the real material basis of human history—genetic continuity—is overlooked. Consequently, in examining the "determinants of human consciousness, the notion of such a phenomenon as *reproductive consciousness* is not seriously entertained," and "the social relations of reproduction are not sought in the process of reproduction."[122]

In attempting to understand the process and relations of repro-

duction, O'Brien isolates what she calls "moments" of the reproductive process. There are ten moments: menstruation, ovula-
tion, copulation, alienation (of the sperm after ejaculation),
conception, gestation, labour, birth, appropriation (of the child)
and nurture. The only voluntary moments are appropriation and
nurture; the others are involuntary, although copulation "is a
halfway house: it has a strong instinctual component, but a great
deal of human effort has been invested historically in demonstrating that it can or at least ought to be controlled by human will."[123]
The experience of the ten moments is not equally shared between
the sexes. The male moments are alienation and appropriation;
shared moments are copulation and nurture; and all the other
moments belong to women. Most importantly, both sexes experience alienation, but the alienation of the male in the reproductive
process is different from that of the female, and it is this fact that
has made the appropriation of the child a male moment.

Female alienation in reproduction occurs at the birth of the
child, but it is overcome or transcended by two characteristics of
that labour. "One, obviously, is the knowledge of this child as in a
concrete sense *her* child, the product of her labour, a *value* that her
labor has created. The second is the experience of integration with
the actual continuity of her species."[124] The experience and understanding—the reproductive consciousness—has both a cultural and
biological base. That is, the alienation represented by the birth of
the child is "mediated involuntarily and naturally in reproductive
labour."[125] The contribution made by men to the reproductive
process is, however, both alienating and *only* culturally mediated.
That is, in the dialectic of reproduction, female labour overcomes
the separation of women from genetic continuity. For men, however, genetic continuity is only an abstract idea.

Men are, of course, included in copulation, but this is the very
point at which they are alienated from the reproductive process.
The alienation of the seed is biologically final. In addition, men
have no way of knowing whether conception has taken place or, if a
child is produced, no certainty that they are the father. Men
therefore have a different reproductive consciousness characterized
by a separation from "nature, from the race and from the continuity of the race over time," and the question is then, "What do men
do about it?"[126]

In the first instance, the reproductive consciousness of men
depends upon the historical discovery of the relationship between

sexual intercourse and conception. But the discovery produces alienation, since paternity can never be anything other than an *idea*. Consequently, men have devised means to overcome this alienation, to attempt to ensure the certainty of their participation in the reproductive process. This has involved the appropriation of the child by the "father" and the confining of women sexually so as to ensure some certainty of paternity. The mechanisms whereby men have attempted to overcome reproductive alienation are, first, cooperative social relations among men, as in "You leave my woman alone and I'll do the same for you." This agreement helps to ensure that the correct child is appropriated. The second means is the confinement of women and the third is asserting dominance over women.

> The exclusive right to a particular woman is therefore buttressed by the physical separation of that women from other men. In creating the right to the appropriation of children, men created that social space which political theorists have called the private realm. Whether mud hut or extended household, the private realm is a necessary condition of the affirmation of particular paternity, while the public realm is the space where men fore-gather to make the laws and ideologies which shape and justify patriarchy.[127]

O'Brien concludes that since traditional political and social theory and practice have generally been constructed in men's interests in order to control women, then they cannot be used unchanged to alter the relations between men and women. The creation of a new theory and practice that can overcome the "man-made" world is especially important in O'Brien's view, given modern contraceptive technology that can transform the process and the relations of reproduction for both men and women. For women, contraceptive technology offers freedom of choice of parenthood, which is "a historical development as significant as the discovery of physiological paternity."[128] Feminists must, however, ensure that this technology is used to integrate the sexes equally into the productive and reproductive realms, and that it is not used, as other technological advances have been in the past, for destructive purposes. For example:

> Contraceptive control can be used by the apostles of potency to accomplish acts of genocide against politically unreliable peoples, or to balance the law of supply and demand as it applies to the ratio

between possible productive capacity and the number of mouths to be fed. It can also be used to create a new class division: women who breed and women who do not.[129]

It is the task of feminists to ensure that the negative possibilities of contraceptive technology are rejected.

The general framework of O'Brien's account is similar to that of Ortner, Chodorow and Dinnerstein in her concern with the dualities of thought that provide the ideological basis for the duality of female/male experiences. It is generally assumed that man's interaction with nature has always been a problem. Men have sought to control and dominate nature rather than experience the connection and continuity that has characterized women's relation to nature. Reproduction is the major means by which women's relationship to nature is both affirmed and differentiated just as it separates and alienates men. The key to changes in sex relations for all of these theorists is to transcend and therefore eliminate the dichotomies or dualities of thought that serve as legitimations of sex inequality and as rationalizations for the despoiling of nature.

Some of the criticisms that have been directed at O'Brien's thesis take the dualistic contention as a problem. Moller Okin claims that activities such as farming, fishing, hunting, and seeing people born and die—in which both men as well as women participate— overcome the difference that O'Brien suggests separates the sexes.[130] But it could also be remarked that the connections that men make with nature through such tasks are always more abstract than the connections experienced by women—especially in their reproductive labour. In addition, the point that men's interaction with nature has generally been problematic is overlooked in this criticism.

Moller Okin also raises another point regarding the uncertainty of paternity. She maintains that this idea carries too great a theoretical burden. She suggests that the institutions of patriarchy have generally been successful in resolving this particular doubt so that it is "extremely difficult to believe that actual historical male consciousness has been obsessed with the issue of paternity . . . Have actual, historical men *really* had no sense of genetic continuity, in spite of having ancestors, in spite of having children that they generally had little cause to doubt were their own biological offspring."[131] In fact, Moller Okin suggests that both men and women have had a sense of genetic continuity and the reason that

men, not women, have created philosophies and political theories
has been because women have not had, until recently, the education
and thus the opportunity to do so. In response, it might be observed
that just as the separation from mother is said, in Dinnerstein's
account, to generate the unconscious motivation for domination, so
the potential uncertainty of paternity, whatever the institutional
and ideological safeguards, may remain a potent, unconscious,
motivating factor for males, as O'Brien suggests.

Neither O'Brien nor the other theorists claim to have developed a
completed metatheory of sex relations. O'Brien does claim, however, that feminism has contributed to a clearer understanding of
the nature of such relations through attempts to transcend the
dualism of "male-stream" thought.

> Feminism presents and represents a fundamentally different experi-
> ence of the relation of people and nature than that posed by male
> dualism. It insists, further, that the principle of integration can form
> the basis for a political praxis which is rational, human and far more
> progressive than any generically one-sided praxis, including Marx-
> ism, can ever be.[132]

The examination of the nature side of the nature/nurture
dualism has been the project of the theorists examined in this
section. The conclusions they have reached for feminist theory and
practice are similar. Feminism must develop both the theoretical
explanation as well as the practical means for a synthesis and
transcendence of the dualism of traditional thought and practice
that has been the source of social conflict, female subordination
and ecological disaster. As O'Brien points out: "The establishment
and growth of feminism as the progressive force in history constitutes a world turned upside down."[133] The practical tasks that
confront feminism are not simply the integration of women into
the productive process, but also the integration of men into the
reproductive process. Rephrasing Marx, O'Brien concludes:

> "In a rational human society, people will be producers in the
> morning, child carers in the afternoon, and critical critics in the
> evening. Only then can men and women abandon a long preoccupa-
> tion with sleeping together in favour of being awake together."[134]

NATURE/NURTURE AND POWER/PATRIARCHY

Thus far we have seen that sex inequality has been a persistent
feature, cross-culturally and historically, of most societies. Expla-

nations for this reality have generally rested upon that basic social incapacity that is assumed to follow from the biological fact that women reproduce. For example, Durkheim, Weber, Marx and Engels regarded women's reproductive capacity as a natural, unchangeable phenomenon, which in itself required no theoretical analysis. Even for Engels, the presumption of a matriarchy that preceded patriarchial society was not recognized as the "political" power of women over men in the same fashion that patriarchy represented the political power of men over women. The development of political power relations was generated only by the institution of private property and the development of class societies. The matriarchal society envisaged by Engels was not a class society, but simply one that traced descent through the mother or the female line because of the "ignorance" of paternity. The biological capacity of women in regard to reproduction was therefore the factor that conferred status, but not political power, on women in a matriarchy.

In general, the Marxist explanation sees the patriarchy/power association as a consequence of economic arrangements and takes for granted the sex differences in the nature/nurture association. But since the transformation of the economic relations does not necessarily alter, in any significant way, the power relations between the sexes, it became clear to many theorists that the "natural" substructure required explanation. That is, why have sexual differences been used to support power differences? In seeking answers to this question, Freud's work has been important. Freud's work reformulated the way in which sexuality could be viewed. From an existence on the margins of culture and nature, sexuality became incorporated into the cultural process. Sex differences in Freud's account are a consequence of the development of the adult psychosexual personality through the Oedipus complex. As a result, normal, that is socially acceptable, development takes a patriarchal form and has always taken such a form since the dawn of civilization.

Feminist theory has taken Freud to task in two ways. First, the assumption of the inevitable patriarchal origins of civilization has been criticized as a historically and culturally contingent account. Secondly, the practical results of psychoanalysis, in western societies, that saw the reinforcement of unequal sex roles and relationships in clinical practice, have been questioned. However, Freud's work has been a positive value in uncovering the significance of the unconscious structures resulting from sex-differentiated socialization. Specifically, consideration of the role of the unconscious and rethinking the universality of patriarchy have made the significance of mothering and the nature of the social practice of reproduction important in feminist analysis. As Angela Miles has pointed out: "The fact that women's oppression is so deeply structured and rationalized in terms of their ability to give birth and that women's resistance is so immediately met by powerful sociobiological opposition means that feminists have dealt centrally with questions of biology."[135]

In this chapter we have examined some of the ways in which biology has been taken into account. Simone de Beauvoir recognized that the nature of the duality that made women the Other stemmed from the reproductive capacity of women. But in her analysis, that biological fact remained immutable; it was men who remained the active participants in history and women who carried the natural burden of reproduction. What de Beauvoir asked for was the inclusion of women in the production of culture. Beyond recognizing the physiological and psychological importance of reproduction for women, de Beauvoir did not incorporate that understanding into her vision of change for *both* sexes.

Firestone's response to Beauvoir's point that the basis for women's subordination lay in their reproductive capacity was to overcome biology. Modern reproductive technology offered, in her view, the means for such transcendence. When the determinism of biology is overcome then the differential power relations between the sexes will have no basis for continuing. Eventually, harmonious, egalitarian social relations would result. Other than observing that reproduction is barbaric in its current form, that the socialization of children, as it is currently practised, is "crippling" for the child, and that children should have full legal, sexual and economic rights along with adults, Firestone does not examine the nature of reproductive practices and socialization techniques that are based on and reinforce the social assumption of biological determinism that is taken as the starting point in her account.

It is precisely the cultural and historical contingency of reproduction and the nurturance of children that is the focus of the other accounts examined in this chapter. Chodorow, Dinnerstein and O'Brien, as well as Ortner, attempt to incorporate the biological differences, the psychological consequences and the social and cultural prescriptions into their examination of socialization and reproduction. In these accounts, the important question—the question of women's compliance—which had been only marginally addressed previously, is tentatively examined.

Ortner reassesses the dualistic patterns of thought and practice that associate women with nature and men with culture. These associations provide the basis for the subordination of women and must be overcome through ideological and structural change. But the possibility of such change would appear remote to the extent that it is not clear how women may come collectively to understand the true nature of their position. Ortner suggests that women also subscribe to the dualistic ways of knowing, and if this is the case, if women's obedience rests on their ideological convictions of the rightness of the division, then social change is questionable. This is particularly true if, as Ortner suggests, the transmission of such ideological beliefs occurs through the early childhood contacts with the mother. At this point the circularity of the situation becomes clear.

The issue of women's mothering is taken up by Chodorow and Dinnerstein. Both of them reject the biological determinism of the Freudian account in the observation that women's mothering is a social, not a biological, construction. Both authors, however, take from Freud his insights into early childhood experiences in the construction of sexually differentiated adults, and use them to examine the implications of women's exclusive mothering in the production of sex inequality. A distinction between the two authors is found in their view of the consequences of mother-dominated childrearing for adult men and women. For Chodorow, women's mothering produces daughters who also want to mother. From this, it must be assumed that it is mothers who socialize daughters into accepting their subordination and sons into their desire to dominate women. For Dinnerstein, both sexes reject the power of the mother. But whereas in males this produces the desire to control and dominate women, in females it produces an identification with male power as a refuge from the all-powerful mother. Again, from either account, it is difficult to understand how change in gender relations might be possible other than through an act of will.

O'Brien's account of the difference produced by reproduction also offers few concrete suggestions for change other than the incorporation of men into the reproductive process. In fact, such incorporation would be problematic on the basis of O'Brien's analysis, since the alienation of the male rests upon the biologically inevitable alienation of the male seed in copulation. The institutional structures of patriarchy are the means by which this alienation has been overcome by males, and it is difficult to see how a restructuring of the subsequent moments of reproduction can overcome that inevitable, biologically invariable alienation that in turn supports the institutions of patriarchy.

In all the accounts examined in this chapter there is one glaring problem that has not been addressed: the major concern with heterosexual relations and the assumption that the biological family of mother, father and children is the general norm. These two features result in a problematic ahistorical and culture-bound analysis of sex relations similar to Freud's and thus hinder the attempt to achieve an integrative general theory.

The emphasis upon heterosexuality in the above accounts has been challenged most notably by Adrienne Rich. Rich claims that heterosexuality "like motherhood needs to be recognized and studied as a *political institution*."[136] Compulsory heterosexuality suggests, in Rich's view, that "large numbers of men could, in fact, undertake child care on a large scale without radically altering the balance of male power in a male identified society."[137] But Rich maintains that by not analyzing the nature of heterosexual relations, the need of men to assure themselves of sexual access to women is obscured, and with it the real nature of male power. Rich's account of the means by which compulsory heterosexuality is enforced provides an alternative perspective on women's compliance with their own subordination. The structures that maintain heterosexuality, and the ideology that claims its normality compared with other sexual preferences, ensure the compliance of the majority of women in their own oppression. This occurs in defiance of the "natural" connections between women that are found in the girl's original love for her mother, according to Rich.

Whether Rich's conceptualization of the coercive nature of heterosexuality is accepted or not, her analysis is important in demonstrating the restrictive nature of much of the work on sexuality and power relations between the sexes. At the same time the debate among feminists over these issues is an indication of the vitality and maturity of the movement. As O'Brien indicates, initially, "feminism's expression of women's interests primarily took the form of refusing the dominant stereotype of women and insisting that women were capable of being the same as men."[138]

Many feminists "accepted the blatantly ideological relegation of reproduction and reproductive work to semi-human status."[139] The re-evaluation of motherhood and the reassessments of the cultural, historical, psychological *and* biological components of the re-productive process have led to the critical analysis of dualistic thinking behind the nature/nurture dichotomy in theorizing about sex relations.

However, the reformulations seem to have examined a previously unexplored area at the expense of another important concept—patriarchy. In general, patriarchy is reified in these accounts and becomes the catchword to express conflict between men and women. Patriarchy becomes "male power" and the unexamined basis for the social-cultural characteristics of women's subordination. But patriarchy requires both social-cultural as well as psychological explanations, especially in the light of women's compliance. It is the unexamined nature of patriarchy as a social-political process that produces the somewhat utopian conclusions regarding future change in gender relations in some of the accounts in this chapter. As Coward suggests, the concept of patriarchy should be treated with caution.

> For the term "patriarchal" implies a model of power as interpersonal domination, a model where all men have forms of literal, legal and political power over women. Yet many of the aspects of women's oppression are constructed diffusely, in representational practices, in forms of speech, in sexual practices. This oppression is not necessarily a result of the literal overpowering of a woman by a man.[140]

This is not to deny that, in nearly all societies, the sexual division confers power on men (irrespective of whether individual men are themselves powerful). Coward's caution, however, does suggest that the uncritical use of the term should be avoided if the complexity of sex relations is to be understood.[141]

The current concern with mothering and the values of cooperation, integration and peaceful and permissive attitudes that have been associated with women's roles is not new. The nineteenth- and early-twentieth-century women's movement also embraced the feminine sphere as a positive transformative possibility. But as Maroney points out, the early movement "made the ideology of difference their own. Women's moral, cultural and practical skills were meant to *extend* the boundaries of differentiated spheres, not break them down: men were not to diaper babies, although women were to read Latin."[142]

The next chapter will summarize the discussions of the work of the sociological fathers in terms of the development of sociological theory and sociological theorizing. The more recent conservative approach taken by sociology is briefly examined as a reaction to feminist theory as well as a continuation of the sociological tradition in the examination of relations between women and men.

CHAPTER 6

Nature/Nurture: The Sociological Fathers and Their Sociobiological Descendants

In pursuing the feminist critique of sociological theory in the work of Durkheim, Weber, Marx, Engels and Freud, we have mentioned the conditions of knowledge and the analysis of the constraints upon knowledge. One of the important themes that underpins the work examined and acts as a constraint on the examination of sex relations is the assumption of the "naturally" unequal power relations between the sexes. As Rosaldo has pointed out, in all societies, whether egalitarian or highly stratified by sex, men appear to be the "locus of cultural value," and "everywhere men have some *authority* over women . . . they have a culturally legitimated right to her subordination and compliance."[1] However, although men may have authority—the legitimate right to make decisions and demand obedience—"in various circumstances male authority might be mitigated, and, perhaps rendered almost trivial, by the fact that women . . . may have a good deal of informal influence and *power*."[2]

The realities of power relations, as opposed to the formal structures of authority, are obscured when both power and authority are assumed to be male preserves. In addition, the possibility that hierarchical arrangements of authority and the competitiveness of power relations are not an invariable form of social organization is also obscured. As Leacock points out:

> data have always been available to show that egalitarian relations between women and men have existed in many cultures, and that if anything, they are more "natural" than the relations of dominance and subordination found in stratified societies. Even those who argue for universal male supremacy have to concede that people who support themselves (or did until recently) by gathering wild vegetable foods, hunting, trapping, collecting wild animals, and/or fishing and collecting sea foods, were generally peaceful and non-aggressive, placed a high value on cooperation and good humor, and were characterized by far greater female independence and equality than societies dependent on agriculture.[3]

The idea of egalitarian sex relations is not dismissed out of hand by the theorists we have examined, but as a general rule such a state of affairs is regarded as pre-social, pre-civilization. Society or civilization requires a division of labour, and the basic, fundamental division of labour is between the sexes.

The second theme pervading the work we examined is that the division of labour between the sexes is understood as universal because of biological differences between women and men. Specifically, that women reproduce is taken to be the factor, recognized by all societies, that separates the sexes in terms of authority and power. As such, the fact that women reproduce is taken as a "natural," logical explanation for the subordination of women to men. Therefore, the idea that biological differences "naturally" produce dichotomized sex relations that cannot be changed, because they are biological, remains unquestioned.

Sociological theory takes society as its object of study. But, as we have seen, given the underlying assumptions or themes, the early theorists accounted for how one half of participants, men, behave and how they believe the other half, women, behave, or ought to behave. Thus, their accounts are partial explanations.

Recognizing the problems involved in the theoretical accounts does not mean that they should be thrown out in their entirety. Theory is an attempt to explain reality through a system of logically connected ideas that can, in some fashion, be validated. In the cases we have examined the explanations advanced follow logically from the initial premises, which, in turn, are a result of how the world appeared to those theorists. Their search for evidence and their interpretation of that evidence were coloured by their initial assumptions about sex relations. Since, in their eyes, women appeared as "Other," their accounts are logically derived but invariably partial representations of social reality. This does not mean, however, that historical hindsight allows us to say of these theorists that they should have known better; in their place and time, they could not have known better.

Similarly, it is not enough to simply add on newly discovered facts, or to reinterpret facts, in order to dismiss the theories, because all facts, including feminist facts, are value-laden. That is, simply to demonstrate the underlying theoretical assumptions and the constraints they generate in the work of the sociological fathers is a necessary but not a sufficient condition for a feminist reformulation of sociological theory. The work is necessary, in the sense that re-examination and reformulation are basic to the process of theorizing. As Kaplan has pointed out, "The aim of theorizing is to unify and systematize knowledge, but even in the happiest circumstances the aim is never completely attained. New knowledge is forever pouring in upon us, carrying with it new tasks for theory to perform."[4] Because the feminist critique opens up the sociological domain so that the former unity and systematization are broken, new explanations, interpretations and sources of knowledge must be sought. For feminists, women must be included as competent observers of social reality—as subjects, not objects, of theory.

The preceding chapters have examined some of the work of the sociological fathers, and it has been demonstrated that the theoretical accounts address only half the human experience. From the standpoint of a history of sociology, the absence of the voice of women, or rather the inability to look beyond the patriarchal principle, seems somewhat surprising. Sociology was very much the product of nineteenth-century western European thought, and its growth as a discipline paralleled the growth and development of the first women's movements. However, sociology as a discipline took very little account of the social movement occurring under its own eyes. Various social science associations may have granted women membership and the right to present papers but they gave little active support to the women's fight for the vote. It is ironic that when many women were protesting the relegation of their interests and needs to some private, domestic sphere, and fighting on all fronts (not simply the political front for the vote) for a stake in the public realm, sociological descriptions, for the most part, either ignored the lives of women or reinforced an idealized patriarchal family on the grounds of social harmony and stability.[5]

Sociological accounts included women as appendages of men, particularly with regard to power and authority. Sociology was supported in its blinkered perspective by evolutionary biology and psychoanalytic theory which understood and documented the "natural" inequality of sex relations and the fact of power as a natural male prerogative. The more recent development of biologically based explanations of natural differences and inequalities by sociobiologists has revived some of the old arguments. As a result, understanding past sociological accounts is a critical necessity for a feminist sociological critique of sociobiology.

In the next section we will summarize the problems in the theoretical accounts examined in the previous chapters. The emphasis will be placed upon the biologically based assumptions in those accounts that rationalize dichotomy and hierarchy in sex relations. We will then briefly examine the work of the sociobiologists and feminist critiques of their work.

PARTIAL PERSPECTIVES

Underlying the accounts of Durkheim, Weber, Marx and Engels, and Freud is the assumption that reproduction is a constraint on all women all of the time. By extension, it is also assumed that women's reproductive capacity automatically or "naturally" makes them responsible for nurturing the young. For Durkheim, Weber, Marx and Engels, the connection between reproduction and child-care was a natural and therefore unchangeable phenomenon that required no analysis, in and of itself, as a social and cultural fact. The connection was problematic, sociologically, only when the socialization process that produced gendered individuals was disrupted.

None of the theorists was sex-blind. On the contrary, the nature of sex relations formed the basis for subsequent speculations on the genesis of society and the nature of the social order. Their partial perspective rested on their assumption that without male control of women, there could be no society, no culture or civilization, but only unorganized hordes of women and children confronted by predatory men.

Important differences among the theorists occur in their thinking on the origin and development of social order or civilization. Weber and Freud rejected the possibility of matriarchy as a viable form of social organization. Engels insisted on a matriarchal period,[6] and Durkheim also suggested that a somewhat disorganized matriarchy was at the origins of social order. But in Durkheim's case, matriarchy simply meant the recognition of the connection between mother and child, which did not necessarily entail any extensive, formal regulation of society in terms of this kinship tie. In fact, "great political societies" are only able to "maintain themselves in equilibrium . . . thanks to the specialization of tasks"; therefore, the division of labour, including especially the sexual division of labour, is the "condition of existence" of social life.[7]

Durkheim's amorphous, androgynous horde was the necessary basis of theorizing about the nature of the division of labour, just as Engels used early matriarchy to explain the economic basis of patriarchy and the formation of the State. For Engels, patriarchy and the attendant monogamy represented the means for the preservation and perpetuation of private property, and it followed that the patriarchal family became the fundamental unit of unequal productive relations. It was also for this reason that Morgan's research was important to Marx and Engels. Morgan had demonstrated that patriarchy represented a specific family form tied to a particular stage in productive relations, and that in more primitive times, mother-right prevailed. In Engels's view, "The rediscovery of the original mother-right gens as the stage preliminary to the father-right gens of the civilized peoples has the same significance for the history of primitive society as Darwin's theory of evolution has for biology, and Marx's theory of surplus value for political economy."[8]

The discovery of father-right at the same time as the development of surplus wealth and the gradual accumulation of that surplus in the hands of a few enabled Engels to relate the patriarchal family form to the development of private property. And it was the need to protect that property that produced the institution of the State. Monogamy was deemed essential to ensure inheritance of the father's wealth. The patriarchal family, and the monogamy imposed on women within that family, "was not in any way the fruit of individual sex love, with which it had absolutely nothing in common . . . It was the first form of the family based not on natural but on economic conditions, namely, on the victory of private property over original, naturally developed common ownership."[9] Monogamy was therefore

> a great historical advance, but at the same time it inaugurated, along with slavery and private wealth, that epoch, lasting until today, in which every advance is likewise a relative regression, in which the well-being and development of the one group are attained by the misery and repression of the other.[10]

It must be remembered that Engels suggested that women themselves started the move towards monogamy, which eventually proved to be so disastrous for them. It was because of their weariness and distaste for multiple sexual partners that women pushed for pairing marriages that led, in turn, to monogamous, patriarchal families. With the development of surplus wealth, men suddenly underwent a psychological change and wanted to possess "their" children in order to pass on their surplus wealth. Because of pairing marriage, men were able to know, with some degree of certainty, which were their children and therefore, in Engels's and Marx's view, the most natural transition to monogamy occurred. The fidelity of the wife was assured by the husband's absolute control and this, in turn, assured him of his paternity. Patriarchy is therefore the structure of male ownership and control of women and children. It is at this point that sex relations become submerged, and the family becomes an undifferentiated unit that can serve, in Marxist terms, as a basic foundation for the social divisions elaborated in the relations between social classes and the state.

> With the division of labour, in which these contradictions are implicit, and which in its turn is based on the natural division of labour in the family and the separation of society into individual families opposed to one another, is given simultaneously the distribution and indeed the unequal distribution, (both quantitative and qualitative), of labour and its products, hence property: the nucleus, the first form, of which lies in the family, where the wife and children are the slaves of the husband.[11]

There are a number of problems with Engels's account of the development of the patriarchal monogamous family, which have been discussed in Chapter 4. The major problem, however, rests with the fact that Engels's explanation presupposes the sexual conflict that it is supposed to explain.

Engels' economic explanation for patriarchy is really no explanation at all, since it presupposes the very male-dominated sexual division of labor it purports to explain . . . The assumption that an interest in the control of property generates an interest in the subordination of women requires the additional assumption of an interest in exclusively male control of property; this assumption, in turn, entails the assumption that a male-dominated sexual division of labor, i.e. patriarchy, already exists.[12]

Abolish property and you abolish patriarchy is the conclusion reached by Marx and Engels. The abolition of patriarchy did not, however, mean that monogamy would necessarily disappear. In Engels's view, if the property basis of patriarchal monogamy were eliminated, then "true sex love" would occur.

With the conversion of the means of production into social property, wage labour, the proletariat, also disappears, and therewith, also, the necessity for a certain—statistically calculable—number of women to surrender themselves for money. Prostitution disappears; monogamy, instead of declining, finally becomes a reality—for men as well.[13]

The simple formula for the development of "true sex love" within a monogamous relationship results from the identification of women with the family and the rejection of the idea that sexual relations under patriarchy are possibly as antagonistic as are class relations under capitalism. According to Coward, "in Engels' work, the sexual and familial bond is thought to override class distinctions; it constitutes men and women as an economic unit in spite of the fact that the imagery used to describe this unit is one of the slave master and his slaves."[14] The abolition of the family as an economic unit supporting capitalist relations does not address the fundamental question of the assumed natural differences between the sexes. As long as women's reproductive capacity is seen to be an essential difference only minimally affected by social and cultural relations, then the presumed equality of "true" love is mythical.

When it comes to the details of sex relations and the family, Marx and Engels remain true to the nineteenth-century idealization of the family. "True sex love" is heterosexual, monogamous and permanent love. In this regard, their ideas are similar to those of Durkheim, who suggested that the modern conjugal family, far from disappearing, was a critical necessity for the moral health of society. However, like Marx and Engels, Durkheim regarded the function of wealth as a problem for the establishment of an equitable society, but the family unit itself was not problematic, at least in terms of sex relations.

Durkheim pointed out that the "inherited fortune loads the scales and upsets the balance" of a society.[15] The inequality that inheritance generates can be eliminated, however, when "the sole economic inequalities dividing men are those resulting from the inequality of their services." This form of inequality would be a "natural" form because it would conform to the natural inequalities between individuals. The removal of any constraints, such as inheritance, would result in the "harmony between the constitution of each individual and his condition."[16] Division of labour would occur "spontaneously" so that each would occupy a "place in the social framework which is compatible with their faculties," with the result that "social inequalities [would] exactly express natural inequalities."[17] It is probable that some individuals would be dissatisfied with the results of the division of labour, but such "men whose desires go beyond their faculties" would be exceptional, "morbid cases," because "normally, man finds happiness in realizing his nature."[18]

Like Marx and Engels, Durkheim recognized the importance of economic structures to the organization of society, but he insisted that social harmony could not be achieved simply by economic reorganization. The abolition of inherited property was necessary to achieve an equitable society, but such a measure would not eliminate division among individuals.

> The moral conditions of our social life are such that societies cannot be maintained unless *extrinsic* inequalities among individuals are evened out. This statement must not be taken to mean that all men ought to become equal. On the contrary, intrinsic inequality will become more and more pronounced. But social inequalities must come to reflect only differences in personal worth without that worth's being exaggerated or debased by some external factor.[19]

With modern industrial society, task differentiation became inevitable, and with it the necessity of ensuring that those differences were appropriately assigned and regulated in the interests of a higher end—the stability and harmony of the society.

> What is needed if social order is to reign is that the mass of men be content with their lot. But what is needed for them to be content, is

not that they have more or less but that they be convinced they have no right to more. And for this, it is absolutely essential that there be an authority whose superiority they acknowledge and which tells them what is right. For an individual committed only to the pressure of his needs will never admit he has reached the extreme limits of his rightful portion.[20]

The only moral power that could say to the individual, "You must go no further,"[21] would be society.

There are social forces, moral authorities, which must exercise this regulating influence, and without which appetites become deranged and economic order disorganized . . . Society alone has the capacity to constrain and only it can do so without perpetually making use of physical restraint . . .[22]

One of the mechanisms that society used in the regulation of such unrestrained appetites was the family, or, more particularly, the conjugal bond.

It is at this point that a contradiction emerges in the Durkheimian account. As we saw in Chapter 2, the preservation of the family was formally an important factor in providing the impetus for men's occupational activities. Without the "capacity to enrich the domestic patrimony [a] powerful moral stimulant" to work activity would be "removed in one fell swoop."[23] Therefore, in the absence of inheritance, something else would be required to motivate men and this could be found in the occupational or professional group. "[T]he termination of the rule of hereditary transmission is not enough. Men must gradually become attached to their occupational or professional life . . . In the hearts of men, professional duty must take over the place formally occupied by domestic duty."[24] This would not mean, however, that marriage would or should be eliminated. On the contrary, because marriage provides the "exclusive basis of kinship," it must be preserved and made indissoluble.

On the one hand, the family is seen to be "increasingly incapable" of performing economic and moral functions and requires replacement. But on the other hand, the family, and especially the conjugal bond, must be strengthened in the interests of the moral health and stability of the society. The strengthening of the conjugal bond can only be accomplished at the expense of women, as Durkheim's investigation of suicide indicated. This would be a lesser evil, however, than the collective harm that marital dissolution, undertaken too readily, could occasion. On this basis, Durk-heim maintained that divorce should not be made available simply because the husband or the wife wished it. Marriage may be contracted voluntarily, but once established, it takes on a signifi-cance apart from the wishes of the couple. Marriage and family constitute basic ordering mechanisms in society, and it is only when a marriage can no longer fulfil its social function that its termination is justified. The judgement of the condition of the marriage cannot be made objectively by the participants because they "see matters only from their own point of view—wholly personal and subjective . . . They feel the shocks, the clashes, of daily life. But as for knowing if those clashes are of such a nature as to contaminate their life together as husband and wife and prevent it from fulfilling its role in society—this is a problem that is beyond their grasp."[25] Only a judge could give an objective opinion of the marriage, being able to take into account the feelings of the couple without regarding such feelings as necessarily "evidence sufficient to sever the bonds of matrimony."[26]

Although men were increasingly likely to find the greater part of their life and interests within professional and occupational groups, they would still require the emotional support of the conjugal family for their complete well-being. Women's well-being was also to be located in the family because this was the locus of her "natural" talents. As the organization of the family seemed to operate negatively for women, then some adjustment was required. The adjustment that Durkheim suggested was that aesthetic func-tions be added to women's activities. Such functions were, in addition, suited to women's nature and temperament.

The sexual division of labour was a natural division for Durk-heim, as it was for Marx and Engels, and predisposed women to domesticity. But whereas Marx and Engels saw the incorporation of women into productive activities as a step towards sex equality, for Durkheim the separation of women from the economic sphere and their increased specialization in domestic and aesthetic tasks would lead to greater equality.

In a review of Marianne Weber's book on the position of women and the history of patriarchy, Durkheim criticized her conclusion that the "patriarchal family brought about the woman's complete subservence." He admitted that such a situation resulted in women having the legal status of minors but this was compensated for by the fact that family life is much more intense and more important than in previous types; the woman's role, which is precisely to preside over life indoors, has also assumed more importance, and the moral scope of the wife and mother has increased. At the same moment and for the same reason, husband and wife have become closer, more directly and more constantly in touch, because the centre of gravity in the life of the male has ceased to be sidetracked away from home as much as in the past.[27]

The closer relationship between husband and wife means that "family matters" increasingly preoccupy men, and when this happens he "falls out of the habit of regarding his wife as an inferior."[28] Patriarchy produces "equality" within the family and household because "the wife is respected by those around her, she shares her husband's position." To call for a situation in which marriages could be "broken simply at the wish, confirmed and duly recorded, of the parties concerned," as Marianne Weber did, was a grave mistake in Durkheim's view. It was too simplistic a solution and held the danger that the high moral status of the wife would be eroded and not compensated for in the acquisition of legal and political reforms.

The contradictions of Durkheim's position on sex relations are derived from his concern for the order and stability of society. However, the contradictions have the same source as the problems the Marxist account confronts, that is, the inability to conceptualize sex and dichotomize sex groups as social constructs. More specifically, by considering women's capacity as reproducers as a collective, natural phenomenon distinguishing them from men, evident when society originated and remaining unchanged ever since, meant that any ideas on the future equality of the sexes would invariably be compromises. The idea of matriarchy, common to Engels's and Durkheim's accounts, is not intended as a contrast to the later patriarchal developments as much as it is an indication of the "natural" basis for subsequent sex dichotomies. In this regard, Weber's account is similar.

For Max Weber, patriarchy was a system of sex relations that formed the foundation for subsequent social and political structures and power relationships. As such, it was an historical form of social relations, limited in scope and structural extension. The origins of patriarchy were not to be found in the subversion or overthrow of a previous matriarchal organization. For Weber, the

"natural" connection between the mother and child was a "biologically based household unit" and lasted only until "the child is able
to search for means of subsistence on his own."[29] Matriarchy as a
social-political form was, in Weber's view, a myth based on the
error of assuming that exclusive property claims did not exist in
early times. Roth quotes Weber on "the villain of matriarchy" in
Weber's criticism of Engels's views and points to the note Weber
attached to Marianne Weber's work on *Fichte's Socialism and its
Relation to the Marxian Doctrine.*

> It is scarcely worth mentioning even vis-a-vis a reader who is not an
> economist that the absence of property in the primeval society is a
> fiction. Only the owners of property, its uses, hence its practical
> importance, have changed. The consumer communism of the con-
> temporary nuclear family is the last remnant of the communism of
> larger associations in matters of property, production and consump-
> tion. Historically, there never was a time when some group did not
> advance exclusive property claims."[30]

Since women under patriarchy are the property of men, and since
property is the mark of collective relations, then there cannot have
been a time when women were not subordinate to men.

For Weber, the origins of society are to be found within a
communistic household. That is, the foundations of social organization are seen to be dependent on the nature of economic activities
rather than on blood ties or sexual connections. In fact, the
household is simply a particular form of economic association that
might also regulate sexual relations and relations between children
"based on the fact of their common parent or parents."[31] Such
regulations can become the "normal, though not the only, bases of
a specific economic organization: the household." The household,
in turn, is not the most primitive institution, but depends upon a
"certain degree of organized cultivation of the soil."

> The household does not seem to have existed in a primitive economy
> of hunters and nomads . . . even under the conditions of a technically
> well-advanced agriculture, the household is often secondary with
> respect to a preceding state which accorded more power to the
> inclusive kinship and neighborhood group on the one hand, and
> more freedom to the individual vis-a-vis the parents, children,
> grandchildren, and siblings on the other hand.[32]

The regulation of sexual relations between men and women and those between father and children are socially constructed regulations that are often the source of "substantial inroads into unmitigated communist house authority."[33] However, it should be noted that the former communist house authority was one that already involved the subjection of women as a collective group to the collective group of men, or "brothers." The "inroads" therefore consisted of regulating sexual access to women on behalf of and among the men.

> Nowhere do we find unregulated, amorphous sexual promiscuity within the house, even if sexual relations between siblings are a recognized institution; at least nowhere on a normative basis. On the contrary, any kind of communist sexual freedom is most thoroughly banished from a house in which there is communist property ownership.[34]

In addition, within such primitive households, with a minimal division of labour, there is still a "differentiation of sex roles."[35]

In contrast to Marx, Engels and Durkheim, but in agreement with Freud, Weber proposed that the beginnings of social organization developed wherever there was patriarchy. As a result, any discussion of power and authority deals with male domination and control. Women are "dealt out" of the structure of authority and exercise of power from the beginning so that the possibility that women might be active participants rather than passive counters in the arrangements among men is ignored. However, as we have seen, the very structure as well as the ideology of traditional domination, exemplified by feudalism, often meant that women were important players in power relations.

In structural terms, in feudal society, the importance of land as a basis for status and power meant that women were a critical part of power negotiations. Keeping the estate intact in order to maintain power and status often meant that female inheritance was preferable to the dispersion of the holding to a far-flung male relative. Ideologically, the ethos of knighthood that rejected any worldly transactions as "undignified and vulgar to the feudal ethic"[36] contributed to the entry of high-status women to the exercise of public power.

More generally, the assumption that the patriarchal principle provided the active ingredient for sex relations at all status levels in traditional society must be rejected. Traditional society was marked by hierarchies of status and relations of superiority-subordination.

As such, it was not necessarily the sex of the position-holder that was of prime importance, but rather the maintenance of correct relations of command and deference in accord with status and tradition. This practice did not ignore the ideal of the natural power of the patriarch, but the very structures developed in accordance with that ideal often meant that practice contradicted theory.

Although the structures of patrimonialism seem to conform to patriarchy in respect to women, this does not mean that women had no resources to power, or that they were passive and compliant. Women could enter into the domain of public power through their sexual attractiveness. The power of women was therefore the precarious power of the harem or the boudoir. This patrimonial master might bow to the requests of a favourite in the heat of passion, but the extension of such "grace and favour" remained in the hands of the master. As a result, the occasional exercise of power by women under this form of domination was not necessarily of any benefit to other women, or a means of setting precedents for other women to exercise power as a legitimate practice.

The exercise of *public* power by women under patrimonial domination might have been unusual and short-lived, but this does not mean that their power within the household and family group was similarly limited. Women may not have had culturally legitimate rights to exercise domination, but they could have exercised power covertly, "behind the scenes." For example, Cronin demonstrates that within the patrimonial tradition of Sicilian society, the cultural expectation of male authority and control and the relegation of women exclusively to the domestic sphere was, in practice, undermined by women's own adaptations to their supposedly powerless position.

> The culture is uniform across the island and there are few who seriously disagree with the value system, but most find it difficult and sometimes impossible to put those values into practice. So another system has grown up that allows the society to adjust to these conflicts and permits the orderly continuance of life."[37]

Although both men and women made adjustments in the attempt to fit the ideals into the practices of day-to-day life, it was women who benefited most from the adjustments.

> In a seeming paradox, cultural powerlessness and low status have become the bases for a freedom not available to men that permits

women to move, operate, and manipulate the daily exigencies of life so that they become not only skilled and crafty but absolutely indispensable to the normal maintenance of affairs.[38]

In general, patrimonial domination relegates women to the household where their power is hidden or disguised. In this sense the public domination exercised by males closely approximates the ideal type elaborated by Weber. Patriarchal domination is, however, confined to the household, so that any extension beyond the household group necessarily weakens the power of the patriarch. In addition, the formalization of household administration creates the means for encroachment upon the power of the patriarch. As Weber pointed out, the essence of patriarchal domination is the belief that the "traditional right of the master" will be exercised in the interests of the members, and in order to maintain this, "it is crucial that . . . there is a complete absence of a personal (patrimonial) staff." The master therefore depends upon the willingness of the subordinates to obey his orders because he has "no machinery to enforce them."[39] Modifications to the patriarch's power develop when patriarchy extends beyond the household and requires an administrative staff. In feudal society, administrative needs produced a status hierarchy that could, and often did, override sex as an organizing principle of power relationships.

In feudal society, pure patriarchy becomes an ideological guide rather than a structural reality in the relations between the sexes. As Weber indicated, "the essence of feudalism is status consciousness, and it increasingly perfects this very characteristic."[40] The combination of status consciousness and the need to maintain the means for the preservation of that status often led to protectionist measures, with the result that,

> When the opportunities for the support of descendants begin to decrease, the monopolization of fiefs and offices . . . sets in with full force. The increasing influence of status conventionalism comes on top of it, and the claim is advanced that the aspirant for a fief or a prebend must not only live like a knight, but also be of knightly descent. That means, he has to be the offspring of a minimum number of knightly ancestors—at first knightly parents, then knightly grandparents: the "four ancestors."[41]

The preservation of status divisions and the need to protect the rights of the lineage meant that some women could exercise powers of the fief.

Our examination of the Weberian ideal type patriarchy and the modifications of this form of domination in traditional societies indicates the importance of understanding the basic assumptions from which the theory proceeds. The assumption of the naturalness of men's control of women rendered the analysis of domination a partial analysis. The various ways in which women had access to the legitimate power, in contradiction to the patriarchal principle, were overlooked. In addition, the assumption that women's place was "naturally" the home and hearth, combined with the assumption of their "natural" subordination to men, meant that power could only be defined in terms of the public power of men. The possibility that such a definition of power is limited as an explanation of social reality is demonstrated in the case of traditional societies in which elaborate distinctions between public and private functions are generally absent and in which complementary relations among women and men *within* status groups, and hierarchical relations *between* status groups independent of sex, are more usual.

Our discussion of ideal type patriarchy also points to another problem with the concept that has generated considerable debate among feminist theorists, as chapter 4 illustrated: the assumption that patriarchy comprises a separate, independent system of sex relations that remains unchanged throughout history. The relations between the sexes may generally be marked by the right of men to some authority over women, but this does not mean that there is only one specific form by which this authority is exercised. If the authority is labelled patriarchy, then it must be recognized that this form varies cross-culturally and historically.

The ideal type construct simply provides one yardstick for the evaluation of the realities of power relations between the sexes. In this light, it is possible that the control men exert over women is far more organized and effective under capitalist relations than under more traditional productive relations that supposedly emerged out of pure patriarchy. Iris Young has argued that male domination under capitalism is not the result of the persistence of a separate set of traditional patriarchal relations that exist independently of economic relations. She suggests that capitalism was "*founded on* gender hierarchy which defined men as primary and women as secondary."[42] Capitalist relations are therefore organized on the basis of sex inequality that governs both public and private spheres.

Capitalism does not merely use or adapt to gender hierarchy as most dual systems theorists suggest . . . the specific forms of the oppression of women which exist under capitalism are essential to its nature. This does not mean, of course, that gender hierarchy did not exist prior to capitalism, nor does it mean that the development of capitalism's gender division of labor did not depend on the prior existence of sexist ideology and a feudal gender division of labor. Many other aspects of capitalism developed out of feudal society, but at a certain point these developments took a specifically new form.[43]

Whatever the specific forms taken by patriarchy, the basic question remains, why is it that women are dominated by men? Weber's ideal type patriarchy simply asserts the domination of the master, and his other comments on the origins of social organization make it clear that men's control over women is a "natural" phenomenon, essential to the generation of organized society. Engels attempted to answer the question but his explanation fell short because of the framework within which it was asked. Durkheim also provided an answer that was compromised by the framework of social evolution he advanced. Freud's answer to the question takes the issue one step back from the assumptions made by the other theorists on the naturalness of sex differences. Freud looked at the issue from the perspective of the *construction* of sexual differentiation as the basis for the subordination of women to men.

In Freud's view, sexual identity is constructed by society on or around the principle of patriarchy, which defined social order and civilization. Human sexuality is initially undifferentiated in terms of the objects to which it is drawn, and heterosexual femininity/masculinity is a consequence of the Oedipus complex. The complex is the process of socialization of females and males into their appropriate roles in patriarchal society. Both sexes therefore learn through the Oedipus complex that the phallus means power. As a result, men define women as inferior, and women learn to accept this view of themselves.

If the acquisition of gender identity is a social process, the question arises as to why it should be one that produces unequal, basically antagonistic relations rather than complementary relations between females and males. Freud's answer is that the construction of gendered sexual identity is the result of the dominant/subordinate relations present at the dawn of civilization. The "beginnings of religion, ethics, society, and art" are the result of the overthrow and murder of the primal patriarch by the "sons."[44] The violent act was the result of the father's exclusive sexual access to all the women and the sons' desire to possess (control) women, also.

This explanation takes for granted that at the dawn of civilization a form of family was already in place. The family was the result of the fact that man realized he could "improve his lot on earth by working" and that it could be further improved by others working with or for him: "in his ape-like prehistory, man had adopted the habit of forming families, and the members of his family were probably his first helpers."[45] The need to work was combined with another need, the "need for genital satisfaction."

> One may suppose that the founding of families was connected with the fact that a moment came when the need for genital satisfaction no longer made its appearance like a guest who drops in suddenly, and, after his departure, is heard of no more for a long time, but instead took up its quarters as a permanent lodger. When this happened, the male acquired a motive for keeping the female or speaking more generally, his sexual objects near him . . .[46]

The female acquiesced in the arrangement not, it seems, because of any reciprocal genital need but because she "did not want to be separated from her helpless young," and as a result, she "was obliged, in their interests, to remain with the stronger male."[47] At this stage of prehistory, women are already subject to male control. Civilization begins with the transference of women from the control of *one* patriarch to the control of *many* patriarchs. The latter situation occurs with the murder of the primal father by the sons.

The Oedipus complex is the result of the actions of the sons, who, having satisfied their hatred of the father, are remorseful because they had also loved the father. Out of the twin aspects of aggression and love, the Oedipus complex emerges. Since the complex allows for cooperation among the brothers, and is therefore the basis for civilization, then both guilt and love are the foundation of society.

> Whether one has killed one's father or has abstained from doing so is not really the decisive thing. One is bound to feel guilty in either case, for the sense of guilt is an expression of the conflict due to ambivalence, of the eternal struggle between Eros and the instinct of destruction or death. This conflict is set going as soon as men are faced with the task of living together.[48]

The Oedipus complex is the reproduction of the original patriarchal foundation of society, and as a result it is men who "make" culture and civilization. Women's contributions to civilization are either minimal or oppositional.

At one point Freud suggested that the only material contribution to the development of civilization by women appeared to be the invention of plaiting and weaving. This singular contribution was the result of women's recognition of their inferiority, compared with men, and their shame at their lack of a penis. The unconscious motivation for the invention was "concealment of genital deficiency."

> Nature herself would seem to have given the model which this achievement imitates by causing the growth or maturity of the pubic hair that conceals the genitals. The step that remained to be taken lay in making the threads adhere to one another, while on the body they stick into the skin and are only matted together.[49]

In general, however, women have a "retarding and restraining influence" on civilization. Because women are concerned with family and sexual life, "the work of civilization has become increasingly the business of men," and this work

> confronts them with ever more difficult tasks and compels them to carry out instinctual sublimations of which women are little capable. Since a man does not have unlimited quantities of psychical energy at his disposal, he has to accomplish his tasks by making an expedient distribution of his libido. What he employs for cultural aims he to a great extent withdraws from women and sexual life.[50]

The cooperation of men in the work of civilization has the effect of also estranging them from their "duties as husband and father." The woman, therefore, "finds herself forced into the background by the claims of civilization and she adopts a hostile attitude towards it."[51]

Whatever the account offered regarding the origins of society or civilization and the nature of sex relations, all of the theorists assumed that sexual differences were basic socially significant differences, and, especially in Freud's case, that genital sex differences were the "natural" foundation for the organization of women and men in society. In addition, the differences led Freud to conclude that men are naturally the major actors in social life. For Engels, it was men who controlled the property that yielded surplus (because of the "natural" division of labour), and it was men who instigated the change in the rules of the game with respect to the inheritance of surplus wealth. Durkheim acknowledged the possible similarities between the sexes at the dawn of civilization, but it was clear that the possibility of society depended upon increasing differentiation, including that, importantly, between the sexes. For Weber, civilization was simply inconceivable without the patriarchal principle that locates women and their children in the context of the social relations of males. And for Freud, it was a band of brothers whose actions inaugurate civilization because of the sexual control of all the women by the primal patriarch.

Direct comments by Marx on the question of sex relations were few, but he did maintain that patriarchy was a precapitalist form that capitalism itself was in the process of destroying.

> The bourgeois clap-trap about the family and education, about the hallowed co-relation of parent and child becomes all the more disgusting, the more, by the action of Modern Industry, all family ties among the proletarians are torn asunder, and their children transformed into simple articles of commerce and instruments of labour.[52]

Because the family, at least the bourgeois version, is based on capital and private gain, this means that there is a "practical absence of family among proletarians."[53] In fact, for the working class as a whole, under capitalism, "differences of age and sex have no longer any distinctive social validity," since all members of that class "are instruments of labour, more or less expensive to use, according to their age and sex."[54]

Marx's key point was that the transformation of sex relations depended upon the destruction of capitalist family relations and the incorporation of women into production. For this reason Engels's account of the "origins" of the family is unsatisfactory. Engels was less concerned with the origins of the family than he was with the origins of private property. With the abolition of private property, the family is to be transformed and the sex inequality that is perpetuated by capitalist family relations will also be transformed. But, as we have noted, the family at the outset was characterized by sex inequality, and neither the theory nor the practice of socialist regimes, for example, has demonstrated the abolition of sex inequality as a result of the transformation of productive relations.

In the theoretical accounts we have examined, women remain the "other," the object of discourse. For this reason, they are partial, flawed accounts of social reality. When an attempt is made to make women the subject of the discourse in the terms set out by the theorists, it becomes clear that the objectivity claimed, in the name of science or valid perspective, by the theorists is highly questionable. In general, the reproductive hazard afflicting women is the rock upon which traditional conceptions of women's "natural" place rest, and this presumption has proved difficult to displace.

Not only have past accounts been problematic regarding the conceptualization of women and sex relations, but current accounts are similarly flawed. A prime example of current research that duplicates, in the name of science, many of the problems we have identified in the preceding discussions is found in the work of the sociobiologists.

SOCIOBIOLOGY

Sociobiology represents a distinct challenge to feminist sociological theory as well as to sociology in general. Sociobiology gives primacy to biology in the analysis of human behaviour and in so doing fundamentally challenges the subject matter of sociology as, for example, Durkheim defined it. As Sahlins points out,

> Sociobiology challenges the integrity of culture as a thing-in-itself, as a distinctive and symbolic human creation. In place of a social constitution of meanings, it offers a biological determination of human interaction with a source primarily in the general evolutionary propensity of individual genotypes to maximize their reproductive success.[55]

In terms of sex relations, sociobiology produces a variation of the "anatomy is destiny" theme, and in this regard sociobiology represents not only a theoretical, but also a political, challenge to feminist theory.

As our preceding discussions have indicated, theories of biological inevitability have been used in the past to justify the social inequality of the sexes (as well as other inequalities such as race and ethnic divisions). The sociobiologists' ideas that social organization is the product of natural selection and that individual behaviour is motivated by genetic self-interest reduce, if not entirely eliminate, human agency in the construction of the social and cultural world. The appeal to biology can thus be used to justify the status quo on the grounds that to oppose or to attempt to alter the situation is to run counter to the power of nature. To the extent that nature decrees the inevitability of male supremacy and female subordination, any attempt to change such relationships would be misguided and ultimately futile. Predictably, feminists have reacted strongly to this sort of political agenda that sociobiology endorses. At the same time, feminist theory, and sociology in general, have not totally dismissed the significance of biology in the analysis of social behaviour. But biology has generally been regarded only as a foundation upon which social, cultural and environmental effects build and modify.

One of the seeming advantages of biological models, however, in contrast to sociological models, is that they appear "to be more testable because their major constructs are derived from tangible physical realities."[56] In contrast, sociological constructs appear to be less precise, cognitive abstractions. This distinction is, in fact, a false distinction because the natural world does not produce descriptive constructs—they are also produced as cognitive abstractions by the scientist. In fact, in contrast to the assumption that biological science, and the natural sciences in general, are more productive of certain knowledge in comparison to sociology, Weber suggested that the search for recurrent sequences that produce hypothetical "laws" could only be one stage in the attainment of knowledge of social and cultural events. The "decisive feature of the method of the cultural sciences" was the analysis of the "phenomena of life in terms of their cultural significance."

> The *significance* of a configuration of cultural phenomena and the basis of this significance cannot however be derived and rendered intelligible by a system of analytical laws . . . however perfect it may be, since the significance of cultural events presupposes a *value-orientation* towards these events.[57]

The analysis of social reality in terms of meanings is very different from an analysis in "terms of laws and general concepts," and Weber's conclusion was that an "objective analysis of cultural events, which proceeds according to the thesis that the ideal of science is the reduction of empirical reality of "laws" is meaningless."[58] It is on this count that a major criticism of sociobiology can be advanced; in that it is the "law-like" behaviour of cells, or more specifically, of genes, that is "understood" to reinforce sex differences and sex inequality. This understanding then provides a political agenda in regard to social policy and social reforms. A brief outline of the sociobiological position on sex relations illustrates the manner in which "objective" research is interpreted or "understood."

Sociobiology regards the genetic structure as the prime motivator of social behaviour. It is suggested that natural selection favours those individuals (human and animal) who maximize their genetic fitness.[59] There are three aspects to genetic fitness: increased personal survival, increased personal reproduction and the improved reproduction and survival of close genetic relatives. In evolutionary terms, that behaviour that maximizes the three aspects is behaviour that survives. A key factor in maximizing genetic fitness is the parental "investment" in the offspring. In this regard, females have a greater investment in offspring than do males, and this difference accounts for the behavioural differences between the sexes as well as for the mutually exploitive relations between women and men.

As Dawkins explains in *The Selfish Gene*,[60] the difference between the sexes in the domestic division of labour can be accounted for by the difference in the size of the male and female sex cells; that is, sperm and eggs may contribute equal numbers of genes, but

> eggs contribute far more in the way of food reserves; indeed sperms make no contribution at all, and are simply concerned with transporting their genes as fast as possible to an egg. At the moment of conception, therefore, the father has invested less than his fair share (i.e., 50 percent) of resources in the offspring.[61]

Because females invest more from the outset, they have a greater interest in protecting their investment and will therefore have a greater interest in post-natal childcare. At the same time, since both parents are influenced by their selfish genes, they will each have an interest in persuading the other to invest more time in the care of the offspring. This is the genesis of the timeless conflict between the sexes.

> If one parent can get away with investing less than his or her fair share of costly resources in each child . . . he will be better off, since he will have more to spend on other children by other sexual

partners, and so propagate more of his genes. Each partner can therefore be thought of as trying to exploit the other, trying to force the other to invest more.[62]

The conflict between the sexes over the maximization of their genetic fitness is also seen to generate different, biologically based evolutionary strategies on the part of the sexes. The female strategy of "coyness" is developed so that the female can assess, before mating, the chances that the male will provide for any resulting offspring. The male strategy of philandering is a response to the lesser investment they have in the offspring. Males who can impregnate as many females as possible increase the possibility of their reproductive success. In addition, they can be sure that any offspring will be cared for by the female because of her greater investment in them. The strategies used by each sex are evolutionary products and are biologically determined; that is, they are genetic. Consequently, Barash could conclude that it is genetically preordained that "Women have almost universally found themselves relegated to the nursery while men derive their greatest satisfaction from their jobs."[63]

The individualistic urge to maximize personal reproductive fitness is combined with the urge to increase the fitness of the common gene pool, and it is in this regard that male aggression, as an innate behaviour, is important. Aggression has several functions according to sociobiologists, all of which are prompted by the attempt to maximize fitness. Among these functions is resolving the competition among males for females.

> Many male vertebrates fight only at mating time, and solely for the possession of females. This points to the existence of a selective advantage associated with fighting between rival males. The advantage to the winners is that they produce more offspring and thus, further the inclusive fitness of their gene pool. Moreover, fighting is reinforced by female reluctance to mate easily or freely with any male. Since females make a much greater investment in the procreation of offspring (i.e., in time and energy), it is in their best interests to await proof of the strongest, healthiest, and most dextrous males.[64]

Male aggression is not only functional in resolving competition among males, but it is also important in the sexual act. Storr suggests that "male sexuality, because of the primitive necessity of pursuit and penetration, does contain an important element of aggressiveness; an element which is both recognized and responded to by the female who yields and submits."[65] Male aggression, which is biologically programmed by the higher levels of testosterone in human males, is functional in advancing the evolutionary survival of the fittest genes. In social terms this means that "the male hormonal system gives men an insuperable 'head start' toward attaining those roles which any society associates with leadership or high status as long as the roles are not ones males are biologically incapable of filling."[66]

There are several critiques of the sociobiology approach that examine in fine detail the theoretical concepts and empirical support of the approach.[67] The present discussion will not treat the issues in depth; rather, the remarks below are concerned with the manner in which sociobiology represents a continuation of the sociological partiality evident in the work of the theorists discussed previously. Durkheim and Freud explicitly, and Weber, Marx and Engels implicitly used biology to explain women's social roles and, in doing so, to justify sex differences and sex inequality. Sociobiology also appeals to natural science as an objective and, by extension unarguable, basis for its conclusions. However, despite all the discussion of selfish genes programming humans and non-humans alike in terms of survival of the fittest, the actual experimental data are scarce and often contradictory.

For example, Leiven points out that the range of behaviours encompassed in the concept of aggression for animals and humans is considerable. This range is linked by sociobiologists to the singular presence of the male hormone testosterone. But there seems to be no evidence of "a correlation between the level of testosterone circulating in different individuals and their levels of 'aggression' (however measured)."[68] In fact, the only study Leiven could find was one that attempted to relate activity levels in neonates with "rough and tumble play" in pre-schoolers, resulting in an "inverse correlation for boys." That is, "the boys who appeared most 'active' at birth (as measured by latency to respond to a bottle being removed from their mouth) were the most 'passive' in the pre-school situation (in the sense of standing quietly watching the other children rather than getting involved in games)."[69]

The essence of sociobiological proof has been based on the discovery of cultural universals. That is, if a behaviour can be found to be common to all known human cultures, it is assumed that it is a result of genetic predisposition. Quite apart from the problematic issue of the identification of identical cross-cultural behaviour, such findings still would not indicate to what degree such behaviours are genetically determined. As Lowe points out, all that could be said in such cases is that the behaviours appear to be "insensitive to environmental variations encompassed by the observed societies," but "these societies certainly do not exhaust the range of human cultural possibilities."[70] In fact, there is a more prosaic difficulty with the appeal to universals and that is that "no behavioural traits have been found that are common to all known cultures."[71] The claim for universals seems to rest entirely on "universal sex differences in behaviour among human beings," and this becomes a problematic basis for the construction of genetically determined sex differences when it is clear that the actual behaviour and roles of the sexes differ greatly among societies. Nevertheless, Barash claims that "ironically, mother nature appears to be a sexist."[72]

The universals that sociobiology seeks are largely confined to sex differences and, as Lowe points out, since every society makes some distinction (although not the same distinctions) between the sexes, this seems the logical place from which to start an analysis of sex relations. However, the result is the elaboration of biologically based social differences simply in terms of sex differences and not, in fact, of species universals. For example, Lowe cites Wilson to the effect that some universal traits include "aggressive dominance systems with males generally dominant over females . . . intensive and prolonged maternal care, with a pronounced degree of socialization in the young; and matrilineal social organization." These are traits based on sex differences not species universals, "since it is argued that males are naturally more aggressive than females."[73] However, the list of traits that follows from these differences are claimed as universals.

> A hierarchal structure to society is explicit in "aggressive dominance systems." A sexual division of labor is related to the aggressive dominance systems and to maternal care. Economics and trade are said to have developed out of this division of labor, through barter between females and males of hunted meat and gathered food. Out of the development of trade came deception and hypocrisy. Territoriality, lust for war, and xenophobia, all alleged universals, are also the result of aggression and dominance systems.[74]

Finally, the tautological reasoning that characterizes the sociobiological argument is compounded by the problem—acknowledged by its advocates and supporters—of the difficulty in separating genetic and environmental effects in human behaviour. The more reasonable assumption that behaviour is a result of a combination of genetic and environmental effects also runs into difficulties because the manner and the effects of such interaction are unknown, and, even if the contribution of the genetic and the environmental could be estimated with some accuracy, this would still "have no predictive value," because "there is no reason to assume that the relative contributions of genetic factors and environment would remain the same."[75] On the contrary, past experience has indicated that knowledge of an interactive effect is itself sufficient to change the process in the future.

Sociobiology marshalls considerable academic credentials to support its arguments. For Lowe and others, it is the weight they carry as political theories rather than as scientific theories of human behaviour that is important and requires the attention of feminist theorists. The questionable scientific status of sociobiology is illustrated by Jessie Bernard's comments.

> How does it happen that so much is made of the fact that the blood of males has more androgen than that of females, but nothing is made of the fact that it also has more uric acid? And how does it happen that the net effect of the vast corpus of research leads to the conclusion that men are superior to women on all the variables that are highly valued in our society; namely, muscular or kinetic strength, competitiveness, power, need for achievement, and autonomy? . . . These are the variables they judge one another by. These are the variables that are rewarded in our society.[76]

Lambert maintains that it is not the "factual inevitability of the biological" that is at issue, but something "more valuational, even moralistic."[77] Whether or not biological differences are thought to be changeable, the argument from biology maintains that they are desirable in that it places a "positive value on the 'natural' in either aesthetic (vive la difference) or religious (God/Nature knows best) terms."[78] Sociobiology takes a less mystical, presumably more scientific, approach to the issue by seeing biological differences as complementary to social institutions, which, in turn, "are also assumed to have roots in human biology." This functionalist, circular argument "assumes the persistence of the status quo and thus the desirability of socialization reinforcing biological predisposition." Tied to this is the further assumption that biological differences can provide "more reasonable bases for unequal social rewards."[79] As Lambert points out, the moral justification for this conclusion is questionable; "one does not deserve one's genes or hormones any more than one deserves other accidents of birth, such as a social class."[80]

The practical and political consequences of the sociobiological approach cannot be overlooked. For feminist theory and practice, however, the first issue in a critique of this reconstruction of the nature/nurture debate is why and how sex differences are used, and have been used in the past, not what causes them. Simply by asking what the causes are, one concedes the first premise of the sociological argument. As Lambert points out, "arguments about sexual equality often get stuck on whether sex differences are socially or biologically caused. This battleground, which feminists generally have not chosen, is strategically unwise. In many cases the question is unanswerable and arguing about it delays social reform."[81] An uncritical social determinism is also unwise and does not protect against the possibility or, given the work we have examined in the previous chapters, the probability that biology will be introduced (even if it is through a back door) to account for women and their reproductive capacity.

Sociobiology is useful to feminist theory because it does make the partiality of some of the sociological accounts transparent. It also sets the terms upon which the issues surrounding sex equality must be confronted. It is clear that

> The problem will not be solved by countering with arguments cast in the same mould—for instance by denying sex differences where they have been shown to exist, or searching for one society in which females hunt as well as males in order to 'disprove' the claims about male 'aggression'.[82]

The basic problem is with the absolute dichotomy between the biological and the social, and the related assumption that "if it's natural, we can't change it." As Leiven points out, humans "manipulate and destroy things we call "biological" in hundreds of different ways each day,"[83] at the same time finding some social behaviours such as crime or poverty difficult to change.

The challenge sociobiology represents to feminist theory and practice may be a variation of an old theme, but it is one of critical importance, especially in the light of some feminist claims regarding women's reproductive capacity. A celebration of women's biological specificity is a potentially reactionary step, especially when sociobiological arguments are extended into the political realm. Nowhere is this more apparent than in the arguments advanced by Alice Rossi in her biosocial approach to reproduction and childcare.[84] Rossi suggests that the female's greater maternal interest and care for the infant are biologically based, and that arguments such as those advanced by Chodorow to include men in parenting are inadequate solutions to restructuring the relations between the sexes. Although she believes men should be encouraged to be more intimate with children from an early age, this cannot replace or alter the natural, biologically programmed need for maternal care in the early years. The restructuring of sex relations should therefore be in terms of greater social support for the biologically important task women have of childbearing *and* childrearing. Once more, women return to that special domestic sphere, but this time "scientifically" proven to be the sphere best suited to their innate, biologically programmed capacities.

The ease with which the sexual dichotomies and sexual hierarchies of subordination and superiority are maintained and revived in social and political theory provides the justification for the examination of "origins," such as we have conducted in this work, as well as setting the terms for a continued critique of the nature/nurture argument. On the nurture side, Shields suggests that there are a variety of moral values that are involved that range from "biology is good; any deviation from it is bad," and the "social structure will inevitably reflect biological predispositions, no matter what efforts are made to circumvent natural inclinations."[85] For feminists, Shields points out, the future looks gloomy because any struggle for change seems a "doomed enterprise." This leads her to ask, "if one acknowledges the biological bases of behaviour, must one also assume their inevitability and immutability?" And, "is a feminist/humanist scientific model nonbiological by definition?"[86]

These are the questions that provide the parameters for some of the feminist attempts at reformulations of sociological theory. One of the ways in which the reformulations have been attempted is to question the manner in which sociological theory has claimed scientific status. This questioning has often been posed in terms of the general status of normal scientific claims, along with the possibility of objectivity and neutrality. The intentions of the feminist critique are expressed in terms of sociology and science being critically informed by feminism. To this endeavour we turn in the concluding chapter.

CHAPTER 7

Feminism and Sociological Theory

Sociological theory attempts to make sense of the social world. The process of theorizing starts with an idea of the nature of society, and out of this idea a conceptual framework is developed that sets out the terms for what is to count as relevant information for a description and explanation of social reality. Sociological theories can then be said to explain social life through a set of logically connected ideas that can be validated, in some manner, by evidence from social reality. Presumably, if the evidence from the real world conflicts with the theory, then the theory is discarded. On this count, the process of theorizing seems to be a fairly coherent activity and one that contains its own corrective mechanism to guard against the acceptance of extreme flights of theoretical fancy. However, the process for sociology, and for scientific theory in general, is less simple than this description suggests.

First, sociologists do not necessarily agree upon what is to count as the subject matter of investigation. That is, how they define society can vary. For example, Durkheim defined society as a moral, normative order. For Weber, society was the product of meaningful interactions of the participants. Marx and Engels defined society according to the nature of productive relations, and Freud understood it as a product of psychic repression and control.

Second, whatever their definition of the nature of society, theorists disagree on the method of its investigation. For example, both Durkheim and Marx were concerned with providing causal explanations of social processes and structures, whereas Weber and Freud stressed understanding and introspection.[1] Third, although sociologists agree that theory development is a process, so that explanations offered cannot be seen as static, timeless truths, they disagree about how "better" theories can be developed. For example, a better theory for Durkheim might be measured by a theory's greater predictability, in contrast to Weber for whom a greater understanding of the meaning of social action would constitute theoretical progress.

Finally, all theorists seek to abstract common features of social existence that will provide them with a basis for generalizations. Again, however, these common features vary with the theorist. For Durkheim, it was social solidarity that provided the important conceptual key; for Weber it was social action; for Marx and Engels it was the nature and distribution of property; and for Freud, psychological development expressed in the Oedipus conflict.

The distinctions between the theorists outlined above have important consequences for the manner in which sociological theory might proceed. In general, these theorists represent different epistemological positions on the nature of sociological theory. Durkheim is usually taken to represent the positivist approach, Weber the idealist approach and Marx, Engels and Freud the realist approach. The three positions emerge out of an understanding of what constitutes the nature of social reality; that is, they represent an "intellectual milieu" that describes the nature of sociology as a science and the subject matter and the methods appropriate to discovery. In Laudan's terms, the three positions represent "research traditions."[2] They refer to "a set of general assumptions about the entities and processes in a domain of study, and about the appropriate methods to be used in investigating the problems and constructing the theories in that domain."[3]

The positivist tradition represented by Durkheim sees society as having structures and processes akin to those in the natural world and therefore as being amenable to discovery by methods similar to those employed in the natural sciences. As he pointed out, sociology simply involves "the principle of causality" applied to social reality. It is on this basis that sociology emancipates itself from philosophy. "Since the law of causality has been verified in the other realms of nature, and since it has progressively extended its authority from the physico-chemical world to the biological, and from the latter to the psychological, we are justified in claiming that it is equally true of the social world."[4] The sociologist must therefore reject metaphysical speculations and "put himself in the same state of mind as the physicist, chemist, or physiologist when he probes into a still unexplored region of the scientific domain."[5]

Like the natural scientist, the sociologist is concerned with the explanatory and predictive knowledge of the social world. Therefore, the sociologist constructs theories that comprise general statements about the regular relationships existing in society. The regular relationships are discovered through observation and experiment, so that "to explain something is to show that it is an instance of these regularities; and we can make predictions only on the same basis."[6] In society as in nature, regularities become known only through sensory experience and "represented in the universal laws of scientific theory." Therefore, in Durkheim's view, "Any attempt to go beyond this representation plunges science into the unverifiable claims of metaphysics and religion, which are at best unscientific, and at worst meaningless."[7]

In contrast to the positivist research tradition, idealism understands the social world as the product of consciousness that can be explained through the analysis of ideas, beliefs and motives. The subject matter is the meaningful nature of social-historical reality, and the discovery of what is meaningful cannot be attained "by means of a "presuppositionless" investigation of empirical data" advanced by positivists. In fact, the meaningfulness of sociological data, according to Weber, "does not coincide with laws as such, and the more general the law the less the coincidence."[8] The major task for sociology is to understand the meaning of social actions. Although this means that the procedures of the natural sciences are inapplicable to sociology, nevertheless, sociology can establish causal links. The key is that the connections between behaviours and events must have "understandable subjective meaning."

The subject matter of sociology distinguishes it from the natural sciences and therefore demands a different methodology. But Weber maintains that this does not mean that sociology is any less objective than the natural sciences.

The type of social science in which we are interested is an *empirical science* of concrete *reality* . . . Our aim is the understanding of the characteristic uniqueness of the reality in which we move. We wish to understand on the one hand the relationships and the cultural significance of individual events in their contemporary manifestations and on the other the causes of their being historically so and not *otherwise*.[9]

An indispensable tool in the research process is the ideal type, because the "pure" conduct exemplified by the type can be used to understand the actions of individuals in the real social world. The function of the ideal type is to enable "the comparison with empirical reality in order to establish its divergences or similarities, to describe them with the *most unambiguously intelligible concepts*, and to understand and explain them causally."[10] The ideal type is the means by which the multitude of individual actions and subjective understandings can be given a meaningful, coherent basis for sociological investigation.

The realist research tradition also uses ideal type constructs, but in contrast to Weber's ideal types, assigns them a different epistemological status. As Keat and Urry demonstrate, the approach differs in two ways. First, Weber's ideal types are those "most useful or appropriate for one's particular scientific purposes at the moment."[11] In contrast, Marx constructed his types in terms of the "essential features" of, for example, capitalism, on the basis that "there is a central structural mechanism within capitalism."[12] Secondly, the development of the type is not the result of the "process of abstraction from, and idealization of, the concrete social relations found within actual societies," because the very structure of relations obscures the "underlying and central mechanisms." Therefore, "any process of concept formation which is based on the way that society presents itself will be inadequate, misleading and ideological."[13] This latter point is central to the realist understanding of social reality.

The realist tradition contends that there are real, but not immediately apprehendable, structures in the social world, and the task of sociology is to uncover these structures. Like the positivist, the realist sees sociology as a science that is "an empirically-based, rational and objective enterprise" that can provide explanatory, predictive knowledge. However, the realist makes a distinction between explanation and prediction, "and it's explanation which must be pursued as the primary objective of science."[14]

> To explain phenomena is not merely to show they are instances of well-established regularities. Instead, we must discover the necessary connections between phenomena, by acquiring knowledge of the underlying structures and mechanisms at work.[15]

The realist, therefore, explains *why* something happens by showing *how* and by *what means* it occurs.[16]

Although the work of Marx and Engels is more representative of sociological realism, Freud's approach is also in line with this research tradition. Consciousness is determined by the invisible unconsciousness; that is, the unconscious represents the underlying structure that has real effects on the apprehendable forms of behaviour and consciousness. Consequently, neuroses are explained as the visible consequence of the repression of instinctual sexual and aggressive desires buried in the unconscious. "Normally, there is nothing of which we are more certain than the feeling of our self, or our own ego. This ego appears to us as something autonomous and unitary, marked off distinctly from everything else."[17] This separation is "deceptive" because the ego is in fact the visible evidence of "an unconscious mental entity which we designate as the id and for which it serves as a kind of facade."[18]

All three research traditions have provided fruitful explanations of society and advanced our understanding of social life, at least for one half of humanity. As we have indicated previously, an examination of the particular theorists within these research traditions carries no presupposition that the theories can be weighed in some epistemological balance and accepted or rejected outright. Rather, the point has been to examine the presuppositions and their implications from the perspective of women as subjects rather than objects of the discourse. It is clear that there are fundamental problems originating with the definition of social reality and the resulting descriptions and explanations. The competing research traditions within which the substantive work of the theorists has been examined unite on the question of sex differences. Women are seen as biologically and, therefore, naturally different and constrained by that difference. It is this basic conception that overrides, in the last analysis, the substantive differences between the various theories in the treatment of sex relations.

Sociologists have disagreed about what society is and what valid sociological knowledge is and how it might be obtained. But in general there is an unquestioned foundation upon which the classical, as well as more recent, theories build—the organizing principle of sex difference. Thus a partial, limited perspective on the nature of social life results, which, in turn, affects the conceptual frameworks and explanations offered by sociologists within the three research traditions.

The feminist critique of sociology has tended to focus on the positivist and Marxist research traditions. Only recently has the idealist tradition been the subject of significant attention.[19] The positivist tradition has received more critical rejection than the Marxist. In general, feminists have been reluctant to abandon the emancipatory promise of Marxism that has generated the sympathy and maintained the relevance of the tradition. Only in the last decade has the idealist tradition received much attention, partly as a response, or an alternative, to positivism and Marxism. The critique of positivism has, however, provided continued debate, which has been conducted at the more general level of a critique of normal science, of which positivism is taken to be the exemplar. To this critique we now turn, followed by a consideration of suggestions for the direction of feminist theory.

DEBUNKING SCIENCE

Science, it would seem, is not sexless; she is a man, a father, and infected too.[20]

Virginia Woolf's comment was made in regard to the nineteenth-century "proofs" provided by craniologists that the female brain was smaller than the male's, and therefore women "were stupider than men." As we saw earlier, Durkheim used some of this "scientific" research to demonstrate the biological as well as the social effects of the progressive division of labour in society.

For the theorists we have discussed, science was an important progressive force in ordering society. Both Marx and Weber believed that the increasing rationalization of life was an inevitable process for western civilization, and that scientific knowledge was an indispensable part of that process. Marx believed in positive results from the march of scientific and technological change, in that they would contribute to both the overthrow of capitalism and the establishment of a more humane future. Weber was more pessimistic about the humanist consequences but did believe that science could "enhance the technical mastery of life." Freud also believed that the progress of civilization was best accomplished through rationality and the renunciation of instinctual impulses such as those embodied in religious beliefs. "Our best hope for the future is that intellect and scientific spirit, reason—may in the process of time establish a dictatorship in the mental life of man."[21]

Bendix suggests that Freud, Weber and Durkheim, along with others, were "discernible as a group by their common concern with the subjective presuppositions of thought."[22] At the same time, "men like Freud, Durkheim, and Weber, while making room for this new awareness," still attempted to retain an enlightened, rationalist heritage.

> Max Weber's essay, "Science as a Vocation" . . . is a document of this generation. It represents a careful blend of rationalist convictions and romantic sensibility. Like the great rationalists before him, but with none of their optimism, Weber commits himself to the scientist's calling.[23]

The origins of faith in science can be traced to the seventeenth-century rejection of "nature" as having purposes and goals like humans and the celebration of mankind's mastery of nature. Nature then became an object that could be controlled by masterful human beings. The man of science could, in Bacon's terms, "mine" nature's secrets and make nature a "slave" to man's needs and desires.[24] The idea of nature as a living, nurturing, growing force was thus replaced with the idea that nature was mere matter to be shaped, moulded and tamed by man, armed with the techniques of science and technology.

In the transformation, nature was frequently thought of as "female." Bacon remarked, "I am come in very truth leading you nature with all her children to bind her to your service and make her your slave."[25] The association of women with nature and the hierarchichal relations between men and women/nature that Chodorow, Ortner and Dinnerstein examined are to be found in the initial philosophical characterization of scientific knowledge.

It is not simply that nature, "like" women, is to be subject to mastery but also that nature, again like women, is understood as a mysterious, unpredictable and, therefore, dangerous Other. To prevent any harm befalling the intrepid investigator (assumed to be male) confronting such a problematic entity, a clear separation had to be maintained between the scientist and nature.

> Having divided the world into two parts the knower (mind) and the knowable (nature) scientific ideology goes on to prescribe a very specific relation between the two. It prescribes the interactions which can consummate this union, that is which can lead to knowledge. Not only are mind and nature assigned gender, but in characterizing scientific and objective thought as masculine, the very activity by which the knower can acquire knowledge is also genderized. The relation specified between knower and known is one of distance and

separation. It is that between subject and object radically divided, which is to say no worldly relation.[26]

The "chaste and lawful marriage between Mind and Nature" promoted by Bacon is one that "is consummated through reason rather than feeling, and observation rather than immediate sensory experience."[27]

When sociology makes its intellectual debut as a science of society it invariably inherits the same system of beliefs that result in a "genderization" of science—that is, a belief that science is male thought and male activity. In addition, sociology makes its debut at precisely the time and place when the dichotomized understanding of sex roles provides the guiding ideal for social and political practice. As we have remarked already, the search for the origins of patriarchy, as well as the concern with the range of sexual behaviours and family structures, were basically motivated by the need to define the most "natural" relations between the sexes. It was generally assumed that the domesticity of women, in contrast to the worldly activities of men, was not only an ideal to be pursued but also the "natural" state of affairs that would make the best, most productive use of the divergent talents of the sexes. Such a dichotomy was also thought to be scientifically established by Darwinian science.

Sociology inherited a sex-dichotomized scientific approach as well as the nineteenth-century cultural ideal of the dichotomized relationship between the sexes as appropriate to their "natural" talents. The sociological concern with uncovering the laws of society and improving it was therefore coloured by this inheritance. In general, the resulting focus was on men in the public world and, when women entered the sociological picture, on the family and socialization tasks of women. This dichotomy was often accompanied, in the nineteenth century, by the idea of the moral superiority of the female because of her exclusion from the public sphere and her closer connection to nature. This doctrine of "separate spheres," however, reinforced the seventeenth-century masculinization of thought that had excluded "feminine modes of knowing, not from culture in general, but from the scientific and philosophical arenas, whose objectivity and purity needed to be guaranteed."[28] The result was that woman was regarded as the mediating form between nature and culture. Woman was "at times saintly and at times evil, but always she seems necessary as the counterpoint to man's self-definition as a being of pure rationality."[29]

Men's pure rationality, in contrast to women's emotional nature, makes them suitable candidates for the pursuit of science. Therefore, science in the western world is a masculine endeavour and as a result,

> the attributes of science are the attributes of males; the objectivity said to be characteristic of the production of scientific knowledge is specifically identified as a male way of relating to the world. Science is cold, hard, impersonal, "objective"; women, by contrast, are warm, soft, emotional, "subjective."[30]

In addition, since science is seen to be a masculine endeavour, then "women in science are perceived as unfeminine," and any discussion of women scientists will usually be accompanied by assurances of their ability to be "graceful and feminine, good housekeepers and mothers."[31]

The association of men with science does not mean that there have not been, or are no, women scientists. On the contrary, but the practice of science and the uses to which its findings have been put have largely been directed at controlling the natural and the social worlds in the interests of men. Ruth Hubbard points out, for example, that the scientific "proof" of women's essential nature was only partially applied to actual women and their work.

> The ideology of women's nature that is invoked . . . would have us believe that a woman's capacity to become pregnant leaves her at all times physically disabled by comparison with men. The scientific underpinnings for these ideas were elaborated in the nineteenth century by the white, university-educated, mainly upper class men who made up the bulk of the new professions of obstetrics and gynecology, biology, psychology, sociology and anthropology.[32]

The idea of physical frailty of women was, however, confined to women of the upper classes, and Hubbard suggests that male professionals used the theory "to disqualify the girls and women of their own race and class who would be in competition with them for education and professional status and might also deprive them of the kinds of personal attention and services they were accustomed to receive from their mothers, wives, and sisters."[33] Poor women as well as black women were noticeably excluded from concern over their possible frailty. In fact, their ability to "work so hard while bearing children was taken as a sign that these women were more animal-like and less highly evolved than upper-class women."[34]

In the comments made above, it should not be assumed that some deliberate Machiavellian process has been involved in restricting science to the male domain. However, science has reinforced racist attitudes on occasion and has always promoted a dichotomized view of the sexes. It is the latter view, as Brown and Jordanov point out, that results in the "association of each sex with universal biological categories, as if all women and all men were really the same regardless of class or other social differences."[35] Through the identification of men with science and women with nature, "women were conceptualized as the passive recipients of scientific manipulation."[36] The question therefore arises, "What interests were, and are, served by elaborating a set of biologically based, opposed categories which deliberately ignored (or conveniently obscured) social divisions?"[37]

This question, in conjunction with the previous discussion, challenges the basic understanding of science as an objective body of knowledge pursued by unbiased, rational individuals. The theories and methods of science are supposed to be subject to continual re-examination and testing to ensure the validity of the knowledge obtained. Consequently, the researcher who follows the abstract rules could claim authority on the basis that the knowledge produced was objective knowledge. But in simply concentrating on the abstract rules of the game, the "scientific method" ignores the social context in which that method is developed and used. As indicated above, the development of science as objective and unbiased is compromised by its origins and unexamined assumptions. In addition, science is compromised by the day-to-day practice of science. The choice of research topic, the nature of the research tools, the interpretation of the data and the manner in which the results reach either the scientific community and/or the general public are some of the ways in which the genderization of science as theory and practice is maintained. As Addelson points out,

> Although the "rationality of science" is supposed to lie in the fact that scientific understanding is the most open to criticism of *all* understanding, a crucial area for criticism was ruled out of consideration: the social arrangements through which scientific understanding is developed and through which cognitive authority of the specialist is exercised.[38]

One of the social arrangements has already been pointed out: the restrictive recruitment pool from which scientists are drawn. This is important to the extent that one of the procedures that supposedly ensures the objectivity of science is the participation of many different scientists from many different societies "all asking their own questions and evaluating the answers independently," so that "whatever personal bias creeps into their individual answers is cancelled out when the large picture is put together." As Ruth Hubbard points out, "This might conceivably be so if scientists were women and men from all sorts of different cultural and social backgrounds who came to science with very different ideologies and interests."[39] But since, in fact, they have been "predominantly university-trained white males from privileged social backgrounds, the bias has been narrow and the product often reveals more about the investigator than about the subject being researched."[40]

The restricted recruitment pool from which most scientists are drawn is important in relation to the assumption that objectivity can be assured by the distance maintained between the holder and the object of knowledge. Durkheim insisted that "all preconceptions must be eradicated," since this is the "basis of all scientific method,"[41] and even Weber, although acknowledging the evaluative content of sociological data, insisted that freedom from values was both a possibility and a necessity for social science through the sociologist's detachment from his research. The distinction between the knower and the known implies a relationship of domination in the sense that "the knowing mind is active, the object of knowledge, passive."[42] This is a relationship that, as we saw in our previous discussions, can be extended to the sexes in the sense that women are like nature—the passive objects of knowledge. The subject-object distinction is regarded as an essential component of objective, and therefore, "true" knowledge.

> The subject-object distinction, the alienation of self as subject from the other as object, is declared to be the essential condition of scientific knowledge. Identified as objectivity, it is epistemologically normative, alienating the knower, the transcendent subject from the known, the transcended object.[43]

Not only are men, as scientists, transcendent over women and nature but, given the cultural and class bias in recruitment, they are often transcendent over other subordinated groups. For example, men are studied by scientists, especially social scientists, but distance is maintained.

The human behaviour that is examined by scientists is either observed in a distanced class or group from which the scientist distinguishes "himself" (prisoners, students, Puerto Ricans, farmers) or it is intellectually abstracted to such a degree that the scientist can avoid making a full human identification with its practice even where in fact it might be human behaviour attributable to "himself" (e.g., voting behavior, rapid eye movement, alcohol abuse).[44]

The objectivity and the distancing that is supposed to be part of the practice of normal science not only removes the scientist from the objects of "his" research but also provides a distance between the production of knowledge and its use. "Pure science" is taken to mean the pursuit of knowledge for its own sake. It is free from value-laden uses, and the scientist is therefore "freed from any social or moral responsibility" for the use made of his findings.[45] The fact that this form of scientific neutrality is frequently compromised by the use of "expert" testimony in a variety of contexts and by the conditions of scientific production that maintain the technological power of industry and the military is often overlooked when the objective neutrality of science is promoted.

Finally, personal feelings have not always been removed from the supposedly objective scientific procedures. For example, Gray suggests that Herbert Spencer's about-face on the question of women's rights had a personal basis. He changed from advocating equality to advocating "discrimination (especially political discrimination) against women."

> At first he was well-disposed towards women. But becoming progressively disillusioned by his relationships with females, Spencer attributed this failure to the deficiencies of the opposite sex. He held women responsible for injury to himself, and the threat that women posed to him was displaced into a threat that women posed to the state. Just as he himself needed to be protected from women, so society as a whole needed to be protected from their pernicious influence.[46]

So much for the rationality and objective sociological observations of one of the foremost social scientists of the nineteenth century.

Feminist critiques have demonstrated in important ways the manner in which science, both theory and practice, and sociology, as a part of that tradition, have excluded women as subjects as well as practitioners. Scientific explanations, and sociological ones in particular, have therefore been hopelessly inadequate, incomplete explanations of both nature and human nature. This does not mean, however, that science or sociology should be abandoned as lost causes. The "corrective," according to Addelson, is to "ferret out all the irrationalities we can find in scientific activity and to expand our understanding of what science and scientific rationality are."[47] Some of the results of the feminist corrective have been apparent in the critical comments brought to bear on the theorists and their work examined in previous chapters. In a positive sense, the "ferreting out" continues, along with attempts to re-conceptualize the scientific enterprise and to understand what the feminist contribution to knowledge represents. It is in this context that the idealist research tradition has been important, although feminist reconstructions have often been highly eclectic in their selections from the three research traditions.

In conclusion to this work we will look at some of the suggestions for the reconstruction of science and sociology from a feminist perspective.

FEMINIST RECONSTRUCTIONS

The creation of knowledge is a central concern to feminism because knowledge creation means power. The issue is not simply the absence of women in knowledge creation or, when they are present, that they participate as marginal members of knowledge creation structure. More to the point, it is that their experiences of the world, and those of other subordinate, disadvantaged groups, have no part in the production of authoritative knowledge of the world. As Smith remarks, "Women do not appear to men as men do to one another, as persons who might share in the common construction of social reality."[48] In sum, women do not "name the world."[49]

One of the tasks of feminist sociology, and feminist scholarship in general, is to assert the validity of women's experience of the world and to find ways of incorporating that experience into the "naming" or the definition of the nature of reality. The act of naming and defining is, as O'Brien points out, a way of organizing reality, and as long as "language and theory . . . are shot through with self-serving masculist assumptions," then feminist redefinition, or renaming, must always constitute "critical analysis."[50] The exercise is both theoretical and practical, because the "images, vocabularies, concepts, knowledge of and methods of knowing the world are integral to the practice of power"[51] and it is a ruling class of men who "produce for women, as well as for other members of society, the means to think and image."[52] For example, the substitution of abstractions for human actions is a way of obscuring reality and ensuring control. Forces, factors, structures, constraints, processes and the like are some of the abstractions that can be used to describe and alter the meaning of human behaviour. The concealment of abstractions allows, for example, foot-binding, which crippled women, to be seen as an "erotic custom," and witch burning to become a "process of religious legitimation."[53] The point is that abstractions mean that "no agent is named," and the scientist's invisibility and, by extension, his "objectivity" is maintained.

In looking at how feminism can reconstruct knowledge creation and use, one important challenge has been the insistence on the visibility of interested parties, whose interests be served by the construction and use of knowledge. The challenge asserts that, "The claim that science is value-free, objective and purely rational is ideology and not reality,"[54] and that what is required is a reassertion of the humanist tradition that insists upon "the centrality of human interests and the primacy of human worth and development."[55] What this means in immediate practical terms is, according to Benston, the "investigation of the effect that the male/female split has had on scientific methodology and practice." The result of such investigations will produce "modes of rationality and scientific investigation that take into account both subjectivity and the interactions between the knower and the known in the context of care and responsibility for both natural processes and other creatures."[56]

Benston does not reject the central feature of the scientific enterprise—objectivity. She maintains that the past and current scientific practices represent a pseudo-objectivity, but that objectivity, correctly understood, is "too important to abandon" because, in Fox Keller's words, it is a "quintessentially human goal."[57] This position is somewhat at odds with another feminist perspective that celebrates women's specificity as a basis for the construction of a more humane, integrative epistemology.

Miles proposes an "integrative feminism" as the alternative to androcentric knowledge production. This involves the "affirmation of female-associated values," such as "caring, sharing, cooperation and solidarity,"[58] as the central features of a feminist epistemology. Miles acknowledges that "we are playing with fire when we accept our special historical identity with reproduction and caring, sharing, nurturing human values as an essential component of our specific political voice, [because] our specificity as women has in the past been inseparable from our oppression as women."[59] Miles is not advocating a glorification or mystification of gynocentric values and behaviours, but she does suggest that the affirmation is the means to the articulation of "new and more universal truths—truths that will end narrow, single-sex definitions of the world, and in the process, feminize and humanize politics."[60]

Hilde Hein concurs with Miles's view and suggests that women's contributions to science, on the basis of their specificity, are essential to the development of a "more universal and genderless science."[61] The most important contribution that women can make will result from women's connectedness and contextual living in contrast to men.

> Partly as a consequence of the status of imminence (as opposed to transcendence) which has been imposed on them; and partly through their own internalization of that status, women have learned to live more contextually than men. Indeed they are more situationally defined than men *deriving* their identity from their environment rather than *distinguishing* themselves from it.[62]

The result of the contextual placing and experiences of women is that the normal science requirement that the scientist exclude self becomes "misplaced, if not meaningless."[63] As a result, if the normal contextual relatedness of women were "to become universally normative, then the ego-detachment now seen as necessary for the very possibility of science and morality would be regarded as pathological."[64] The celebration of ego, and the problem of alienation that it generates, would then become "deviations from an ideal of integrationism," and "ego-involvement would be a symptom of immaturity or incomplete organic development."[65]

The incorporation of women's values associated with their biological specificity is, to some extent, in the idealist research tradition. For example, Weber insisted that value-relevance was integral to the selection of sociological topics: "as soon as we attempt to reflect about the way in which life confronts us in immediate concrete situations, it presents an infinite multiplicity of successively and coexistently emerging and disappearing events, both 'within' and 'outside' ourselves."[66] This multiplicity means that in the study of "infinite reality" by the "finite human mind," only a part of it is seen to be "worthy of being known," and the selection of what is important or significant is the result of a "value-orientation towards these events." "The concept of culture is a *value-concept*. Empirical reality becomes "culture" to us because and insofar as we relate it to value ideas."[67]

The objectivity of social science is secured, in Weber's view, by the fact that once the object of sociological interest has been selected in terms of values, then values cease to enter into the causal explanations offered regarding the behaviours and events.

If it were simply a matter of value-relevance in the Weberian sense then the claims advanced for an integrative feminist approach to science could possibly be incorporated into a multi-paradigmatic conception of sociology. However, the claims go further than this, to encompass not only the "objects" of knowledge, but also the process by which they can be known. The "recognition of one's values, interests, intersubjectivity and status as a historical agent" is what enables feminists to gain a "more accurate view of the world."[68] In fact, it is "the recognition that no knowledge is ever separate from its context or is ever absolute" that "enables a fuller understanding of reality."[69] Integrative feminism is not simply the substitution of a female understanding for the current male viewpoint. Feminism escapes such relativism, according to Miles, by virtue of the fact that it is the viewpoint of outsiders to power, who therefore have a more accurate view of reality because they have no stake in mystifying that reality. In addition, because the "perspective on the world forged by a powerless group in struggle must necessarily be tested in practice for its accuracy and usefulness,"[70] then "limiting bias" is avoided.

Despite the strong claims for the non-relativity of an integrative feminism, several feminists have reservations about this position. Fox Keller maintains, "The essential goal of theory in general I take to be to represent our experience of the world in as comprehensive and inclusive a way as possible."[71] In progressing towards that goal, she suggests that it is necessary to give up the simplistic "objective realist's dream of providing an error-free description of the world "out there.""[72] But in doing so it is not necessary to "give up on objectivity as a process." Consequently, changes will depend "less on the introduction of a specifically female culture into science than on a rethinking of sexual polarities and the abandonment of a sexual division of intellectual labor."[73] Fox Keller agrees

that feminists are in a privileged position in regard to the epistemological critique of science, but that the result cannot simply be
changing the definition of science "to include more of what
actually women do."[74]

> I would prefer to adhere to the traditional uses of the word science
> and argue instead that what is at issue is what is called "good"
> science. In effect I am arguing for changes in both the acculturation
> of women (and men) and in the definition of "good" science, and I
> see them as proceeding together.[75]

Elizabeth Fee has also been cautious about the idea that the
incorporation of female values, based on the reproductive specificity of women, into the scientific, theoretical enterprise is a sufficient, or even wise, course for feminism. Such theories, she suggests, are based on an acceptance of the traditional sex dichotomy
that associates science with masculinity. The problem becomes
"not one of making women more scientific, but of making science
less masculine."[76] This general aim becomes problematic to the
extent that objectivity, associated with the masculine pursuit of
knowledge, tends to get thrown out absolutely. However, as Fee
remarks,

> We need not . . . go so far as to reject the whole human effort to
> comprehend the world in rational terms, nor the idea that forms of
> knowledge can be subjected to critical evaluation and empirical
> testing. The concept of creating knowledge through a constant
> process of practical interaction with nature, the willingness to
> consider all assumptions and methods as open to question, the
> expectation that ideas will be subjected to the most unfettered critical
> evaluation, all these are aspects of scientific objectivity which should
> be preserved and defended.[77]

As a result, the feminist critique of science, and theory production
in general, should not abandon "the ideal that we can come to an
ever more complete understanding of the natural [and social] world
through a collective and disciplined process of investigation and
discovery."[78]

Although Fee would preserve a feminist objectivity that allows
for open exchanges, nevertheless, the intentions and character of
those exchanges are seen as basically integrative. A feminist science
has not yet been created in her view, and to imagine what a feminist
science would be like means to imagine a feminist society, which is

"rather like asking a medieval peasant to imagine a theory of genetics. . . ." However, some characteristics of such a science can be described as follows:

> We can say that feminist science should not create artificial distinctions between the production and uses of knowledge, between thought and feeling, between subject and object, or between expert and non-expert. It would not be based on the divorce between subjectivity and objectivity, but would rather seek to integrate all aspects of human experience into our understanding of the natural world.[79]

It is clear that the debates among the feminist community on theory and epistemology do not present a unified, and therefore monolithic, front. Indeed, the vitality of feminism is captured in the diversity of these debates. In addition, the fact that the preceding discussion has taken the comments of a range of non-sociological "specialists" is a further indication of the rejection of traditional boundaries and hence of the stimulating nature of the feminist enterprise. Although the feminist critiques that challenge the mainstream ideas of what constitutes knowledge continue to take place more on the fringes of academic disciplines, increasingly the issues cannot be ignored. But current academic myopia is not crushing because feminism is not constrained by, or confined to, the academy with its specializations and separation of theory from practice. Dorothy Smith's point that feminism demands the construction of "a sociology for women rather than of women"[80] is a central tenet for feminism and has the effect of initiating a discourse among women that transcends the traditional academic and knowledge boundaries. "The discourse of women opposes the development of forms of knowledge which presuppose the isolation of the subject, of knower, from the lived historical process of the everyday world—an isolation which the academy has been created to provide."[81]

In many ways the feminist discourse in sociology continues the traditions of the "founding fathers." Their discourse also transcended the barriers and specialties characteristic of current academic knowledge creation. The works of the sociological fathers examined in this text represent the tip of the iceberg. There remains a potentially fruitful mine of information in other works by the same authors that is tantalizing in, for example, the manner in which they referred to and used each other's ideas. The dialogues among feminists represent a continuation of this theoretical tradition. What detractors might view as eclecticism seems to be more true of the initial presuppositions of the founding fathers. As such, those fathers, like many of their modern counterparts, would be amazed to find that it is the daughters rather than the sons who represent the most active and vital researchers at the present time. The "mothers" would be less surprised, and very proud.

Notes

PREFACE

1. Kate Millet, *Sexual Politics* (New York: Avon Books, 1969), 363.
2. It should be noted that not all feminists were optimists; in fact, several suggested that only total revolution by women for women could resolve the issue.
3. Dorothy Smith, "A Peculiar Eclipsing: Women's Exclusion from Man's Culture," *Women's Studies International Quarterly* 1(4), 1978: 281.
4. Politics and knowledge are supposed to be separated in the interests of "objectivity" within the academy. Feminists, however, insist that such a separation is in fact not made because of the male monopoly on knowledge production and dissemination and, furthermore, that the separation is impossible.
5. Strictly speaking, only Weber and Durkheim can be identified as sociologists, but the work of Marx, Engels and Freud has been appropriated by sociology from the outset and so they are ranked with the "fathers."
6. Dorothy Smith, "The Renaissance of Women." In *Knowledge Reconsidered: A Feminist Overview* (Ottawa: Canadian Research Institute for the Advancement of Women, 1984), 13.

CHAPTER 1

1. T. Hobbes, *Leviathan* (London: J.M. Dent and Sons, n.d.).
2. J. Locke, *Two Treatises of Government* (Cambridge, England: Cambridge University Press, 1963).
3. L.M.G. Clark, "Women and Locke: Who Owns the Apples in the Garden of Eden?" In L.M.G. Clark and L. Lange (eds.), *The Sexism of Social and Political Theory* (Toronto: University of Toronto Press, 1979), 19. Emphasis added.
4. *Ibid.*, 38.

5. For the Frankfurt school the domination of nature that was seen as central to the development of social thought in the West becomes domination over "social" nature, and the control of men over the environment becomes the control of men over men. For Weber, the increasing rationality of the West, in the interests of efficiency, results in control of the natural and social worlds by the technical rationality of the bureaucratic process. It is this process that leads Weber to a certain pessimism about the future of western society.

6. Quoted in Rosemary Agonito, *History of Ideas on Women* (New York: G.P. Putman's Sons, 1977), 47.

7. G.E.R. Lloyd, *Polarity and Analogy: Two Types of Argumentation in Early Greek Thought* (Cambridge: Cambridge University Press, 1971).

8. I. MacLean, *The Renaissance Notion of Women* (Cambridge: Cambridge University Press, 1980), 43-44.

9. M. Ficino, *The Letters of Marsilio Ficino*. 3 vols. (London: Shepheard-Walwyn, 1975) 1: 44.

10. *Ibid.*, 1: 44-45.

11. Ficino, *Letters*, 3: 69.

12. *Ibid.*, 3: 71.

13. J. O'Faolain and L. Martinese (eds.), *Not in God's Image* (New York: Harper Colophon Books, 1973), 208-09.

14. *Ibid.*

15. *Ibid.*

16. Ficino, *Letters*, 3: 70.

17. L.B. Alberti, *The Family in Renaissance Florence* (Columbia, South Carolina: University of Carolina Press, 1969), 207.

18. Agonito, *History of Ideas on Women*, 166-67.

19. *Ibid.*, 206.

20. *Ibid.*, 199. Emphasis in the original.

21. D. Morris, *The Naked Ape* (London: Jonathan Cape, 1967), 84.

22. M. Zimbalist Rosaldo and L. Lamphere (eds.), *Woman, Culture and Society* (Stanford, California: Stanford University Press, 1974), 20.

23. K. Sacks, "Engels Revisited: Women, the Organization of Production and Private Property." In Rosaldo and Lamphere, *Woman, Culture and Society*, 207-22.

24. Rosaldo and Lamphere, *Woman, Culture and Society*, 39.

25. Simone de Beauvoir, *The Second Sex* (New York: Vintage Books, 1974).

26. *Ibid.*, 39.

27. A. Oakley, *The Sociology of Housework* (London: Martin Robertson, 1974), 17.

28. T. Caplow, *The Sociology of Work* (New York: McGraw-Hill, 1961), 261.

29. A more critical examination of the situation that separates for analysis house*work* and implications of house*wifery*, as well as the mothering role, indicates that there are important differences in how these activities are understood and acted upon according to social class, ethnic background and other dimensions.
30. T. Parsons, "Age and Sex in the Social Structure of the United States." In T. Parsons (ed.), *Essays in Sociological Theory* (New York: The Free Press, 1964).

CHAPTER 2

1. Thompson remarks that "Durkheim can be considered as one of the first professional, university-based, sociologists." Kenneth Thompson, *Emile Durkheim* (Sussex, England: Ellis Horwood, 1982), 50.
2. Emile Durkheim, *The Rules of Sociological Method*. 8th edition. (New York: The Free Press, 1964), ix. Hereafter referred to as *The Rules*.
3. *Ibid.*, xxxvii.
4. Emile Durkheim, *The Division of Labor in Society* (New York: The Free Press, 1964), 43.
5. *Ibid.*, 37.
6. *Ibid.*, 62.
7. *Ibid.*, 64.
8. *Ibid.*, 65.
9. *Ibid.*, 69. (Original emphasis.)
10. *Ibid.*, 89.
11. *Ibid.*, 79.
12. *Ibid.*, 130.
13. *Ibid.*, 121.
14. *Ibid.*, 227.
15. *Ibid.*, 226.
16. *Ibid.*, 228.
17. *Ibid.*
18. *Ibid.*, 407-08.
19. *Ibid.*, 387.
20. *Ibid.*
21. *Ibid.*, 124.
22. George Simpson, "A Durkheim Fragment: The Conjugal Family," *The American Journal of Sociology* LXX (5) 1965: 527-36.
23. *Ibid.*, 531.
24. *Ibid.*, 532, footnote 15 by Marcel Mauss.
25. Durkheim, *The Division of Labor in Society*, 175.
26. *Ibid.*

27. Simpson, "A Durkheim Fragment." 533.
28. *Ibid.*
29. *Ibid.*
30. Emile Durkheim, *Suicide* (New York: The Free Press, 1966), 185.
31. Simpson, "A Durkheim Fragment," 530-31.
32. *Ibid.*, 529.
33. Durkheim, *Suicide*, 202.
34. Simpson, "A Durkheim Fragment," 534.
35. *Ibid.*, 535.
36. Durkheim, *The Division of Labor in Society*, 207.
37. *Ibid.*, 58.
38. *Ibid.*, 61.
39. Simpson, "A Durkheim Fragment," 535.
40. *Ibid.*, 555.
41. *Ibid.*, 535.
42. *Ibid.*, 536.
43. *Ibid.*
44. Emile Durkheim, *The Elementary Forms of the Religious Life.* (New York: Collier Books, 1961), 126, footnote 24.
45. Durkheim, *The Division of Labor in Society*, 59.
46. *Ibid.*, 57.
47. *Ibid.*
48. *Ibid.*, 57-58.
49. *Ibid.*, 58.
50. *Ibid.*, 60.
51. *Ibid.*
52. *Ibid.*
53. *Ibid.*, 61.
54. *Ibid.*, 56.
55. *Ibid.*
56. Georges Davy, *Sociologues d'hier et d'aujourd'hui* (Paris: Alcan, 1931), 153-54.
57. Durkheim, *The Division of Labor in Society*, 233.
58. *Ibid.*, 250.
59. *Ibid.*, 247.
60. *Ibid.*, 406.
61. *Ibid.*, 365.
62. Steven Lukes, *Emile Durkheim: His Life and Work* (London: Allen Lane, The Penguin Press, 1973) 191.
63. *Ibid.*, 195-96.
64. Durkheim, *Suicide*, 38.
65. *Ibid.*
66. *Ibid.*, 299.
67. *Ibid.*

68. *Ibid.*, 209.
69. *Ibid.*, 214-15.
70. *Ibid.*, 209.
71. *Ibid.*, 221.
72. *Ibid.*, 219.
73. *Ibid.*, 227.
74. *Ibid.*, 258.
75. *Ibid.*
76. *Ibid.*, 255.
77. *Ibid.*, 257.
78. *Ibid.*
79. *Ibid.*, 269.
80. *Ibid.*, 275.
81. *Ibid.*, 270.
82. *Ibid.*
83. *Ibid.*, 270-71.
84. *Ibid.*, 271.
85. *Ibid.*
86. *Ibid.*, 272.
87. *Ibid.*
88. *Ibid.*
89. *Ibid.*
90. *Ibid.*, 275.
91. *Ibid.*, 276.
92. *Ibid.*, 370.
93. *Ibid.*, 373.
94. *Ibid.*, 374.
95. *Ibid.*, 372.
96. *Ibid.*, 377.
97. *Ibid.*, 378.
98. *Ibid.*, 379.
99. *Ibid.*, 382.
100. *Ibid.*, 274.
101. *Ibid.*, 384.
102. *Ibid.*
103. *Ibid.*, 385.
104. *Ibid.*
105. *Ibid.*
106. *Ibid.*
107. *Ibid.*, footnote 16.
108. *Ibid.*
109. *Ibid.*, 386.
110. *Ibid.*
111. *Ibid.*

112. Durkheim, *The Elementary Forms of the Religious Life*, p. 298.
113. *Ibid.*, 299.
114. Emile Durkheim, "The Dualism of Human Nature and its Social Conditions." In Kurt H. Wolff (ed.), *Essays on Sociology and Philosophy* (New York: Harper and Row, 1964), 327. Hereafter referred to as "The Dualism."
115. *Ibid.*, 328.
116. *Ibid.*, 329.
117. *Ibid.*, 328.
118. *Ibid.*, 330.
119. Durkheim, *The Elementary Forms of the Religious Life*, 466.
120. *Ibid.*
121. Durkheim, "The Dualism," 335.
122. *Ibid.*, 337.
123. *Ibid.*, 338.
124. *Ibid.*
125. *Ibid.*, 339.
126. Emile Durkheim, *Education and Sociology* (Glencoe, Illinois: The Free Press, 1956), 90.
127. Durkheim, *The Division of Labor in Society*, 130.
128. *Ibid.*, 131.
129. Durkheim, "The Dualism," 339.
130. Durkheim, *The Division of Labor in Society*, 239.
131. *Ibid.*
132. *Ibid.*, 239-40.
133. *Ibid.*, 240.
134. Emile Durkheim, *Selected Writings* (Cambridge: University Press, 1972), 110.
135. Durkheim, *The Division of Labor in Society*, 239.
136. Durkheim, *Selected Writings*, 110-11.
137. *Ibid.*, 111.
138. *Ibid.*
139. *Ibid.*, 217.
140. Lukes, *Emile Durkheim*, 533.
141. Durkheim, *The Division of Labor in Society.*, 58.
142. *Ibid.*, 57.
143. Durkheim, "Sociology," p. 378.
144. *Ibid.*, 377.
145. Durkheim, *Suicide*, 38.
146. *Ibid.*, 38. Emphasis in original.
147. Durkheim, *The Rules*, lvii.
148. *Ibid.*, 32.
149. *Ibid.*, 10.

150. *Ibid.*
151. *Ibid.*, 110.
152. *Ibid.*, 44.
153. *Ibid.*, 95.
154. *Ibid.*
155. *Ibid.*, 111.
156. *Ibid.*, 61.
157. Emile Durkheim, *Contributions to l'Année sociologique* (New York: The Free Press, 1980), 209. Emphasis added. Hereafter referred to as *Contributions*.
158. *Ibid.*
159. Durkheim, *The Division of Labor in Society*, 399.
160. *Ibid.*, 401.
161. Durkheim, *Suicide*, 215.
162. *Ibid.*
163. *Ibid.*, 216.
164. Durkheim, *Contributions*, 296.
165. *Ibid.*, 288.
166. *Ibid.*
167. *Ibid.*, 288-89.
168. *Ibid.*, 414.
169. Richard Bendix, "Two Sociological Traditions." In Reinhard Bendix and Guenther Roth (eds.), *Scholarship and Partisanship: Essays on Max Weber* (Berkeley, California: University of California Press), 1971, 286.
170. *Ibid.*

CHAPTER 3

1. Laurel Walum Richardson, *The Dynamics of Sex and Gender*, 2nd ed. (Boston: Houghton Mifflin, 1981), 15.
2. Juliet Mitchell, *Woman's Estate* (New York: Vintage Books, 1973).
3. The debates over this question are numerous and form an important basis for the continuing vitality of feminist scholarship. Some of the critical dimensions are discussed throughout the book, especially in chapter 3.
4. Durkheim, *The Rules of Sociological Method*, 102.
5. Max Weber, *The Theory of Social and Economic Organization* (New York: The Free Press, 1964), 88.
6. *Ibid.*
7. *Ibid.*, 103-04.
8. *Ibid.*, 99.
9. *Ibid.*, 100.

10. Max Weber, *Economy and Society: An Outline of Interpretive Sociology.* 3 vols. (New York: Bedminster Press, 1968), 1: 19.
11. W.G. Runciman (ed.), *Weber: Selections in Translation* (New York: Cambridge University Press, 1978), 23. Emphasis in the original.
12. N. Chodorow, *The Reproduction of Mothering* (California: University of California Press, 1978), 12.
13. Guenther Roth and Claus Wittich (eds.), *Max Weber, Economy and Society.* 3 vols. (New York: Bedminster Press, 1968), 1: 53.
14. *Ibid.,* 3: 943.
15. *Ibid.,* 3: 946.
16. H.H. Gerth and C. Wright Mills (eds.), *From Max Weber: Essays in Sociology* (New York: Oxford University Press, 1946), 296.
17. Roth and Wittich, *Max Weber,* 3: 1006.
18. *Ibid.* 1: 231.
19. *Ibid.,* 1: 357.
20. *Ibid.*
21. *Ibid.*
22. *Ibid.,* 1: 359.
23. *Ibid.,* 1: 363-64.
24. *Ibid.,* 1: 359.
25. *Ibid.,* 3: 1007.
26. *Ibid.,* 3: 1009.
27. *Ibid.,* 3: 1007.
28. *Ibid.,* 3: 1009.
29. *Ibid.,* 1: 363-64. Emphasis added.
30. *Ibid.,* 1: 358.
31. *Ibid.*
32. *Ibid.*
33. *Ibid.,* 360.
34. *Ibid.,* 364.
35. *Ibid.,* 365.
36. *Ibid.,* 367.
37. *Ibid.,* 368.
38. *Ibid.*
39. Talcott Parsons (ed.), *Max Weber: The Theory of Social and Economic Organization* (London: Collier-Macmillan, 1947), 346.
40. Gerth and Mills, *From Max Weber,* 254.
41. Roth and Wittich, *Max Weber,* 1: 371.
42. *Ibid.,* 1: 372.
43. *Ibid.,* 3: 1011.
44. This tension is well documented historically and cross-culturally in an aged ruler's fear of the ambition of his young heir.
45. Roth and Wittich, *Max Weber,* 3: 1001.

46. *Ibid.*
47. *Ibid.*, 3: 1012.
48. *Ibid.*
49. Frances Geis and Joseph Geis, *Women in the Middle Ages* (New York: Barnes and Noble Books, Harper and Row, 1978), 22.
50. Parsons, *Max Weber*, 255.
51. Roth and Wittich, *Max Weber*, 1: 255.
52. *Ibid.*, 306.
53. Amy Kelly, *Eleanor of Aquitaine and the Four Kings* (Cambridge, Mass.: Harvard University Press), 1978, 1-2.
54. Geis and Geis, *Women in the Middle Ages*, 28.
55. Shulamaith Shahar, *The Fourth Estate* (London: Methuen), 40.
56. Margaret King suggests that the incompatibility of marriage and scholarship for women meant that those who rejected marriage in favour of learning had little alternative than to retire to the "book-lined cell" of the convent. There the learning they displayed was admired because it was a rarity in a woman. They were "prodigies," who were not "quite male, not quite female," but some "third and amorphous sex." Margaret King, "Book-Lined Cells: Women and Humanism in the Early Italian Renaissance." In Patricia H. Labalme, *Beyond Their Sex* (ed.) (New York: New York University Press, 1980), 66-90.
57. The nature of women according to the clergy of the Middle Ages was problematic, to the extent that some debated whether women could be considered human beings. In general, woman was inferior to man, having been constructed from Adam's crooked rib and consequently incapable of having any authority over him as would be the case, according to Aquinas, if she had been produced from Adam's head. In general, order in the family is "wanting if some were not governed by others wiser than themselves . . . women is naturally subject to man, because in man the discretion of reason predominates." Thomas Aquinas, quoted in Rosemary Agonito, *History of Ideas on Women*, 85.
58. Roth and Wittich, *Max Weber*, 3: 1078. Emphasis in the original.
59. Shahar, *The Fourth Estate*, 170.
60. Roth and Wittich, *Max Weber*, 3: 1078.
61. Geis and Geis, *Women in the Middle Ages*, 125.
62. One of the requirements of such Christian knights was supposed to be the renunciation of sexual relations. The monk Guibert of Nogent wrote approvingly in 1108 of King Baldwin, who undertook a crusade to the Holy Land and "sent his wife to a convent so that thus protected against inflammatory desires, emancipated from the necessity to fight against flesh and blood, he could devote himself

entirely to the struggle against the princes of the world." Georges
Duby, *The Three Orders: Feudal Society Imagined* (Chicago: University of Chicago Press, 1978), p. 221.

63. Daniel Waley, *Later Medieval Europe* (New York: Longman, 1964),
151.
64. Roth and Wittich, *Max Weber*, 3: 1105.
65. *Ibid.*
66. Duby points out that the great number of "wandering youth" that
appear in the chronicles of the Middle Ages was a consequence of
primogeniture. Although heirs of the knightly group might take to
wandering from tournament to tournament while waiting for their
inheritance, younger sons who did not enter the Church were almost
forced to wander in search of adventure and, more importantly, of a
rich heiress to marry. "Youth" defined the period between being
dubbed a knight and becoming a husband and father, so that for
many errant knights their youth could comprise a considerable
portion of their adult life. This "pack let loose by noble houses to
relieve their surplus of expansive power" set off to "conquer glory,
profit, and feminine prey." Georges Duby, "In Northwestern
France: The 'Youth' in Twelfth-Century Aristocratic Society." In
Frederic L. Cheyette (ed.), *Lordship and Community in Medieval
Europe* (New York: Holt, Rinehart and Winston, 1968), 206.
67. Roth and Wittich, *Max Weber*, 3: 1106.
68. *Ibid.*
69. *Ibid.*
70. Norman David (ed.) *The Paston Letters* (Oxford/New York: Oxford
University Press, 1983).
71. Muriel St. Clare Byrne (ed.), *The Lisle Letters* (Chicago: University
of Chicago Press, 1981). See pages 335-50 for the dispute with
Cromwell.
72. Shahar, *The Fourth Estate*, 151.
73. Jo- Ann McNamara and Suzanne F. Wemple, "Sanctity and Power:
The Dual Pursuit of Medieval Women." In Renate Bridenthal and
Claudia Koonz, *Becoming Visible: Women in European History*
(Boston: Houghton Mifflin, 1977), 104.
74. See, for example, Shahar, *The Fourth Estate*, especially pages 127-
73; Jo Ann McNamara and Suzanne Wemple, "The Power of
Women through the Family in Medieval Europe: 500-1100." In
Mary S. Hartman and Lois Banner (eds.), *Clio's Consciousness
Raised* (New York: Harper Torchbooks, 1974); Geis and Geis,
Women in the Middle Ages.
75. Shahar, *The Fourth Estate*, 128. Emphasis added.
76. J. Huizinga, *The Waning of the Middle Ages* (New York: Doubleday
Anchor Books, 1954).

77. Shahar, *The Fourth Estate*, 129.
78. Georges Duby, *The Early Growth of the European Economy* (New York: Cornell University Press, 1974), 171.
79. Georges Duby, *The Chivalrous Society* (London: Edward Arnold, 1977), 75.
80. Keith Wrightson points out that in a sample of first marriages for London craftsmen and tradesmen in the fifteenth century that 25 per cent of them married widows, "thereby ensuring a good start for themselves." Keith Wrightson, *English Society, 1580-1680* (London: Hutchinson, 1983), 81.
81. Rodney Hilton, *Bond Men Made Free* (New York: The Viking Press, 1973), 38.
82. Geis and Geis, *Women in the Middle Ages*, 149.
83. *Ibid.*, 149-50.
84. *Ibid.*, 232.
85. *Ibid.*
86. Roth and Wittich, *Max Weber*, 3: 1081.
87. Duby, *The Three Orders*, 166.
88. Frank Parkin, *Max Weber* (London: Tavistock Publications, 1982), 83.
89. Peter Laslett, *The World We Have Lost* (London: Methuen, 1965), 183.
90. Barbara W. Tuchman, *A Distant Mirror* (New York: Ballantine Books, 1978), 19.
91. *Ibid.*, 216.
92. Roberta Hamilton, *The Liberation of Women* (London: George Allen and Unwin, 1978), 25.
93. Geis and Geis, *Women in the Middle Ages*, 147.
94. Max Weber, *The Methodology of the Social Sciences* (New York: The Free Press, 1949), 92.
95. *Ibid.*, 81.
96. *Ibid.*, 84.
97. *Ibid.*
98. Lawrence Stone, "The Rise of the Nuclear Family in Early Modern England." In Charles E. Rosenberg (ed.), *The Family in History* (Pennsylvania: University of Pennsylvania Press, 1975), 34.
99. Constance Cronin, in her analysis of Sicilian peasant society, which approximates the society described by Stone, indicates that women have various strategies that subvert the accepted ideal of gender behaviour and that, in fact, such strategies are essential to the smooth functioning of the society. Constance Cronin, "Illusion and Reality in Sicily." In Alice Schlegel (ed.), *Sexual Stratification: A Cross-Cultural View* (New York: Columbia University Press, 1977), 67-93.

100. Roth and Wittich, *Max Weber*, 1: 372.

101. *Ibid.*

102. As Duby remarks, over time, "The knighthood thus became a society of heirs, all the more solid and shut in because, in order to maintain their position of wealth, families attempted to limit births mainly by strictly controlling marriage." Duby, *The Chivalrous Society*, 87.

103. Women's participation in nearly all of the crafts and trades undertaken by men across various societies and their membership in various guilds did not ensure equality in the workplace. Guilds themselves were often the source of restrictions on women's labour, and in some instances women were denied membership in the guilds relevant to their craft or trade.

104. Women's wages were usually lower than men's even for comparable work. J.G. d'Avenal has calculated that in 1326-1350, "the average female wage was 68 percent of the male wage for the same work." Quoted in Shahar, *The Fourth Estate*, 243.

105. *Ibid.*, 250.

106. Heidi Hartmann, "The Unhappy Marriage of Marxism and Feminism: Towards a More Progressive Union." In L. Sargent (ed.), *Women and the Revolution* (Montreal: Black Rose Books, 1981), 14-15.

CHAPTER 4

1. Karl Marx and Frederick Engels, *Collected Works*. 10 vols. (New York: International Publishers, 1975), 3: 296.

2. Heidi Hartmann, "The Unhappy Marriage of Marxism and Feminism: Towards a More Progressive Union." In Lydia Sargent (ed.), *Women and Revolution* (Montreal: Black Rose Books), 1981, 2.

3. Charnie Guettel, *Marxism and Feminism* (Toronto: The Women's Press, 1974), 50.

4. The debate regarding the "correct" identification of revolutionary potential, whether in the traditionally defined working class or the women's movement, is an ongoing one and the specific issues are addressed at the close of this chapter as well as in the subsequent chapters on power and legitimations.

5. Karl Marx and Frederick Engels, *The German Ideology* (New York: International Publishers, 1947), 17.

6. David McLellan, *The Thought of Karl Marx*. 2nd edition. (London: The Macmillan Press, 1980).

7. Karl Marx, *Capital: A Critique of Political Economy*. 3 vols. (Chicago: Charles H. Kerr 1909), 3: 1031.

8. Karl Marx and Frederick Engels, *Manifesto of the Communist Party* (Moscow: Foreign Languages Publishing House, 1959), 45.

9. Marx and Engels, *The German Ideology*, 17. Emphasis in the original.
10. *Ibid.*
11. Marx and Engels, *Manifesto of the Communist Party*, 45-46.
12. Marx, *Capital*, 1: 715.
13. In describing various historical manifestations of such conflict, Marx often used multiple class models but the transformation of any society was always the result of a conflict between two classes.
14. Marx and Engels, *Manifesto of the Communist Party*, 46.
15. Karl Marx, "Value, Price and Profit." In Eleanor Marx Aveling (ed.), *The Essential Left* (London: Unwin Books, 1962), 81-82. Emphasis in the original.
16. Marx, *Capital*, 1: 40-41.
17. Christine Delphy, *Close to Home* (London: Hutchinson in association with The Explorations in Feminism Collective, 1984), 160.
18. Marx and Engels, *The German Ideology*, 20.
19. *Ibid.*, 21.
20. Frederick Engels, *The Origin of the Family, Private Property, and the State* (New York: Pathfinder Press, 1972), 25. Hereafter referred to as *The Origin*.
21. L.H. Morgan, *Ancient Society* (New York: Henry Holt, 1877).
22. Engels, *The Origin*, 49.
23. *Ibid.*, 60.
24. *Ibid.*, 60-61.
25. *Ibid.*, 61.
26. *Ibid.*, 64.
27. *Ibid.*
28. *Ibid.*, 66.
29. *Ibid.*, 67.
30. *Ibid.*, 66.
31. *Ibid.*
32. *Ibid.*, 72. Emphasis in the original.
33. *Ibid.*, 67-68. Emphasis in the original.
34. *Ibid.*, 75.
35. *Ibid.*, 82.
36. *Ibid.*
37. *Ibid.*, 25-26.
38. *Ibid.*, 26.
39. *Ibid.*, 67. The suggestion in the quote is that the predominance of the father as opposed to the mother is right and natural and this then suggests that the matrilineal society celebrated in Engels's account is, in fact, unnatural when questions of property—the material conditions of existence—come into play.
40. Engels states, "this revolution—one of the most decisive ever experi-

enced by mankind—need not have disturbed one single living member of a gens . . . The simple decision sufficed that in the future the descendents of the male members should remain in the gens, but that those of the females were to be excluded from the gens and transferred to that of their father. The reckoning of descent through the female line and the right of inheritance through the mother were hereby overthrown." *Ibid.,* p. 67.

41. *Ibid.,* 151-52.
42. Marx, *Capital,* 1: 351. Emphasis added.
43. Engels, *The Origin,* 149.
44. *Ibid.,* 151.
45. Both anthropological data as well as historical data from our own society indicate that physical strength has rarely been a consideration in separating the tasks appropriate to either sex, unless such a basis for separation has been in the interests of men.
46. Juliet Mitchell, *Woman's Estate* (Middlesex, England: Penguin Books, 1971), 105.
47. Several of the articles found in Rosaldo and Lamphere (eds.), *Woman, Culture and Society* illustrate these two points. For example, Peggy Sanday in "Female Status in the Public Domain" points out that Somali women undertake most of the work in the society, including the heavy work, as the men "consider it beneath their dignity to tend anything but camels, cattle, and ponies—the most valuable economic assets of the Somali" (p. 202). In contrast, Rosaldo in her "Theoretical Overview" indicates that in Ilongot society the division of labour between the sexes is not a strict one and the work of men and women is regarded as complementary. The only activity that sets men apart is head hunting, associated with the transition to manhood. But head hunting is "not felt to be obligatory, nor is it desirable for a man to take a head more than once." (p. 40)
48. For a discussion of the "dangers" attendant on any tampering with the sex/gender division of labour, see Lionel Tiger and Robin Fox, *The Imperial Animal* (New York: Holt, Rinehart and Winston, 1971).
49. Marx, *Capital,* 1: 294.
50. Engels, *The Origin,* 152.
51. *Ibid.,* 88.
52. *Ibid.,* 79.
53. *Ibid.,* 88.
54. Zillah Eisenstein, "Developing a Theory of Capitalist Patriarchy and Socialist Feminism." In Zillah Eisenstein (ed.), *Capitalist Patriarchy and the Case for Socialist Feminism* (New York: Monthly Review Press, 1979), 14.

55. Marx saw women's productive labour as a reserve form of labour under capitalism that could be used to undercut the wages of men and/or meet the short-term needs of the productive process after which they would be let go. The possible threat that women, and children, represented to men was recognized during the period in which Marx and Engels wrote and the frequent attempts to establish a "family wage" on the part of men were attempts to contain the threat posed by women's paid labour. For an examination of this issue, see Heidi Hartmann, "Capitalism, Patriarchy, and Job Segregation by Sex," in Eisenstein (ed.), 1979; and Jane Humphries, "The Working-Class Family: A Marxist Perspective," in Jean Bethke Elshtain (ed.), *The Family in Political Thought*, 1982.
56. Guettel, *Marxism and Feminism*, 52.
57. Rosalind Coward, *Patriarchal Precedents: Sexuality and Social Relations* (London: Routledge and Kegan Paul, 1983), 156.
58. *Ibid.*
59. Anthony Giddens, *The Class Structure of the Advanced Societies* (London: Hutchinson, 1973), 288.
60. Marx, *Capital*, 1: 572.
61. *Ibid.*
62. *Ibid.*, 1: 509.
63. Margaret Benston, "The Political Economy of Women's Liberation," *Monthly Review* 21 (4), 1969: 16.
64. Mariarosa Dalla Costa and Selma James, *The Power of Women and the Subversion of the Community* (Bristol, England: Falling Wall Press, 1973), 7.
65. *Ibid.*, 33.
66. See Jean Gardiner, "Women's Domestic Labour," *New Left Review* 8 (1), 1975: 89, 1975; Maxine Molyneux, "Beyond the Domestic Labour Debate," *New Left Review* 9 (3), 1979; and the articles in Bonnie Fox (ed.), *Hidden in the Household* (Toronto: The Women's Press, 1980).
67. Wally Seccombe, "The Housewife and her Labor Under Capitalism," *New Left Review* 7 (1), 1974.
68. *Ibid.*, 12.
69. Jean Gardiner, "Women's Domestic Labour." In Eisenstein, *Capitalist Patriarchy*, 188.
70. *Ibid.*, 183.
71. *Ibid.*, 178.
72. Seccombe, "The Housewife," 21.
73. *Ibid.*, 22-23.
74. Roberta Hamilton, "Working at Home," *Atlantis* 7 (1), 1981: 115.
75. Meg Luxton, *More Than a Labour of Love* (Toronto: The Women's Press, 1980), 142.

76. Ann Oakley, *The Sociology of Housework* (New York: Pantheon Books, 1974), 50.
77. *Ibid.*, 183.
78. *Ibid.*, 106.
79. Luxton, *More Than a Labour of Love*, 131.
80. Oakley, *The Sociology of Housework*, 184.
81. Luxton, *More Than a Labour of Love*, 170.
82. Luxton, *More Than a Labour of Love*, 190.
83. As many authors have indicated, the majority of married women in paid labour in industrialized countries are there because one wage is insufficient for the needs of the family. See Pat Armstrong and Hugh Armstrong, *The Double Ghetto*, (Toronto: McClelland and Stewart, 1984), for a discussion of the Canadian situation.
84. For some international comparisons of time budgets, see Martin Meissner, "Sexual Division of Labour and Inequality." In Marylee Stephenson (ed.), *Women in Canada* (Don Mills: General Publishing, 1977).
85. Martin Meissner, "Women and Inequality," *Our Generation* 11 (2), 1976: 64.
86. *Ibid.*, 67.
87. *Ibid.*, 68.
88. *Ibid.*
89. Dorothy Smith, "A Sociology for Women." In J. Sherman and T. Beck (eds.), *The Prism of Sex: Essays in the Sociology of Knowledge* (Madison: University of Wisconsin Press, 1979), 168.
90. Delphy, *Close to Home*, 95.
91. *Ibid.*
92. *Ibid.*, 97.
93. Herbert Spencer, *The Principles of Sociology* (New York: Appleton, 1898), 743.
94. Coward, *Patriarchal Precedents*, 12.
95. Simone de Beauvoir, *The Second Sex* (New York: Alfred A. Knopf, 1952), 41.
96. Mitchell, *Woman's Estate.*
97. *Ibid.*, 14.
98. *Ibid.*, 148.
99. Juliet Mitchell, *Psychoanalysis and Feminism* (New York: Vintage Books, 1975), 391.
100. Mitchell, *Woman's Estate*, 156.
101. Hartmann, "The Unhappy Marriage," 11.
102. Barbara Sinclair Deckard, *The Women's Movement*. 3rd edition (New York: Harper and Row, 1983), 326.
103. *Ibid.*, 327.
104. Eisenstein, "Developing a Theory of Capitalist Patriarchy," 22.

105. *Ibid.*, 25. It should be noted that why men should have so chosen and why women allowed the process to proceed are not addressed here. The questions are raised in those accounts dealing with the significance of women's reproduction, which we examine in some detail elsewhere in the text.
106. *Ibid.*, 28.
107. *Ibid.*, 31.
108. Hartmann, "The Unhappy Marriage," 3-4.
109. Hartmann, "Capitalism, Patriarchy, and Job Segregation by Sex," 207.
110. *Ibid.*
111. Hartmann, "The Unhappy Marriage," 15.
112. *Ibid.*, 18.
113. *Ibid.*, 32.
114. *Ibid.*, 33. Emphasis in the original.
115. *Ibid.*
116. Iris Young, "Beyond the Unhappy Marriage: A Critique of Dual Systems Theory." In Sargent, (ed.), *Women and the Revolution*, 49.
117. Isaac D. Balbus, *Marxism and Domination: A Neo-Hegelian, Feminist Psychoanalytic Theory of Sexual, Political and Technological Liberation* (Princeton, New Jersey: Princeton University Press, 1982), 71.
118. Carol Ehrlich, "The Unhappy Marriage of Marxism and Feminism: Can it be Saved?" In Sargent (ed.), *Women and the Revolution*, 109-33.
119. Sandra Harding, "What is the Real Material Base of Patriarchy and Capital?" In Sargent (ed.), *Women and the Revolution*, 135-63.
120. *Ibid.*, 159.
121. Shulamith Firestone, *The Dialectic of Sex* (New York: Bantam Books, 1970), 13.

CHAPTER 5

1. Rosalind Coward, *Patriarchal Precedents, Sexuality and Social Relations* (London: Routledge and Kegan Paul, 1983), 12.
2. *Ibid.*, 97.
3. The phallic stage represents the realization on the part of both sexes of the importance of the penis. As Freud remarked in his lecture "Anxiety and Instinctual Life", during this phase the girl wishes to possess a penis, but this "entirely unfeminine wish . . . is normally transformed into a wish for a baby, and then for a man as the bearer of the penis and the giver of the baby." Sigmund Freud, *New Introductory Lectures on Psychoanalysis* (New York: W.W. Norton 1965), 101.

4. Freud, *New Introductory Lectures,* 129.
5. *Ibid.,* 125.
6. *Ibid.,* 124.
7. *Ibid.,* 128.
8. *Ibid.,* 129.
9. Sigmund Freud, *On Sexuality* (Harmondsworth: Penguin, 1977), 342.
10. *Ibid.*
11. Sigmund Freud, *Totem and Taboo.* (New York: Vintage Books, 1946).
12. *Ibid.,* 183.
13. *Ibid.,* 186.
14. *Ibid.,* 185.
15. *Ibid.*
16. *Ibid.,* 186.
17. Sigmund Freud, *The Standard Edition of the Complete Psychological Works of Sigmund Freud* (London: Hogarth Press, 1874), vol. 23:99.
18. Freud, *New Introductory Lectures,* 135.
19. *Ibid.,* 125.
20. *Ibid.,* 116.
21. Karen Horney, *New Ways in Psychoanalysis* (New York: W.W. Norton 1939), 113.
22. *Ibid.,* 119.
23. *Ibid.,* 118-19.
24. Alfred Adler, *Understanding Human Nature* (New York: Greenberg, 1927), 134.
25. *Ibid.,* 123.
26. Freud, *New Introductory Lectures,* 131.
27. *Ibid.,* 132.
28. B. Malinowski, *Sex and Repression in Savage Society* (London: Routledge, 1926).
29. Coward, *Patriarchal Precedents,* 250.
30. *Ibid.,* 246.
31. The classic exponent of this Freudian perspective was Talcott Parsons. See Talcott Parsons and Robert Bales, *Family, Socialization and Interaction Process* (New York: The Free Press, 1955).
32. Simone de Beauvoir, *The Second Sex* (New York: Vintage Books, 1974), xv.
33. *Ibid.,* xvii.
34. *Ibid.,* xix.
35. *Ibid.*
36. *Ibid.,* xxi.
37. *Ibid.,* xxii.

38. *Ibid.*, xxiv.

39. For example, women, especially young women, still assume marriage will provide them with security and happiness despite the divorce statistics and the poverty of single female parents. At the same time, for many women marriage does represent a better, or more congenial possibility, than the alternatives in the world of paid labour.

40. de Beauvoir, *The Second Sex*, xxv.

41. *Ibid.*, 301.

42. *Ibid.*

43. *Ibid.*, 36.

44. *Ibid.*, 39.

45. *Ibid.*, 41.

46. *Ibid.*, 61.

47. *Ibid.*, 64.

48. *Ibid.*, 64-65.

49. *Ibid.*, 46.

50. *Ibid.*, 48.

51. De Beauvoir suggests that "the doll, incarnating the promise of the baby that is to come in the future, can become a possession more precious than the penis." *Ibid.*, 54.

52. *Ibid.*, 56.

53. *Ibid.*, xx.

54. *Ibid.*, 66.

55. *Ibid.*, 813.

56. Sheila Rowbotham, *Woman's Consciousness, Man's World* (Harmondsworth: Penguin, 1973), 21.

57. Shulamith Firestone, *The Dialectic of Sex* (New York: William Morrow 1970), 7.

58. de Beauvoir, *The Second Sex*, 452.

59. *Ibid.*, 454. De Beauvoir's point here is that the lesbian preference is a reaction against masculine domination. As men set themselves up as the subject then women become their prey, and the lesbian, along with "every adolescent female," is said to fear penetration and feels a "certain repulsion for the male body." As we will see later in this chapter, more recent work has also made the claim for the homosexuality of women as a natural phenomenon and heterosexuality as a socially imposed necessity for women. But the claim is largely with regard to the link between women, as mothers and daughters, that their common reproductive capacity generates. See Adrienne Rich, 1980, pp. 630-60, and Luce Irigaray, 1981, pp. 60-67.

60. de Beauvoir, *The Second Sex*, 540.

61. Firestone, *The Dialectic of Sex*, 4.

62. *Ibid.*, 7.

63. *Ibid.*, 8.
64. *Ibid.*, 12.
65. *Ibid.*, 10.
66. *Ibid.*
67. *Ibid.*, 11. Emphasis in the original.
68. *Ibid.*
69. *Ibid.*, 59.
70. *Ibid.*, 198. Emphasis in the original.
71. *Ibid.*, 200.
72. *Ibid.*, 202.
73. Roberta Hamilton, *The Liberation of Women* (London: George Allen and Unwin, 1978), 87.
74. *Ibid.*, 88.
75. Mitchell, *Woman's Estate*, 89.
76. *Ibid.*, 89-90.
77. Firestone, *The Dialectic of Sex*, 190.
78. Jean Bethke Elshtain, *Public Man, Private Woman* (Princeton: Princeton University Press, 1981), 221.
79. Firestone, *The Dialectic of Sex*, 68-69.
80. Gayle Rubin, "The Traffic in Women: Notes on the 'Political Economy' of Sex." In Rayna R. Reiter (ed.), *Toward an Anthropology of Women* (New York: Monthly Review Press, 1975), 196.
81. *Ibid.*, 184.
82. It must be recognized that many women were protesting, rebelling and refusing to take second place as the nineteenth-century women's movement demonstrates. It is significant that those theorists whose work we consider here—Durkheim and Weber—more or less ignored the movement other than to caution women against "excessive" demands.
83. Sherry B. Ortner, "Is Female to Male as Nature is to Culture?" In M.Z. Rosaldo and L. Lamphere (eds.), *Woman, Culture and Society* (Stanford: Stanford University Press, 1974), 67.
84. *Ibid.*, 72.
85. *Ibid.*
86. *Ibid.*, 73.
87. *Ibid.*
88. *Ibid.*
89. *Ibid.*, 79.
90. *Ibid.*, 74.
91. *Ibid.*, 76.
92. Nancy Chodorow, "Mother, Male Dominance, and Capitalism." In Zillah R. Eisenstein (ed.), *Capitalist Patriarchy and the Case for Socialist Feminism* (New York: Monthly Review Press, 1979), 87.

93. *Ibid.*, 87. Emphasis in the original.
94. Nancy Chodorow, *The Reproduction of Mothering* (Berkeley: University of California Press, 1978), 33.
95. Nancy Chodorow, "Family Structure and Feminine Personality." In M.Z. Rosaldo and L. Lamphere (eds.), *Woman, Culture and Society*, 46.
96. *Ibid.*
97. *Ibid.*, 47.
98. *Ibid.*, 50.
99. *Ibid.*
100. *Ibid.*, 51 (paraphrased).
101. Chodorow, *The Reproduction of Mothering*, 175-76.
102. Chodorow, "Family Structure and Feminine Personality," 53.
103. Chodorow, "Mothering, Male Dominance, and Capitalism," 95.
104. Chodorow, "Family Structure and Feminine Personality," 54.
105. Chodorow, "Mothering, Male Dominance, and Capitalism," 102.
106. Dorothy Dinnerstein, *The Mermaid and the Minotaur* (New York: Harper and Row, 1977), 95.
107. *Ibid.*, 53.
108. *Ibid.*, 161.
109. *Ibid.*, 175.
110. *Ibid.*, 155.
111. *Ibid.*, 108.
112. *Ibid.*, 103.
113. *Ibid.*
114. Janet Sayers, *Biological Politics* (London: Tavistock Publications, 1982), 160.
115. Chodorow, *The Reproduction of Mothering*, 218.
116. Ortner, "Is Female to Male as Nature is to Culture?" p. 87.
117. Frederick Engels, *The Origin of the Family, Private Property, and the State* (New York: Pathfinder Press, 1972), 25-26.
118. Mary O'Brien, "Reproducing Marxist Man." In Lorenne M.G. Clark and Lynda Lange (eds.), *The Sexism of Social and Political Theory: Women and Reproduction from Plato to Nietzsche* (Toronto: University of Toronto Press, 1979), 104.
119. Mary O'Brien, "Reproductive Labour and the Creation of Value," *Atlantis* 8 (2), 1983: 6.
120. *Ibid.*, 3.
121. Mary O'Brien, *The Politics of Reproduction* (London: Routledge and Kegan Paul, 1981), 44.
122. O'Brien, "Reproducing Marxist Man," 104. Emphasis in the original.
123. O'Brien, *The Politics of Reproduction*, 47.

124. Mary O'Brien, "Feminist Theory and Dialectical Logic," *Signs: Journal of Women in Culture and Society* 7 (1), 1981: 151. Emphasis in the original.

125. *Ibid.*

126. O'Brien, *The Politics of Reproduction*, 53.

127. *Ibid.*, 56.

128. *Ibid.*, 22.

129. O'Brien, "Feminist Theory and Dialectical Logic," 157.

130. Susan Moller Okin and Mary O'Brien, "The Politics of Reproduction, A Review," *Resources for Feminist Research* XI (4), 1982-83: 443-44.

131. *Ibid.*, 444. Emphasis in the original.

132. O'Brien, *The Politics of Reproduction*, 166.

133. *Ibid.*, 197.

134. *Ibid.*, 210.

135. Angela Miles, "Feminist Radicalism in the 1980's," *Canadian Journal of Political and Social Theory* IX (1-2), 1985: 18.

136. Adrienne Rich, "Compulsory Heterosexuality and Lesbian Existence," *Signs: Journal of Women in Culture and Society* 5 (4), 1980: 637.

137. *Ibid.*, 638.

138. Mary O'Brien, "Feminist Praxis." In Geraldine Finn and Angela Miles (eds.), *Feminism in Canada: From Pressure to Politics* (Montreal: Black Rose Books, 1982), 214.

139. *Ibid.*, 214-15.

140. Coward, *Patriarchal Precedents*, 272.

141. The question of the definition of patriarchy as a viable concept for feminist analysis will be addressed in more detail in the final chapter of this work.

142. Heather Jon Maroney, "Embracing Motherhood: New Feminist Theory," *Canadian Journal of Political and Social Theory* XI (1-2), 1985: 58.

CHAPTER 6

1. Michelle Zimbalist Rosaldo, "Woman, Culture, and Society: A Theoretical Overview." In M. Z. Rosaldo and L. Lamphere (eds.), *Woman, Culture and Society* (Stanford, California: Stanford University Press, 1974), 21.

2. *Ibid.*

3. Eleanor Leacock, "Ideologies of Male Dominance as Divide and Rule Politics: An Anthropologist's View." In Marian Lowe and Ruth Hubbard (eds.), *Woman's Nature: Rationalizations of Inequality* (New York, Pergamon Press, 1983), 115.

4. Abraham Kaplan, *The Conduct of Inquiry* (San Francisco, California: Chandler, 1964), 310.

5. Kathleen McCrone points out that the British National Association for the Promotion of Social Science, founded in 1857, always included women and provided a platform for their papers. But "one is left with the uneasy feeling that women were accorded full membership in the SSA by the grace of men who, despite the best of intentions, did not regard them as equals." Male support was made easier because of the "world-improving philosophy" of the association and also because of the "inoffensiveness of feminist claims and claimants." Kathleen E. McCrone, "The National Association for the Promotion of Social Science and the Advancement of Victorian Women," *Atlantis* 8 (1), 1982: 58.

6. Matriarchy was not seen as something to be reinstated, despite Engels's seemingly positive view of its earlier manifestation. Nor was it seen as providing some structural or evaluative basis for future reconstructions of sex relations. Like Durkheim, he felt that once matriarchy was succeeded by patriarchy, there was no going back.

7. Durkheim, *The Division of Labor in Society*, 62-63.

8. Engels, *The Origin*, 36.

9. *Ibid.*, 74.

10. *Ibid.*, 75.

11. Marx and Engels, *The German Ideology*, 21.

12. Isaac D. Balbus, *Marxism and Domination: A Neo-Hegelian, Feminist, Psychoanalytic Theory of Sexual, Political, and Technological Liberation* (Princeton, New Jersey: Princeton University Press, 1982), 83.

13. Engels, *The Origin*, 83.

14. Rosalind Coward, *Patriarchal Precedents*, 156.

15. Emile Durkheim, *Professional Ethics and Civic Morals* (Glencoe, Ill.: The Free Press, 1958), 214.

16. Durkheim, *The Division of Labor in Society*, 376.

17. *Ibid.*, 377.

18. *Ibid.*, 376.

19. George Simpson, "A Durkheim Fragment," *American Journal of Sociology* LXX (5), 1965: 534.

20. Emile Durkheim, *Socialism.* (New York: Collier Books, 1962), 242.

21. *Ibid.*, 243.

22. *Ibid.*, 244.

23. Simpson, "A Durkheim Fragment," 534.

24. *Ibid.*, 535-36.

25. Emile Durkheim, review of Alfred Valensi, *L'Application de la loi du divorce en France.* In *Emile Durkheim: Contributions to L'année sociologique* (New York: The Free Press), 430.

26. *Ibid.*, 431.

27. Emile Durkheim, review of Marianne Weber, *Ehefrau und Mutter in der Rechtsentwicklung.* In Durkheim, *Contributions to L'année sociologique,* 288.

28. *Ibid.*

29. Weber, *Economy and Society,* 1: 357.

30. Guenther Roth, "The Historical Relationship to Marxism," In R. Bendix and G. Roth, *Scholarship and Partisanship* (Berkeley, Los Angeles: University of California Press, 1971), 241.

31. Weber, *Economy and Society,* 1: 358.

32. *Ibid.*

33. *Ibid.*, 363.

34. *Ibid.*, 364.

35. Weber, *The Theory of Social and Economic Organization,* 225.

36. Weber, *Economy and Society,* 3: 1105.

37. Constance Cronin, "Illusion and Reality in Sicily." In Alice Schlegel (ed.), *Sexual Stratification: A Cross-Cultural View* (New York: Columbia University Press, 1977), 91.

38. *Ibid.*

39. Weber, *Economy and Society,* vol. 1, 231.

40. *Ibid.*, vol. 3, 1081.

41. *Ibid.*

42. Iris Young, "Beyond the Unhappy Marriage," 61. Emphasis in the original.

43. *Ibid.*

44. Freud, *Totem and Taboo,* 202.

45. Freud, *Civilization and its Discontents,* 46.

46. *Ibid.*

47. *Ibid.*

48. *Ibid.*, 79.

49. Freud, *New Introductory Lectures on Psychoanalysis,* 132.

50. Freud, *Civilization and its Discontents,* 50-51.

51. *Ibid.*, 51.

52. Marx and Engels, *Manifesto of the Communist Party,* 69.

53. *Ibid.*

54. *Ibid.*, 55.

55. M. Sahlins, *The Use and Abuse of Biology* (Ann Arbor, Michigan: University of Michigan Press, 1976), 4.

56. Stephanie A. Shields, "The Variability Hypothesis: The History of a Biological Model of Sex Differences in Intelligence," *Signs: Journal of Women in Culture and Society* 7 (4), 1982: 796.

57. Weber, *The Methodology of the Social Sciences,* 77. Emphasis in the original.

58. *Ibid.*, 80.

59. W.D. Hamilton, "The Genetic Evolution of Social Behaviour," *Journal of Theoretical Biology* 7 (1) 1964: 1-52.
60. Richard Dawkins, *The Selfish Gene* (London: Oxford University Press, 1976).
61. *Ibid.*, 153.
62. *Ibid.*, 151.
63. D. P. Barash, *Sociobiology and Behaviour* (New York: Elsevier, 1977), 301.
64. R. Paul Shaw, "Humanity's Propensity for Warfare: A Sociobiological Perspective," *The Canadian Review of Sociology and Anthropology* 22 (2), 1985: 165.
65. Anthony Storr, "Aggression in the Relations between the Sexes." In Alison M. Jaggar and Paula Rotherberg Struhl (eds.), *Feminist Frameworks: Alternative Theoretical Accounts of the Relations Between Women and Men* (New York: McGraw-Hill, 1978) 278.
66. Steven Goldberg, "The Inevitability of Patriarchy." In Jaggar and Struhl, *Feminist Frameworks*, 93.
67. See, for example, Janet Sayers, *Biological Politics* (London: Tavistock Publications, 1982); Carol Tavris and Carole Offir, *The Longest War: Sex Differences in Perspective* (New York: Harcourt Brace Jovanovich, 1977); Jessie Bernard, *Women, Wives, Mothers* (Chicago: Aldine, 1975); M. Sahlins, *The Use and Abuse of Biology* (London: Tavistock, 1977); A. Montagu (ed.), *Sociobiology Examined* (Oxford: Oxford University Press, 1980).
68. Elena Leiven, "If it's natural, we can't change it." In The Cambridge Women's Study Group, *Women in Society: Interdisciplinary Essays* (London: Virago Press, 1981), 208.
69. *Ibid.*
70. Marian Lowe, "Sociobiology and Sex Differences," *Signs: Journal of Women in Culture and Society* 4 (1), 1978: 121.
71. *Ibid.*
72. Barash, *Sociobiology and Behaviour*, 122.
73. Lowe, "Sociobiology and Sex Differences," 122.
74. *Ibid.*, 122-23.
75. *Ibid.*, 120.
76. Bernard, *Women, Wives, Mothers*, 10 (see note 67).
77. Helen H. Lambert, "Biology and Equality: A Perspective on Sex Differences," *Signs: Journal of Women in Culture and Society* 4 (1), 1978: 113.
78. *Ibid.*, 114.
79. *Ibid.*
80. *Ibid.*, 114-15.
81. *Ibid.*, 116.
82. Leiven, "If it's natural, we can't change it," 221.

83. *Ibid.*, 222.
84. Alice Rossi, "A biosocial perspective on parenting," *Daedalus* 106 (2), 1977: 1-31.
85. Shields, "The Variability Hypothesis," 796.
86. *Ibid.*, 797.

CHAPTER 7

1. The methodological position of all the theorists is more complex than this description suggests, but the characterization in terms of their general thrust is accurate.
2. L. Laudan, *Progress and its Problems: Towards a Theory of Scientific Growth* (Berkeley, California: University of California Press, 1977).
3. *Ibid.*, 81.
4. Durkheim, *The Rules of Sociological Method*, 141.
5. *Ibid.*, xiv.
6. Russell Keat and John Urry, *Social Theory as Science* (London: Routledge & Kegan Paul, 1982), 4.
7. *Ibid.*, 4-5.
8. Max Weber, *The Methodology of the Social Sciences* (New York: The Free Press, 1949), 76.
9. *Ibid.*, 72.
10. *Ibid.*, 43.
11. Keat and Urry, *Social Theory as Science*, 112.
12. *Ibid.*
13. *Ibid.*, 113.
14. *Ibid.*, 5.
15. *Ibid.*
16. *Ibid.*, 31.
17. Freud, *Civilization and its Discontents*, 13.
18. *Ibid.*
19. Some of the more interesting feminist research within this tradition is found in literary studies. See, for example, G.C. Spivak, "Subaltern Studies: Deconstructing Historiography." In E.D. Ranajit Guha (ed.), *Subaltern Studies: Writings in South Asian History and Society* (Delhi: Oxford University Press, 1985).
20. Virginia Woolf, *Three Guineas* (Harmondsworth, England: Penguin Books, 1977), 159.
21. Freud, *New Introductory Lectures on Psychoanalysis*, 171.
22. Reinhard Bendix, "Sociology and the Distrust of Reason." In R. Bendix and G. Roth (eds.), *Scholarship and Partisanship: Essays on Max Weber* (Berkeley, California: University of California Press, 1971), 92.
23. *Ibid.*

24. Francis Bacon, *The Philosophy of Francis Bacon* (Liverpool, England: Liverpool University Press, 1964).
25. *Ibid.*, 62.
26. Evelyn Fox Keller, "Gender and Science." In Sandra Harding and Merrill B. Hintikka (eds.), *Discovering Reality: Feminist Perspectives on Epistemology, Metaphysics, Methodology, and the Philosophy of Science* (Dordrecht, Holland: D. Reidal, 1983), 190-91.
27. *Ibid.*
28. Susan Bordo, "The Cartesian Masculinization of Thought." *Signs: Journal of Women in Culture and Society* 11 (3), 1986: 456.
29. Elizabeth Fee, "Women's Nature and Scientific Objectivity." In Marian Lowe and Ruth Hubbard, *Woman's Nature: Rationalizations of Inequality* (New York: Pergamon Press, 1983), 12.
30. *Ibid.*, 13.
31. *Ibid.*, 14.
32. Ruth Hubbard, "Social Effects of Some Contemporary Myths About Women." In Lowe and Hubbard, *Women's Nature*, 4.
33. *Ibid.*
34. *Ibid.*, 5.
35. Penelope Brown and L.J. Jordanov, "Oppressive Dichotomies: The Nature/Culture Debate." In The Cambridge Women's Studies Group, *Women in Society* (London: Virago Press, 1981), 238.
36. *Ibid.*, 239.
37. *Ibid.*
38. Katherine Pyne Addelson, "The Man of Professional Wisdom." In Harding and Hintikka, *Discovering Reality*, 166.
39. Ruth Hubbard, "Have Only Men Evolved?" In Sandra Harding and Merrill B. Hintikka, *Discovering Reality*, 65.
40. *Ibid.*
41. Durkheim, *The Rules of Sociological Method*, 31.
42. Elizabeth Fee, "Is Feminism a Threat to Scientific Objectivity?", *International Journal of Women's Studies* 4 (4), 1981: 386.
43. Hilde Hein, "Women and Science: Fitting Men to Think about Nature," *International Journal of Women's Studies* 4 (4), 1981, 371.
44. *Ibid.*, 372.
45. Fee, "Is Feminism a Threat to Scientific Objectivity?", p. 384.
46. T.S. Gray, "Herbert Spencer on Women: A Study in Personal and Political Disillusion," *International Journal of Women's Studies* 7 (3), 1984: 218.
47. Addelson, "The Man of Professional Wisdom," 182.
48. Dorothy E. Smith, "An Analysis of Ideological Structures and How Women are Excluded: Considerations for Academic Women," *Canadian Review of Sociology and Anthropology* 12 (4), 1975:365.
49. Mary Daly, *Gyn/Ecology: The Meta-Ethics of Radical Feminism* (Boston: Beacon Press, 1978).

50. Mary O'Brien, "Feminist Praxis: Feminism and Revolution," 259.
51. Smith, "An Analysis," 354.
52. *Ibid.*, 357.
53. Daly, *Gyn/Ecology: The Meta-Ethics of Radical Feminism*, 29.
54. Margaret Benston, "Feminism and the Critique of Scientific Method." In Miles and Finn, *Feminism in Canada*, 64.
55. *Ibid.*, 52.
56. *Ibid.*
57. *Ibid.*, 60.
58. Angela Miles, "Ideological Hegemony in Political Discourse: Women's Specificity and Equality." In Miles and Finn, *Feminism in Canada*, 222.
59. *Ibid.*, 217-18.
60. *Ibid.*, 226.
61. Hein, "Women and Science," 376.
62. *Ibid.*, 373. Emphasis in the original.
63. *Ibid.*, 374.
64. *Ibid.*, 375.
65. *Ibid.*
66. Weber, *The Methodology of the Social Sciences*, 72.
67. *Ibid.*, 76.
68. Angela Miles, "Sexuality, Diversity and Relativism in the Women's Liberation Movement," *Resources for Feminist Research* XIV (3), 1985: 9.
69. *Ibid.*, 9-10.
70. *Ibid.*, 10.
71. Evelyn Fox Keller, "Women, Science, and Popular Mythology." In Joan Rothschild (ed.), *Machina Ex Dea* (New York: Pergamon Press, 1983), 134.
72. *Ibid.*, 135.
73. *Ibid.*, 143.
74. Evelyn Fox Keller, "Women and Science: Two Cultures or One?", *International Journal of Women's Studies*, 4 (4), 1981, 417.
75. *Ibid.*
76. Elizabeth Fee, "Is Feminism a Threat to Scientific Objectivity?", p. 382.
77. *Ibid.*, 383.
78. *Ibid.*, 384.
79. *Ibid.*, 389.
80. Smith, "An Analysis," 367.
81. Dorothy E. Smith, "The Renaissance of Women." In *Knowledge Reconsidered: A Feminist Overview* (Ottawa: Canadian Research Institute for the Advancement of Women, 1984), 10.

A Select
Bibliography

Addelson, Katherine Pyne
1983 "The Man of Professional Wisdom." In Sandra Harding and Merrill B. Hintikka (eds.), *Discovering Reality: Feminist Perspectives on Epistemology, Metaphysics, Methodology, and the Philosophy of Science.* Dordrecht, Holland: D. Reidal.

Adler, Alfred
1927 *Understanding Human Nature.* New York: Greenburg.

Agonito, Rosemary
1977 *History of Ideas in Women.* New York: G.P. Putman's Sons.

Alberti, L.B.
1969 *The Family in Renaissance Florence.* Trans. by R. Neu Watkins. Columbia, South Carolina: University of Carolina Press.

Armstrong, Pat and Hugh Armstrong
1984 *The Double Ghetto.* Rev. ed. Toronto: McClelland and Stewart.

Bacon, Francis
1964 *The Philosophy of Francis Bacon.* Edited and translated by Benjamin Farrington. Liverpool: Liverpool University Press.

Balbus, Isaac D.
1982 *Marxism and Domination: A Neo-Hegelian, Feminist, Psychoanalytic Theory of Sexual, Political and Technological Liberation.* Princeton, New Jersey: Princeton University Press.

Bendix, Reinhard and Guenther Roth (eds.)
1971 *Scholarship and Partisanship: Essays on Max Weber.* Berkeley, California: University of California Press.

Benston, Margaret
1969 The Political Economy of Women's Liberation. *Monthly Review* 21 (4).
1982 Feminism and the Critique of Scientific Method. In Angela R. Miles and Geraldine Finn (eds.), *Feminism in Canada: From Pressure to Politics*. Montreal: Black Rose Books.

Bordo, Susan
1986 The Cartesian Masculinization of Thought. *Signs: Journal of Women in Culture and Society* 11 (3), Spring.

Bridenthal, Renate and Claudia Koonz (eds.)
1977 *Becoming Visible: Women in European History* Boston: Houghton Mifflin.

Brown, Penelope and L.J. Jordanov
1981 Oppressive Dichotomies: The Nature/Culture Debate. In The Cambridge Women's Studies Group, *Women in Society*. London: Virago Press.

Caplow, T.
1961 *The Sociology of Work*. New York: McGraw-Hill.

Cheyette, Frederick L. (ed.)
1968 *Lordship and Community in Medieval Europe*. New York: Holt, Rinehart and Winston.

Chodorow, Nancy
1974 Family Structure and Feminine Personality. In M. Z. Rosaldo and L. Lamphere (eds.), *Woman, Culture and Society*. Stanford: Stanford University Press.
1978 *The Reproduction of Mothering*. California: University of California Press.
1979 Mothering, Male Dominance, and Capitalism. In Z. R. Eisenstein (ed.), *Capitalist Patriarchy and the Case for Socialist Feminism*. New York: Monthly Review Press.

Clark, L.M.G.
1979 Women and Locke: Who Owns the Apples in the Garden of Eden? In L.M.G. Clark and L. Lange (eds.), *The Sexism of Social and Political Theory*. Toronto: University of Toronto Press.

Coward, Rosalind
1983 *Patriarchal Precedents: Sexuality and Social Relations*. London: Routledge and Kegan Paul.

Cronin, Constance
1977 Illusion and Reality in Sicily. In Alice Schlegel (ed.), *Sexual*

Stratification: A Cross-Cultural View. New York: Columbia University Press.

Dalla Costa, Mariarosa and Selma James
1973 *The Power of Women and the Subversion of the Community*. Bristol, England: Falling Wall Press.

Daly, Mary
1978 *Gyn/Ecology: The Meta-Ethics of Radical Feminism*. Boston: Beacon Press.

Darwin, Charles
1950 *The Origin of Species and the Descent of Man*. New York: The Modern Library.

David, Norman (ed.)
1983 *The Paston Letters*. Oxford: Oxford University Press.

Davy, Georges
1931 *Sociologues d'hier et d'aujourd'hui*. Paris: Alcan.

de Beauvoir, Simone
1952 *The Second Sex*. Trans. by H.M. Parshley. New York: Alfred A. Knopf.

Deckhard, Barbara Sinclair
1983 *The Women's Movement*. 3rd ed. New York: Harper and Row.

Delpy, Christine
1984 *Close to Home*. Translated and edited by Diana Leonard. London: Hutchinson, in association with The Explorations in Feminism Collective.

Duby, Georges
1968 In Northwestern France: The "Youth" in Twelfth-Century Aristocratic Society. In Frederic L. Cheyette (ed.), *Lordship and Community in Medieval Europe*. New York: Holt, Rinehart and Winston.
1974 *The Early Growth of the European Economy* (Trans. by Howard B. Clarke). New York: Cornell University Press.
1977 *The Chivalrous Society*. Trans. by Cynthia Postan. London: Edward Arnold.
1978 *The Three Orders: Feudal Society Imagined*. Trans. by A. Goldhammer. Chicago: University of Chicago Press.

Durkheim, Emile
1950 *The Rules of Sociological Method*. 8th ed. Translated by S.S. Solovay and John Mueller, edited by G. Catlin. New York: The Free Press.

1956 *Education and Sociology.* Trans. by Sherwood D. Fox. Glencoe, Illinois: The Free Press.
1961 *The Elementary Forms of the Religious Life.* Trans. by Joseph Ward Swain. New York: Collier Books.
1964 *The Division of Labor in Society.* Trans. by George Simpson. New York: The Free Press.
1966 *Suicide.* Trans. by John A. Spaulding and George Simpson, edited by George Simpson. New York: The Free Press.
1972 *Selected Writings.* Edited and translated by Anthony Giddens. Cambridge: Cambridge University Press.
1980 *Contributions to l'année sociologique.* Edited by Yash Nandan. New York: The Free Press.

Ehrlich, Carol
1980 The Unhappy Marriage of Marxism and Feminism: Can It Be Saved? In Lydia Sargent (ed.), *Women and Revolution.* Montreal: Black Rose Books.

Eisenstein, Zillah
1979 Developing a Theory of Capitalist Patriarchy and Socialist Feminism. In Eisenstein (ed.), *Capitalist Patriarchy and the Case for Socialist Feminism.* New York: Monthly Review Press.

Eisenstein, Zillah (ed.)
1979 *Capitalist Patriarchy and the Case for Socialist Feminism.* New York: Monthly Review Press.

Elshtain, Jean Bethke
1982 *Public Man, Private Woman.* Princeton: Princeton University Press.

Elshtain, Jean Bethke (ed.)
1982 *The Family in Political Thought.* Amherst: The University of Massachusetts Press.

Engels, Frederick
1972 *The Origin of the Family, Private Property and the State.* New York: Pathfinder Press.

Fee, Elizabeth
1981 Is Feminism a Threat to Scientific Objectivity? *International Journal of Women's Studies* 4 (4), Sept./Oct.
1983 Women's Nature and Scientific Objectivity. In Marian Lowe and Ruth Hubbard (eds.), *Women's Nature: Rationalizations of Inequality.* New York: Pergamon Press.

Ficino, Marsilio
1975 *The Letters of Marsilio Ficino.* London: Shepheard-Walwyn. 3 volumes.

Firestone, Shulamith
1970 *The Dialectic of Sex*. New York: Bantam Books.

Freud, Sigmund
1946 *Totem and Taboo*. Trans. by A.A. Brill. New York: Vintage Books.
1961 *Civilization and Its Discontents*. Translated and edited by James Strachey. New York: W.W. Norton.
1964 *New Introductory Lectures on Psychoanalysis*. Translated and edited by James Strachey. New York: W.W. Norton.
1974 *The Standard Edition of the Complete Psychological Works of Sigmund Freud*. London: Hogarth Press.
1977 *On Sexuality*. Harmondsworth: Penguin.

Fox, Bonnie (ed.)
1980 *Hidden in the Household*. Toronto: The Women's Press.

Fox Keller, Evelyn
1981 Women and Science: Two Cultures or One? *International Journal of Women's Studies* 4 (4), Sept./Oct.
1983 Women, Science and Popular Mythology. In Joan Rothschild (ed.), *Machina Ex Dea*. New York: Pergamon Press.
1983 Gender and Science. In S. Harding and M.B. Hintikka (eds.), *Discovering Reality: Feminist Perspectives on Epistemology, Metaphysics, Methodology, and the Philosophy of Science*. Dordrecht, Holland: D. Reidal.

Gardiner, Jean
1975 Women's Domestic Labour. *New Left Review* 8, (1).

Geis, Frances and Joseph Geis
1978 *Women in the Middle Ages*. New York: Barnes and Noble.

Gerth, H.H. and C. Wright Mills (Translators and editors)
1946 *From Max Weber: Essays in Sociology*. New York: Oxford University Press.

Giddens, Anthony
1973 *The Class Structure of Advanced Societies*. London: Hutchinson.

Gray, T.S.
1984 Herbert Spencer on Women: A Study in Personal and Political Disillusion. *International Journal of Women's Studies* 7 (3), May/June.

Guettel, Charnie
1974 *Marxism and Feminism*. Toronto: The Women's Press.

Hamilton, Roberta
1978 *The Liberation of Women*. London: George Allen and Unwin.

1981 Working at Home. *Atlantis* 7 (1).

Harding, Sandra
1981 What is the Real Material Base of Patriarchy and Capital? In Lydia Sargent (ed.), *Women and Revolution*. Montreal: Black Rose Books.

Hartmann, Heidi
1979 Capitalism, Patriarchy, and Job Segregation by Sex. In Z. Eisenstein (ed.), *Capitalist Patriarchy and the Case for Socialist Feminism*. New York: Monthly Review Press.
1981 The Unhappy Marriage of Marxism and Feminism: Towards a More Progressive Union. In Lydia Sargent (ed.), *Women and Revolution*. Montreal: Black Rose Books.

Hein, Hilde
1981 Women and Science: Fitting Men to Think About Nature. *International Journal of Women's Studies* 4 (4), Sept./Oct.

Hilton, Rodney
1973 *Bond Men Made Free*. New York: The Viking Press.

Hobbes, Thomas
n.d. *Leviathan*. London: J.M. Dent and Sons.

Horney, Karen
1939 *New Ways in Psychoanalysis*. New York: W.W. Horton.

Hubbard, Ruth
1983 Have Only Men Evolved? In S. Harding and M. B. Hintikka (eds.), *Discovering Reality: Feminist Perspectives on Epistemology, Metaphysics, Methodology and the Philosophy of Science*. Dordrecht, Holland: D. Reidal.
1983 Social Effects on Some Contemporary Myths About Women. In Marian Lowe and Ruth Hubbard (eds.), *Women's Nature: Rationalizations of Inequality*. New York: Pergamon Press.

Huizinga, J.
1954 *The Waning of the Middle Ages*. New York: Doubleday Anchor.

Humphries, Jane
1982 The Working-class Family: A Marxist Perspective. In J. Elshtain (ed.), *The Family in Political Thought*. Amherst: University of Massachusetts Press.

Irigaray, Luce
1981 And One Doesn't Stir Without the Other. Trans. by H. V. Wenzel. *Signs: Journal of Women in Culture and Society* 7 (1), Autumn.

Keat, Russell and John Urry
1932 *Social Theory as Science*. London: Routledge and Kegan Paul.

Kelly, Amy
1978 *Eleanor of Aquitaine and the Four Kings.* Cambridge, Mass.: Harvard University Press.

King, Margaret
1980 Book-lined Cells: Women and Humanism in the Early Italian Renaissance. In Patricia H. Labalme (ed.), *Beyond Their Sex.* New York: New York University Press.

Labalme, Patricia H.
1980 *Beyond Their Sex.* New York: New York University Press.

Laslett, Peter
1965 *The World We Have Lost.* London: Methuen.

Laudan, L.
1977 *Progress and Its Problems: Towards a Theory of Scientific Growth.* Berkeley: University of California Press.

Leacock, Eleanor
1983 Ideologies of Male Dominance as Divide and Rule Politics: An Anthropologist's View. In M. Lowe and R. Hubbard (eds.), *Woman's Nature: Rationalizations of Inequality.* New York: Pergamon Press.

Lloyd, G.E.R.
1971 *Polarity and Analogy: Two Types of Argumentation in Early Greek Thought.* Cambridge: Cambridge University Press.

Locke, John
1963 *Two Treatises of Government.* Edited by P. Laslett. Cambridge: Cambridge University Press.

Lukes, Steven
1973 *Emile Durkheim: His Life and Work.* London: Allen Lane, The Penguin Press.

Luxton, Meg
1980 *More Than a Labour of Love.* Toronto: The Women's Press.

MacLean, Ian
1980 *The Renaissance Notion of Women.* Cambridge: Cambridge University Press.

Malinowski, Bronislaw
1926 *Sex and Repression in Savage Society.* London: Routledge.

Marx, Karl
1909 *Capital: A Critique of Political Economy.* 3 vols. Edited by Frederick Engels and translated by Ernest Untermann. Chicago: Charles H. Kerr.

1962 Value, Price and Profit. In Eleanor Marx Aveling (ed.), *The Essential Left*. London: Unwin Books.

Marx, Karl and Frederick Engels
1947 *The German Ideology*. Edited by R. Pascal. New York: International Publishers.
1959 *Manifesto of the Communist Party*. Moscow: Foreign Languages Publishing House.
1975 *Collected Works*. 10 vols. New York: International Publishers.

Marx, Karl, Frederick Engels and N. Lenin
1960 *The Essential Left: Four Classic Texts on the Principles of Socialism*. London: Unwin Books.

McLellan, David
1980 *The Thought of Karl Marx*. 2nd ed. London: Macmillan Press.

McNamara, JoAnn and Suzanne F. Wemple
1977 Sanctity and Power: The Dual Pursuit of Medieval Women. In Renate Bridenthal and Claudia Koonz (eds.), *Becoming Visible: Women in European History*. Boston: Houghton Mifflin.

Meissner, Martin
1976 Women and Inequality. *Our Generation* 11 (2), Winter.
1977 Sexual Division of Labour and Inequality. In Marylee Stephenson (ed.), *Women in Canada*. Rev. ed. Don Mills: General Publishing.

Miles, Angela
1982 Ideological Hegemony in Political Discourse: Women's Specificity and Equality. In Angela R. Miles and Geraldine Finn (eds.), *Feminism in Canada: From Pressure to Politics*. Montreal: Black Rose Books.
1985 Feminist Radicalism in the 1980's. *Canadian Journal of Political and Social Theory* XI (1-2).
1985 Sexuality, Diversity and Relativism in the Women's Liberation Movement. *Resources for Feminist Research* XIV (3) November.

Millet, Kate
1969 *Sexual Politics*. New York: Avon Books.

Mitchell, Juliet
1973 *Women's Estate*. New York: Vintage Books.
1975 *Psychoanalysis and Feminism*. New York: Vintage Books.

Moller Okin, Susan
1982-3 Mary O'Brien: The Politics of Reproduction, A Review. *Resources for Feminist Research* XI (4), Dec./Jan.

Morgan, L.H.
1877 *Ancient Society*. New York: Henry Holt.

Morris, Desmond
1967 *The Naked Ape*. London: Jonathan Cape.

Oakley, Ann
1974 *The Sociology of Housework*. New York: Pantheon Books.

O'Brien, Mary
1979 Reproducing Marxist Man. In Lorenne M.G. Clark and Lynda Lange (eds.), *The Sexism of Social and Political Theory: Women and Reproduction from Plato to Nietzsche*. Toronto: University of Toronto Press.
1981 Feminist Theory and Dialectical Logic. *Signs: Journal of Women in Culture and Society* 7 (1), Autumn.
1982 Feminist Praxis. In Angela Miles and Geraldine Finn (eds.), *Feminism in Canada: From Pressure to Politics*. Montreal: Black Rose Books.
1983 Reproductive Labour and the Creation of Value. *Atlantis* 8 (2), Spring.

O'Faolain, J. and L. Martinese (eds.)
1973 *Not in God's Image*. New York: Harper Colophon Books.

Ortner, Sherry B.
1974 Is Female to Male as Nature is to Culture? In M. Z. Rosaldo and L. Lamphere (eds.), *Woman, Culture and Society*. Stanford: Stanford University Press.

Parkin, Frank
1982 *Max Weber*. Tavistock Publications.

Parsons, Talcott (ed.)
1947 *Max Weber: The Theory of Social and Economic Organization*. London: Collier-Macmillan.
1964 Age and Sex in the Social Structure of the United States. In T. Parsons (ed.), *Essays in Sociological Theory*. New York: The Free Press.

Parsons, Talcott and Robert Bales
1955 *Family, Socialization and Interaction Process*. New York: The Free Press.

Reiter, Rayna (ed.)
1975 *Toward an Anthropology of Women*. New York: Monthly Review Press.

Rich, Adrienne
1980 Compulsory Heterosexuality and Lesbian Existence. *Signs: Journal of Women in Culture and Society* 5 (4), Summer.

Richardson, Laurel Walum
1981 *The Dynamics of Sex and Gender.* 2nd ed. Boston: Houghton Mifflin.

Rosaldo, M. Zimbalist and L. Lamphere (eds.)
1974 *Woman, Culture and Society.* Stanford: Stanford University Press.

Rosenberg, Charles E. (ed.)
1975 *The Family in History.* Pennsylvania: University of Pennsylvania Press.

Rowbotham, Sheila
1973 *Woman's Consciousness, Man's World.* Harmondsworth: Penguin Books.

Rubin, Gayle
1975 The Traffic in Women: Notes on the 'Political Economy' of Sex. In Rayna R. Reiter (ed.), *Toward an Anthropology of Women.* New York: Monthly Review Press.

Runciman, W.G. (ed.)
1978 *Weber: Selections in Translation.* Trans. by Eric Matthews. New York: Cambridge University Press.

Sargent, Lydia (ed.)
1981 *Women and the Revolution.* Montreal: Black Rose Books.

Sayers, Janet
1982 *Biological Politics.* London: Tavistock Publications.

Schlegel, Alice (ed.)
1977 *Sexual Stratification: A Cross Cultural View.* New York: Columbia University Press.

Seccombe, Wally
1974 The Housewife and Her Labor Under Capitalism. *New Left Review,* 83, Jan-Feb.

Shahar, Shulamaith
1983 *The Fourth Estate.* Trans. by Chaya Galai. London: Methuen.

Sherman, J. and T. Beck (eds.)
1979 *The Prism of Sex: Essays in the Sociology of Knowledge.* Madison: University of Wisconsin Press.

Simpson, George
1965 A Durkheim Fragment: The Conjugal Family. *American Journal of Sociology* LXX, (5), March.

Spencer, Herbert
1898 *The Principles of Sociology.* New York: Appleton.

Spivak, Chakravorty
1985 Subaltern Studies: Deconstructing Historiography. In E. D. Ranajit Guha (ed.), *Subaltern Studies: Writings in South Asian History and Society.* New Delhi: Oxford University Press.

Smith, Dorothy
1975 An Analysis of the Ideological Structures and How Women are Excluded: Considerations for Academic Women. *Canadian Review of Sociology and Anthropology* 12 (4), November.
1978 A Peculiar Eclipsing: Women's Exclusion from Man's Culture. *Women's Studies International Quarterly* 1 (4).
1979 A Sociology for Women. In J. Sherman and T. Beck (eds.), *The Prism of Sex: Essays in the Sociology of Knowledge.* Madison: University of Wisconsin Press.
1984 The Renaissance of Women. In *Knowledge Reconsidered: A Feminist Overview.* Ottawa: Canadian Research Institute for the Advancement of Women.

Stephenson, Marylee (ed.)
1977 *Women in Canada.* Rev. ed. Don Mills: General Publishing.

St. Clare Byrne, Muriel (ed.)
1981 *The Lisle Letters.* Chicago: University of Chicago Press.

Stone, Lawrence
1975 The Rise of the Nuclear Family in Early Modern England. In Charles E. Rosenberg (ed.), *The Family in History.* Pennsylvania: University of Pennsylvania Press.

Thompson, Kenneth
1982 *Emile Durkheim.* Sussex, England: Ellis Horwood.

Tiger, Lionel and Robin Fox
1971 *The Imperial Animal.* New York: Holt, Rinehart and Winston.

Tuchman, Barbara W.
1978 *A Distant Mirror.* New York: Ballantine Books.

Young, Iris
1981 Beyond the Unhappy Marriage: A Critique of Dual Systems Theory. In Lydia Sargent (ed.), *Women and Revolution.* Montreal: Black Rose Books.

Waley, Daniel
1964 *Later Medieval Europe.* New York: Longman.

Weber, Max
1949 *The Methodology of the Social Sciences.* Translated and edited by Edward A. Shils and Henry A. Finch, with a foreword by Edward A. Shils. New York: The Free Press.

1964 *The Theory of Social and Economic Organization*. Trans. by A.M. Henderson and Talcott Parsons (ed.). New York: The Free Press.
1968 *Economy and Society: An Outline of Interpretive Sociology*. Edited by Guenther Roth and Claus Wittich. 3 vols. New York: Bedminster Press.

Wolff, Kurt H. (ed.)
1964 *Essays on Sociology and Philosophy by Emile Durkheim et al.* New York: Harper and Row.

Woolf, Virginia
1977 *Three Guineas*. Harmondsworth, England: Penguin Books.

Wrightson, Keith
1983 *English Society, 1580-1680*. London: Hutchinson.

Index

identification of women with, 3,
4, 205
inadequacy of scientific and
sociological explanations
of, 210-11
as Other, 205
Nature/culture dichotomy, 3-4
Durkheim on, 38
Freud on, 148
in the patriarchal household
(Weber), 59-60
woman as mediating force in,
206-7
Nature/nurture debate (Freud),
126, 161-66
feminist reformulations of, 142-
61

Oakley, Ann, 8, 9, 107-8, 108-9
Object relations approach
(Chodorow and Dinnerstein),
154
O'Brien, Mary, 163, 164-65, 165
on contraceptive technology,
159-60
critique of Marx and Engels,
156-61
on dialectical method, 157
Moller Okin's critique of, 160-61
moments of the reproductive
process, 158
on naming and defining, 211
on reproductive consciousness,
157-59
Occupational group (Durkheim),
31-32, 177
Occupational status, of
housewives (Parsons), 9
Oedipus complex (Freud), 126-33,
186-87
Oedipus Rex (Sophocles), 127
Organic solidarity (Durkheim), 15,
16, 25, 37
*The Origin of the Family, Private
Property and the State*
(Engels), 90, 95, 98, 140, 156
production/reproduction in, 98

Ortner, Sherry B., 156, 163-64, 205
on nature/culture dichotomy,
148-49, 164

Parkin, Frank, 81
Parsons, Talcott, 9, 48
Pascal, Blaise, 36
Patriarchy, Freud on, 125, 161-66
as realm of superego, 127, 129
explanations for, 166
Patriarchy, Marx and Engels on,
97, 113, 162, 172-75, 187-88
and capitalism, 115-20
and class, 115-20
Patriarchy, Weber on, 51, 55-64,
115, 122, 179-85 *passim*
defined, 56, 62
and male/female relations, 57,
58-59
and relations between men, 85
Patrilineal descent:
Marx and Engels on, 96
Weber on, 61, 63
Patrimonial domination (Weber),
64-67, 182-83
Positivism (Durkheim), 48, 200-
201
Power, 169-70
in mainstream sociological
theory, 10
Weber on, 51, 54, 86, 181, 182
Pre-cultural horde:
Durkheim on, 18, 173
Freud on, 130-33, 185-86
Primogeniture (Weber), 77
"Private Property and
Communism" (Marx), 89
Private property (Marx and
Engels), 98, 175, 194
Production (Marx and Engels), 98
women's and men's differing
relations to, 121
Proletariat (Marx and Engels), 90,
92
Property law (Weber), 85
Public sphere/private sphere: *see*
Division of labour, sexual

DuD CAMPUS
18